Seeking Customers

The Harvard Business Review Book Series

Seeking Customers

Edited, with
an Introduction by
**Benson P. Shapiro and
John J. Sviokla**

A Harvard Business Review Book

HF
5438.25
.S434
1993

Library of Congress Cataloging-in-Publication Data

Seeking customers / edited, with an introduction by Benson P. Shapiro and
  John J. Sviokla.
      p. cm. — (The Harvard business review book series)
    Includes bibliographical references and index.
    ISBN 0-87584-332-8 (acid-free paper)
      1. Selling. 2. Consumers' preferences. 3. Consumer satisfaction.
  I. Shapiro, Benson P. II. Sviokla, J. J. III. Harvard business review. IV.
Series.
    HF36862.S434 1993
    658.8'343—dc20   92-36862
                                                                          CIP

The *Harvard Business Review* articles in this collection are available as individual reprints. Discounts apply to quantity purchases. For information and
ordering contact Operations Department, Harvard Business School Publishing Corporation, Boston, MA 02163. Telephone: (617) 495-6192, 9 a.m. to 5
p.m. Eastern Time, Monday through Friday. Fax: (617) 495-6985, 24 hours
a day.

Contents

By combining traditional and evolving communications
approaches, marketers can design more flexible and
cost-efficient marketing programs. The "marketing-
oriented income statement" provides a powerful tool
for combining the best of the traditional methods, such
as personal selling and media advertising, with the
best of the new techniques, such as telemarketing and
national account management.

Marketing and sales costs average 15% to 35% of total
corporate costs. Marketing and sales productivity
(MSP) systems harness the power of the computer to
improve productivity by coordinating the complete
range of sales and marketing activities. Carefully
planned automation systems will increase a company's
competitive advantage, leading to higher profits.

In today's complex environment, selling efforts must often be coordinated across product lines, functions, and geographic locations, to customers with similarly decentralized purchasing processes. Executives need to focus training, compensation systems, and goal-setting programs to encourage commitment to the team. Well-managed team relationships will translate into customer satisfaction, profitable sales, and a long-term competitive edge.

Part II   Understand Your Prospects and Customers
A great deal of market research is wasted because it is done to confirm a chosen plan of action that will be taken regardless of the findings, or because it provides interesting but not implementable results. Participating in research design and focusing on how the research will be used before it is undertaken will help companies capture its benefits.

Effective market segmentation has tremendous profit implications but is very difficult to achieve, especially in industrial markets. This article provides a process for segmentation that begins with the simplest, most external variables, such as demographics, before considering more ambiguous, intimate variables, such as situational factors and buyers' personal characteristics. Using this "nested" approach, marketers can segment the market along several dimensions and target the most promising prospects and customers most effectively.

organization. The company featured in this article used the occasion of losing its biggest customer to improve its focus and redesign its presentation, ultimately winning back the customer.

The eight-step format provided in this article can help companies learn to cope creatively with large, complex selling tasks and achieve lasting results. The nuts-and-bolts approach can energize the novice salesperson or provide a valuable refresher for the seasoned veteran.

Crafting a customer relationship takes an extraordinary commitment of time, energy, and resources. The detailed recommendations in this article show how to sell the company and its capabilities before selling a specific product or service. This process builds a deeper, more lasting relationship and sets the stage for long-term profits.

Nothing creates as much anxiety among salespeople as the phrase, "Your price is way too high—what's my discount?" A demand for a lower price may signal an erosion of the seller-customer relationship at a deeper level. This article, which includes commentary by several business leaders, shows how to benefit from these demanding interactions with customers.

manager can significantly reduce turnover and
improve sales performance.

Effective compensation system design is at the heart of
managing a sales force. Designing the right
combination of commissions, salary, bonuses, and
fringe benefits can be a complex task. This article
provides benchmarks and practical ideas on how to
create these vital management systems.

This article emphasizes the enduring power of strong
relationships. Distributors are not only people to sell
through, they are people to see *to*. Creating, nurturing,
and monitoring relationships with distributors will
provide tremendous short- and long-term leverage in
the marketplace.

In today's competitive marketplace, companies are
enhancing their sales and marketing departments with
a wide array of vendors, agents, and distributors.
These hybrid systems offer flexibility and cost-
efficiency, but are difficult to manage. This article
explains how to minimize unnecessary conflict, while
maximizing market coverage at minimum cost.
Information technology is a vital tool in coordinating
these efforts.

Preface

Benson P. Shapiro and John J. Sviokla

In an increasingly complex and competitive business environment, having a terrific new product or service is no longer sufficient for achieving success. Technological, organizational, and institutional advances have created a marketplace where greater producer capacity chases each dollar of customer spending. Differentiating your product has become increasingly a function of the selling process itself, in addition to product features, price, and delivery schedule.

This two-volume set (*Seeking Customers* and *Keeping Customers*) focuses on improving the competitiveness with which companies attract customers and develop profitable, long-term relationships. The articles we have culled from the *Harvard Business Review* move beyond the popular rhetoric of "market orientation" as an end in itself to a philosophy that market orientation is a primary management task on the road to better corporate performance. While *Seeking Customers* is concerned primarily with attracting and acquiring customers, its companion, *Keeping Customers*, concentrates on developing relationships that remain profitable over time.

Efficient selling increases value to the customer (relative to price) as well as to the seller (relative to costs). At every stage in the process of seeking and keeping customers—for example, identifying prospects, initiating and cultivating relationships, setting prices, closing the sale, monitoring the order management cycle, offering post-sales product support—sellers have the opportunity to add value to the customer. However, tight coordination within the selling company is necessary to ensure that the costs of investing resources in customer value creation do not outweigh the benefits of making the sale.

These two books highlight the many ways in which sellers can increase the value of their products or services efficiently. We must caution the reader that much of the advice offered in these volumes is not easy to execute. Value creation requires persistence and creativity. The process begins with understanding the needs and goals of each potential customer and demonstrating how you as the seller are best qualified to satisfy those demands. You must be aware of how the customer perceives the benefits from doing business with you rather than with your competitors. At the same time, you cannot lose sight of your interests; satisfying customers must not be pursued at the expense of long-term profitability.

Fortunately, some of the factors contributing to the complex and competitive nature of the business environment actually help sellers pursue customers more profitably. For example, information and communication technologies have vastly improved the abilities of a company to track and share important customer-related information. New distribution channels and support services enable companies to better coordinate product development, production, delivery, service, and support. Most important, today's intense competition has provided the motivation for organizational changes, such as cross-functional teams, that would have been considered impossible even a few years ago.

In this environment of rapid change and intense competition, *Seeking Customers* and *Keeping Customers* will help make the 1990s a decade of profitable customer satisfaction for your company.

Introduction

Benson P. Shapiro and John J. Sviokla

"Selling is dead; there was respect, and courtship, and gratitude in it. Today it's all cut and dried, and there's no chance for bringing friendship to bear or personality."

Thus Arthur Miller's immortal salesman, Willy Loman, bemoaned the demise of selling. However, reports of the death of selling are exaggerated. Selling is not dead; rather, it has evolved to meet the challenges of an increasingly competitive environment. In fact, for companies to sell effectively and efficiently today, they cannot subscribe to the static approach described by Willy Loman in 1949. Instead, they must recognize that selling is a complex, dynamic process that requires the commitment of the entire company.

The purpose of this book is to explore and illuminate major changes in the customer-seeking process, and to clarify the relationships among selling and several closely related activities, such as understanding customers, sales force management, distribution, pricing, marketing, and, above all, account selection. This unique collection of *Harvard Business Review* articles highlights the interplay among these elements, preserving important enduring themes, while leveraging them with the latest approaches to this complex topic.

Our primary theme is not making sales or managing salespeople. It is, instead, more basic and central to the goals of business—**generating profits.** Throughout this book, we will concentrate on how each element of the customer-seeking process contributes to profit generation. Understanding the full scope of this process will help managers allocate resources more efficiently, making investments that will increase value to the customer often while enhancing profits.

Achieving this balance between value and costs has become increasingly challenging as technological, organizational, and institutional development have created a more competitive marketplace. Several trends illustrate the changing demands on the seller:

1. *There are more competitors going after each piece of business.* With freer trade, deregulation, privatization, technological advances, and worldwide economic development, there is greater producer capacity chasing each dollar of consumer spending.

2. *There is a smaller margin between producer costs and customer value.* As business has grown more competitive, producers can no longer enjoy the luxury of inefficient selling. In fact, productivity, value, and competitiveness are increasingly being gained through marketing- and sales-related activities rather than through lower costs of materials and labor.

3. *Selling has become more integrated with other company functions.* Through the customer-seeking process the seller must identify and select customers who will be profitable in the long term to the whole company. The relationship with a customer is not owned exclusively by the sales force, but by everyone—from product development to finance—who has a stake in the company's profitability.

4. *There is less differentiation among competitors.* Traditionally, with a great new product a seller could determine its customer base and selling price. Today, having a great product or service is only an entry into the game. It is a necessary condition, but not sufficient. Differentiating a product—increasing its value to the customer, relative to competitive products—is increasingly a function of the sales process itself.

Given these developments in the selling environment, an effective selling effort must:

1. Provide more value to the customer.
2. Be more connected to the rest of the company.
3. Continue to fulfill all its traditional roles, only more efficiently.

Competitive and profitable selling demands that everyone in the organization be working at peak efficiency, peak effectiveness, and peak commitment. The seller must look *outward* to the market, but also *inward* into its own networks, conventions, capabilities, and resources. The articles in this volume provide a practical and conceptual framework for addressing these issues. We have arranged the articles to highlight six principal themes in the customer acquisition process.

"Seeking" customers is more than selling—it is a system of closely linked activities that range from screening prospects to establishing distribution networks. In order for this system to work effectively, it is necessary to **Build Channels of Communication** (Part I). Two-way communication between seller and customer allows sellers to understand the customer's needs and let the customer know how the seller can meet these needs. Communication within the selling organization enables coordination across company functions and operating units, which in turn encourages companywide commitment to profitable selling.

In a marketplace comprised of diverse companies and diverse individuals, profitable selling is largely a function of understanding buyer behavior, segmenting the market, and selecting the most promising prospects. Personal selling enables you to segment the market at the individual buying influence—a single person. To take full advantage of the personalized marketing approach, you must **Understand Your Prospects and Customers** (Part II), whether through broad-based market research or through more intimate interaction with individual buyers. In this section, we consider ways to relate market research to implementable decisions, and demonstrate several approaches to understanding the human element of business interaction.

Next, we engage the challenges of understanding different types of selling situations, from simple single transactions to complex strategic-account relationships. Each type of selling requires different assumptions, approaches, time investments, and resource allocations. When the account is diverse and dispersed, the sales team must be tightly coordinated and focused. Long-term profits can be realized when you **Close the Sale and Open the Relationship** (Part III). For more complex accounts, closing the sale is only one step toward profitability: commitment to nurturing, building, and continuing a two-way relationship is necessary to achieve lasting results.

During the selling process, price inevitably becomes a major issue. Few customers have the luxury and willingness to buy at any price. At the same time, the seller wants to achieve sales at the highest price possible, to ensure a healthy profit. Although price is often the major source of conflict between buyers and sellers, it is actually only one of many variables contributing to customer value.

It is important to **Balance Price and Value** (Part IV) in order to create a package that maximizes consumer value without sacrificing seller profits.

Willy Loman and countless other salespeople have presented challenges to their managers and to the marketing executives who use the sales force as a competitive weapon. **Energize the Selling Effort** (Part V) by motivating the sales force to achieve the company's marketing and business goals. Top-level sales executives must create a clear sales task, use relevant salesperson selection criteria, emphasize important performance evaluation standards, enhance field sales management quality, and utilize well-directed compensation and reward plans.

As improving the sales effort has become more important and more difficult to achieve, sales forces are increasingly being enhanced and complemented with outside distributors and agents that are both customers to be satisfied and nurtured, and team members that help create value for the end customers. Distributors are just one element of today's "hybrid" marketing systems, where an entire array of vendors and subcontractors can be called upon to perform different tasks in the customer-seeking process. To achieve maximum coverage at minimum cost it is necessary to **Manage the Selling System** (Part VI) with intelligence, vigor, and foresight.

All six sections and virtually every article in this collection convey four underlying themes: profits, focus, relationships, and combining art and science.

Profit generation is the primary theme. The popular rhetoric about being "customer-oriented" and making sales a "value-added" process can easily obscure the central importance of profits. Certainly, increasing value to the customer will likely result in more sales. But customer orientation should not be viewed as an end in itself; it is only a means for achieving profits. Profits are a function of sales volume, the costs of creating value for the customer, operating costs, and price. It is important to recognize that price and value are not necessarily equivalent: price is the mediator among value, cost, and profitability. Each section in this book cautions the manager to consider whether the value-added to the customer exceeds the cost incurred at each step of the selling process.

Secondly, unfocused companies are not very profitable. This book stresses focus in selecting a target group of customers to serve, defining a meaningful sales task that creates value for those customers, and designing a sales effort that effectively accomplishes the task. Focusing involves the ability to recognize your own underlying motivations, needs, and goals, as well as those of the customer. In order to allocate resources efficiently, you must be able to see the big picture, to evaluate how a given transaction or longer-term relationship will benefit the company. Not all customers are created equal, and in this regard, it is important to recognize when the costs of pursuing a customer may outweigh the benefits. By focusing on overall objectives you encourage creative, cooperative, and profitable solutions to challenges.

Our third theme is relationships. Much of this volume is concerned with understanding, creating, and managing customer relationships. However, these are not the only important relationships in the selling effort. For example, the approach to an account that covers different geographical locations, organizational jurisdictions, or levels of hierarchy must be meticulously coordinated to ensure an effective selling and servicing program. Furthermore, the sales force depends upon its relationships with other parts of the company for guidance, support, and cooperation. Strong internal relationships are necessary for closing orders efficiently and satisfying customers.

It is important here to clarify what we mean by relationships. Not every interaction between seller and customer involves establishing a relationship. Despite the increasing complexity of the marketplace, a lot of business still takes the form of a traditional one-time transaction. A relationship that requires an investment in intimacy and longevity is, by definition, distinct from a discrete transaction. Nevertheless, even a single transaction requires coordination and commitment between buyer and seller. It is important to understand the nature and demands of each connection to allocate the appropriate resources where it is profitable to invest.

Finally, we consider the creative tension between art and science. Despite Willy Loman's concerns, selling and sales management *are* human endeavors that require respect, courtship, gratitude, and friendship. Many of the articles in this book stress this "soft" side of the sales effort. Meanwhile, scientific advancements, especially in communications and information technology, have provided salespeople, sales managers, and marketers with a whole new set of tools and approaches to enhance focus, improve relationships, and increase profitability. Behavioral science has also contributed useful insights about the dynamics of buying, selling, and sales management. Nevertheless, sophisticated economic formulas, state-of-the-art computers, and comprehensive market research cannot replace the art that develops from intuition, experience, and common sense. While science may be encroaching upon the venerable art of selling, today's effective and efficient selling effort is managed by a dynamic combination of both.

Seeking Customers

PART

I

Build Channels of Communication

Introduction

The articles in this section provide a broad introduction to the elements of profitable selling. These articles also express the four underlying themes running throughout the volume: profits, focus, relationships, and combining art and science. On the surface, these three articles may seem disparate: one describes new communications approaches; another focuses on the benefits of automation systems; the third illustrates the need for sales coordination across geography, product lines, and departmental functions.

Nevertheless, all three articles argue one fundamental point: the foundation of good selling is good communication. In order to create an efficient and effective sales program, the seller must establish channels of communication along three important dimensions:

1. *With the Customer.* Attracting a customer relies on the seller's ability to understand the customer's needs and to let the customer understand what the seller can provide. Communication between seller and buyer must flow in both directions; the best salespeople are not good talkers but good listeners, who recognize the interests and demands of the entire purchasing organization.
2. *Within the Company.* Sales is not an isolated function; an effective sales effort requires input from and feedback to all company functions and departments.
3. *Within the Team.* Complex account management often involves selling across product lines and from different geographic locations, to customers with decentralized purchasing processes. Competitive selling requires team commitment to a coordinated and integrated sales effort.

The first article in this collection, "New Ways to Reach Your Customers," by Benson Shapiro and John Wyman, was one of the early articles to suggest that seeking customers could be a highly disciplined process. Focusing on several communications techniques that evolved during the 1970s and early 1980s, the authors argue that national account management, demonstration centers, industrial stores, telemarketing, and new forms of catalog selling can be integrated with traditional tools (media advertising, direct mail advertising, telephone selling, trade shows, and face-to-face selling) to create "a more integrated, tailored, and cost-effective communications program than was previously possible." Furthermore, the authors argue that investing in an integrated communications program can be done rationally and efficiently, where the costs of developing a program are weighed against the benefits of more flexible and focused marketing.

In addition to describing the applications of each new communications technique, "New Ways" proposes a four-step approach for developing an effective communications program:

1. Analyze the communications costs.
2. Specify the communications needs.
3. Formulate a coherent program.
4. Monitor the total system.

The centerpiece of this approach is the "marketing-oriented income statement," which identifies fixed and variable communications costs and relates them to profits, thereby allowing the investor to analyze communications costs at a strategic level.

New communications techniques evolved largely in response to the increased need for persuasive impact, customization, speed, and customer convenience in attracting customers competitively. Harnessing these new techniques can improve the precision and impact of the marketing program, reducing communications costs by saving time and improving coordination of sales activities. Recently, the opportunities to reach customers have grown more complex, to include outside distributors and agents—a topic discussed in greater detail in Part VI. Given the wide range of communications approaches, the authors stress that careful planning is essential for designing "mix and match" programs that maximize efficiency and productivity.

The other two articles, "Automation to Boost Sales and Marketing," by Rowland Moriarty and Gordon Swartz, and "Teamwork for Today's Selling," by Frank Cespedes, Stephen Doyle, and Robert Freedman, focus on increasing efficiency by improving communications within the selling company. "Automation" illustrates the power of computerization in improving sales and marketing productivity. In fact, the technology available in computer hardware and software can be used to implement, coordinate, and enhance the types of communications approaches described in "New Ways."

Marketing and sales costs often represent one-quarter to one-third of total corporate costs. Automation of these functions, through marketing and sales productivity (MSP) systems, can increase the effectiveness and efficiency of seeking customers by streamlining operations, reducing operating costs, and improving customer service. The authors argue that MSP systems, such as data bases and networks designed to track leads, maintain mailing lists, and report expenses, decrease both the fixed and variable costs of seeking customers, allowing sellers to focus on the most profitable market segments, products, and accounts. As in "New Ways," the authors argue that investment in new programs and systems must be pursued wisely, with a clear vision of the costs weighed against the benefits. It does not make sense to invest in an MSP system if it does not add value to the sales effort.

Moriarty and Swartz argue that "marketers can get competitive advantage in two ways: by lowering costs and by enhancing the differentiation of the product or service offering." A commitment to communication enables sellers to compete in both ways. Well-planned communications programs allow sellers to represent their capabilities adequately and respond quickly and flexibly to customers' needs. Sellers can then coordinate and direct sales resources toward the highest priority prospects and customers. Efficient resource allocation improves sales productivity and lowers costs, making the selling company more competitive.

While "Automation" considers the contributions of information technology, "Teamwork" focuses on the human component, arguing that sales can be made more profitably when the sales force is motivated to work toward common goals as a team. This coordination is especially vital to managing major and national accounts competitively.

National account management was described in "New Ways" as "the ultimate form of both personal selling and management of the personal selling process." This approach evolved to handle the largest, most geographically dispersed, complex, and demanding customers. These accounts tend to have a disproportionate impact on revenues, costs, prices, and profits. Meanwhile, the internal mechanisms designed to service and manage these accounts have become increasingly decentralized. For these accounts, "selling depends on the vendor's ability to marshal its resources effectively across a range of buying locations, buying influences, product lines, and internal organizational boundaries."

In order to ensure that the sales effort is focused and coordinated, managers, salespeople, and support staff must be motivated to work as a unified team. Perhaps the simplest way to dissipate resources is to have members of the sales force working at cross-purposes or duplicating each other's efforts, adding significantly to costs, hurting revenue generation, and, of course, reducing profits. "Teamwork" argues that compensation, task clarity and goal setting, performance measurement, recruiting, and training programs should be designed to encourage team commitment. The authors stress, however, that the investment in sales coordination depends on the complexity of the account, the company's products, and the way it sells. Not every account requires a highly disciplined team effort: "The more complex the selling task, the more information must be exchanged between vendor and customer and the more information passed around among the vendor's salespeople working on a common account." As the other two articles do, "Teamwork" emphasizes the importance of carefully planning investments in sales improvement. The costs of investment should not exceed the increase in revenues resulting from the investment.

These three articles set the stage for the book, illuminating the central themes of profits, focus, relationships, and the integration of art and science. Despite the tremendous contributions of information and communications technology, selling is still largely a function of interpersonal relations, which are guided by the artful ability to recognize motivations, needs, and perceptions. From here, we will move through all the critical steps of managing a profitable customer-seeking process, including understanding customers, closing the sale, balancing price and value, and managing communications and distribution systems.

1

New Ways to Reach Your Customers

Benson P. Shapiro and John Wyman

From farther back than any of us can remember, personal selling, advertising, and sales promotion have been the essential marketing approaches. But these tested and proved methods for reaching customers also have their limitations, particularly in the light of two significant changes that have taken place in the business picture over the past decade.

1. The costs of communication climbed radically. Media costs skyrocketed. And the cost of a sales call, as estimated by McGraw-Hill, rose from $49 in 1969 to $137 in 1979.
2. A new set of options evolved, giving marketers a wider array of communications tools.

These developments mean that the marketing manager can make the best use of the newer methods, as well as the older ones, to respond to increasing top management demand for efficient and effective communication. In particular, the evolving options offer opportunities to improve the precision and impact of the marketing program, sometimes at great cost savings over the traditional methods.

There is no need for us to belabor the all too familiar change in communications costs. On the other hand, little note has been made of the newer options. Thus, in the first section of this article, we will focus on them. Then, in the second section, we will provide a four-step approach for developing a marketing program that makes the best use of both the newer and the older communications tools.

Evolving Options

In the past, the marketer's primary communications tools were *media advertising, direct mail advertising, telephone selling, trade shows*, and *face-to-face selling.* These traditional methods differed in impact and cost per message, with media advertising at the low end and personal selling at the high end. Telephone and personal selling offered flexibility in tailoring the message to the target prospect and in having two-way contact but at a substantial cost, particularly for the field sales force. Trade shows added the excitement and impact of product demonstration but were competitive and temporary in nature.

Whereas the opportunities to "mix and match" the five traditional approaches into a coherent, synergistic marketing program were limited, we believe that the increase in the number of available tools gives the marketing manager the ability to develop a more integrated, tailored, and cost-effective communications program than was previously possible.

The newer tools include *national account management, demonstration centers, industrial stores, telemarketing*, and new forms of *catalog selling.* These tools, used together and with the traditional methods, are leading to a new economics of selling. Let us look first at these five evolving options individually and then at the opportunities they offer when combined with the traditional methods.

NATIONAL ACCOUNT MANAGEMENT

A few large accounts comprise a disproportionately large percentage of almost any company's sales (industrial as well as consumer goods and services). National account management can often be applied: (a) if these large accounts are geographically or organizationally dispersed, (b) if the selling company has many interactions with the buying company's operating units, and (c) if the product and selling process are complex. National account management thus is an extension, improvement, and outgrowth of personal selling. In essence, this method is the ultimate form of both personal selling and management of the personal selling process.

National account management responds to the needs of the customer for a coordinated communications approach while giving the seller a method of coordinating the costs, activities, and objectives of the sales function for its most important accounts. It is expensive, but the value to customer and seller alike is high if the situation is appropriate and the concept well executed.

Many people and companies use other names for this approach. Banks (as well as some other companies) call it *relationship management* because it draws attention to the primary objective of creating and developing an enduring relationship between the selling and buying companies. Others call it *corporate account management* because the accounts are managed at the corporate level, although the customers buy from several divisions in a multidivisional corporation. Yet others prefer the term *international account management* because the relationships transcend national boundaries. We prefer to use *national account management* because it appears to be the most popular and descriptive term.

National account management programs share certain characteristics, depending on the sales situation.

First, the accounts managed are large relative to the rest of the company's accounts, sometimes generating more than $50 million each.

Second, the national account manager is often responsible for coordinating people who work in other divisions of the selling company or in other functional areas. (This raises a great many issues of conflicting objectives and priorities.)

Third, the national account manager often has responsibility for a team that includes support and operations people.

Finally, the manager calls on many people in the buying company in addition to those in the formal buying function (e.g., engineering, manufacturing, finance) and often gets involved in highly conceptual, financially oriented systems sales.

The first issue that confronts companies considering national account management is how many accounts to involve. At this point the marketing managers need to understand the difference between "special handling" for a few select accounts and a real national account management program. Almost any company can develop a way to give special attention to a few accounts. But a full-blown national account management program requires fundamental changes in selling philosophy, sales management, and sales organization. Often the special handling of a few select accounts by top-level sales and marketing managers will lead to a formal program because the managers involved cannot find enough time for both the accounts and their regular duties.

Once the program begins, the selection of national accounts is an important phase. American Can Co., for example, found that careful account selection helped to define the nature of the program and to ease its implementation. Many companies, including IBM, separate their programs into different account categories depending on size, geographical dispersion, and servicing needs.

National accounts need special support, as do the managers responsible for them. All of the standard issues of sales management arise: selection, training, supervision, and compensation. The job requires people with both selling and administrative skills. Training and supervision must be keyed to the need for both depth and breadth in skills. And compensation—both amount and form (salary, commission, or both)—becomes important.

But often the most sensitive matter is how to organize. Some companies organize their national account managers with line authority over a large, dispersed sales and support team. Some go so far as to create separate manufacturing operations for each account, and the account team becomes a profit center. Other companies prefer to view the national account managers as coordinators of salespeople who report to different profit centers or divisions. There is a myriad of choices between these two extremes.

DEMONSTRATION CENTERS

Specially designed showrooms, or demonstration centers, allow customers to observe and usually to try out complex industrial equipment. The approach supplements personal selling and works best when the equipment being demonstrated is complex and not portable. Demonstration centers have been used in many industries including telecommunications, data processing, electronic test gear, and machine tools. A variant of the approach is a traveling demonstration center in which the equipment (or process) for sale is mounted in a trailer truck or bus. Rank Xerox, for example, once used a railroad train to demonstrate its equipment all over Europe.

The demonstration center also supplements trade shows, with three major differences between them.

1. The demonstration center is permanent and thus can more easily be fitted in a company's marketing and sales schedule. Trade shows, on the other hand, are temporary and are not scheduled for the convenience of any single company.
2. The company can determine the location of the demonstration center, unlike trade shows.
3. Demonstration centers are designed to provide a competition-free environment for the selling process. Trade shows, of course, are filled with competitors.

But the primary benefit to the seller comes from demonstration—often to high-level executives who are unavailable for standard sales presentations. Demonstration centers in some situations, furthermore, replace months of regular field selling. The economic trade-off then becomes partially a comparison of the cost of the center versus the cost of traveling salespeople. Demonstrating equipment or processes often has more impact than describing them. The most effective demonstration centers relate directly to the customer's needs and include a custom-designed demonstration.

An outstanding example of the concept involved the use of trailer-mounted, demonstration-sized versions of Union Carbide's UNOX waste water treatment system by the company's Linde division. In the early 1970s, Linde used these models (costing $100,000 each) to demonstrate that its system could handle the waste water of an industrial plant or even a particular municipality.

Linde had available to it all of the traditional communications approaches. UNOX sales, however, had been slow and difficult. After carefully considering the time and effort involved in selling, Linde executives decided that the demonstration units would speed sales, generate some sales that otherwise would be lost, and save the substantial expense of traditional approaches. And the demonstration units in fact accomplished all these objectives.

INDUSTRIAL STORES

This approach also involves a demonstration of equipment or a process with the emphasis generally on cost reduction, not the creation of seller benefits. Stores are permanent, but the same concept is used by companies that present customer seminars and demonstrations in hotels, trade shows, or other temporary facilities. Here too the idea is to bring the customer to the salesperson. Boeing Computer Services, for example, has used hotel room demonstrations effectively in selling structural analysis computer time-sharing services to engineering firms. The store approach works well when:

> The sale is too small to justify sales calls. A substantial percentage (often as high as two-thirds) of industrial salespeople's time is spent traveling and waiting to see customers. If the sale is small, personal selling is not economical. One way around the problem is to ask the prospect to do the traveling. Thus, the customer comes to the salesperson's location, not vice versa.
>
> The product or process is complex and lends itself to demonstration.
>
> The company does not sell many products to the same customer. (If, on the other hand, the company has a large, active account with the same customer, the cost of a sales call can be amortized over the sale of many products.)

The store approach has been successful in the small business computer industry, where Digital Equipment has more than 20 stores in operation and development. IBM uses a similar approach but promotes it differently, using office space instead of retail space and encouraging appointments instead of drop-ins. In November 1980, however, IBM announced a commitment to develop stores more along the evolving concept used by Digital and other competitors. Xerox has made stores a major part of its marketing strategy.

Industrial stores vary widely according to product lines offered and approach used to attract people to visit. Xerox carries a wide variety of items, including many *not* made by Xerox; other stores offer limited lines produced only by the owners. Some, especially those in prime retail locations, can generate walk-in traffic. Others are in more office-oriented settings. For management, the stores certainly raise retail-oriented questions—location, fixtures, sales staffing—concerning their operations. In addition to display and sales service, stores can also provide physical distribution and service facilities to customers.

Economics has played a large part in the development of the store concept. As selling and travel costs escalate, the use of stores will become even more popular.

TELEMARKETING

Telephone marketing is an important emerging trend that companies can exploit in five ways—as a less costly substitute for personal selling, a supplement to personal selling, a higher-impact substitute for direct mail and media advertising, a supplement to direct mail and other media, and a replacement for other slower, less convenient communications techniques.

COST SAVINGS.   Telephone selling has traditionally provided a highly customized means of two-way communication. Greater sophistication in telecommunications equipment and services, new marketing approaches, and broader applications have turned telephone selling into telemarketing. It still does not provide the quality of a personal visit but is much cheaper. While a commercial or industrial salesperson might average perhaps 5 or 6 fast personal sales calls per day, he or she can average perhaps 30 long telephone calls. The costs are much lower because of the lack of travel. Personal sales calls tend to cost upward of $100 each, while normal-length telephone sales calls cost generally under $10 each.

The cost advantage makes telemarketing a good substitute for visits to small accounts. Fieldcrest, for example, has been using telemarketing in conjunction with catalogs to introduce and sell bed and bath fashions to stores in sparsely settled areas.

SUPPLEMENT TO PERSONAL VISITS.   Some selling situations require periodic sales visits. Often the cost of the required call frequency is greater than the sales volume justifies and, in these cases, telephone calls can supplement personal visits. The visits might be made two to four times per year and the telephone calls eight to ten times per year for a total frequency of one per month—but at a cost substantially lower than twelve visits. Personal visits would be used for the opening presentation of, say, a new line of apparel or furniture or the sale of equipment, while telephone calls would be used for fill-in orders or supply sales.

SUBSTITUTE FOR DIRECT MAIL.   Some insurance salespeople who wish to keep in touch with their customers have switched from using direct mail to the telephone, which gives greater impact—at an admittedly higher cost. For the economics to work well, the person called must be either an existing customer or a good prospect, not just a random name from the phone book. Telemarketing has been successful in selling subscription renewals and other continuity sales and could also aid sales of large consumer durables such as automobiles, swimming pools, and appliances. A Cadillac salesperson might, for example, telephone owners of Lincoln Continentals or Mercedes that are a few years old.

AS A SUPPLEMENT.   Telemarketing can add to as well as replace direct mail and media advertising. Many companies have effectively used 800 telephone numbers in direct mail, television, and print media advertising. Such a program has three advantages over mail replies:

1. The prospect can make an immediate commitment to purchase while the idea is fresh and the desire for action greatest—and, perhaps more important, he or she can get an immediate reply;
2. It is easier for most people to telephone than to fill in a coupon and mail it;
3. The selling company can become actively involved in supplying product information to aid the customer's decision making, and the customer can also express concerns to be responded to by the telephone salespeople in future media communication or even in later product development.

The combined media/telemarketing approach has been successful for a variety of products, including specialty coffees, smokeless tobacco, books, and records. AT&T uses the approach to sell many of its products and services. An additional advantage is the quick generation of data about media effectiveness. Within a few days a company or its advertising agency can determine the effectiveness of a new advertising campaign. With mail response, the time lag slows the analysis so that a campaign is generally run longer before review.

CUSTOMER-COMPANY COORDINATION.   Finally, the telephone can be used as a part of a communications program to tie companies to their constituencies. The responsiveness and convenience of the telephone, combined with its two-way message content, make it particularly appropriate for this use. A dissatisfied customer, for example, can get a quick response to a problem.[1]

Confused customers who need product information can get it when they need it most, thus preventing product misuse and abuse.

O.M. Scott & Sons Co. uses this approach to good advantage in its lawn and garden care business. Problems with the product or its distribution become clear to the seller and can be rectified quickly without much loss of the expensive time of dealers and salespeople. A manufacturer can use the telephone to gather information from salespeople or dealers to find, for example, whether a new product is selling well or whether competitors met a price increase.

The use of the telephone in marketing can create junk phone calls much like junk mail in direct mail advertising. For both economic and customer relations reasons, we advocate the use of selective telemarketing, showing good judgment and good taste. Otherwise, the attention-getting quality of the telephone in uncontrolled situations can irritate consumers.

The telephone's particular mix of benefits and growing cost-effectiveness versus other media make it an increasingly important part of the communications mix. Ongoing telephone contact with customers or prospects can produce important information through close communication. And once the line is open, there are ever-increasing opportunities to creatively cross-sell complementary products and services.

CATALOG SELLING

An old approach in the consumer goods market, catalog selling is an evolving method in industrial and commercial markets. Companies active in the office- and computer-supply businesses have found catalogs to be an efficient way of generating the relatively small dollar sales typical of their businesses. The Drawing Board, an office supply company in Dallas, apparently relies solely on its catalog for communication with customers.

Wright Line, Inc., a $50 million vendor of computer-related supplies and capital equipment for computer rooms, programmers and analysts, and small businesses, has developed an elaborate communications system that includes personal selling, telemarketing, and catalogs. The 140-person sales force makes visits for the larger capital equipment sales and for developing systems sales. The quarterly catalog generates both fill-in sales of capital equipment and supplies for already-sold systems, as well as orders from customers whose size would not justify a personal call. Customers can place orders by mail, through the salespeople, or by telephone.

Most orders come in by telephone and mail. The catalog—a new approach at Wright Line—has improved sales volume more than Wright Line executives had expected.

Wright Line's integrated approach developed through a combination of careful analysis and trial-and-error testing. Management has been willing and able to try new approaches, carefully analyze the results, and commit resources to the successful experiments.

Other industries have also used catalogs, particularly in conjunction with telephone order centers or telemarketing centers. Sigma Chemical Co., for example, uses a catalog to sell enzymes for laboratory use, although competitors generally use sales forces. Other catalog applications include electronic components and industrial supplies. The approach is highly cost-effective in transmitting a great deal of information to selected prospects and customers in a usable, inexpensive format.

It is interesting to relate the development of the five evolving options to the more traditional approaches. Personal selling led to national account management. Demonstration centers and industrial stores are variations on the trade show. Telemarketing developed from telephone selling and the early inside order desks of industrial distributors. And industrial stores and catalog selling are based on retail stores and consumer catalogs, such as those used by Sears, Roebuck and Co., that date from the nineteenth century.

Economics and technology are driving the evolution, and the need for more precise communications programs is encouraging it.

Creating a Program

The newer ways of selling, when combined with the traditional communications approaches, enable marketers to make precise choices in developing their communications programs. Four major steps are necessary for developing an effective program:

1. Analyze the communications costs.
2. Specify the communications needs.
3. Formulate a coherent program.
4. Monitor the total system.

ANALYZE CURRENT COSTS

The basic device for understanding marketing costs is a marketing-oriented income statement that divides all costs into three primary categories—manufacturing, physical distribution, and communication—and two generally smaller categories—nondivisible overhead and profit (see Exhibit I).

This income statement differs from the company's income statement. To be useful, it should begin with the price the customer pays. Distributor discounts are allocated to communications cost (the value of the retail and/or wholesale salespeople, display, advertising, trade show attendance) and physical distribution cost (order processing, inventory carrying, transportation). If the distributor customizes the product in the field (e.g., adds accessories, cuts to shape, mixes), the cost of doing so should be allocated to the manufacturing task.

The well-designed marketing-oriented income statement helps marketers determine the role of each set of costs (manufacturing, distribution, and communication) in their businesses. Marketers can then ask questions such as:

Where should I concentrate my cost-cutting activities?

What do I get and, more important perhaps, what does my customer get from each of the three functions?

Do the benefits provided by each function justify the costs?

Marketing executives can thus categorize their businesses as communications-intensive, distribution-intensive, or manufacturing-intensive and can then analyze competitors from the same viewpoints. Avon Products, for example, trades off higher physical distribution costs (sending its cosmetics and toiletries in small packages to its several hundred thousand salespeople) against the higher communications costs of its competitors, which place more emphasis on advertising but use more efficient distribution methods (large sales to supermarket and drug chains that depend on the customer to pick up the order and transport it home).

The marketing-oriented income statement helps to analyze communications costs at a strategic, but not a tactical, level. We cannot consider the detailed costs without first specifying marketers' communications needs or objectives.

Exhibit I. A Marketing-Oriented Income Statement

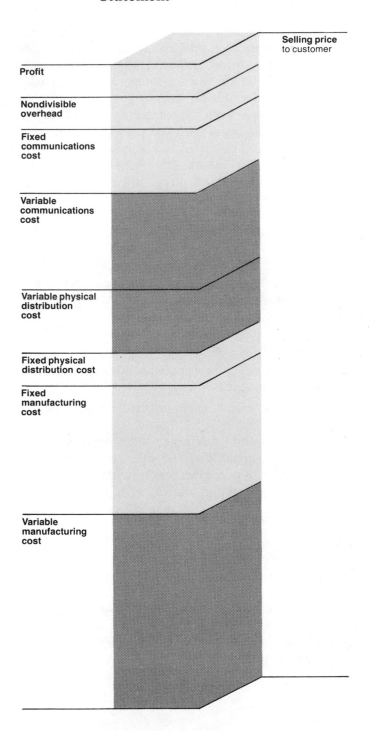

Selling price
to customer

Profit

Nondivisible
overhead

Fixed
communications
cost

Variable
communications
cost

Variable physical
distribution
cost

Fixed physical
distribution cost

Fixed
manufacturing
cost

Variable
manufacturing
cost

SPECIFY NEEDS

Marketing executives must state precisely the objectives of the communications program and also understand the costs of achieving each objective. There are many different types of communication between a company and its marketing constituencies. Companies may wish to strive for four major goals in specifying their needs:

1. *Persuasive Impact.* Two-way communication is more effective than one-way communication. Media advertising by itself, for example, tends to be one way—from the seller to the buyer—while methods such as telemarketing allow a two-way dialogue.
2. *Customization.* Different people, even within the same buying unit, desire different information, and opportunities for customization vary. Two-way communication, of course, enables the seller to tailor a message to the precise needs of a specific customer at a given moment.
3. *Speed.* Some information is much more time sensitive than others. An order to a commodities broker, for example, is urgent. And because we live in an era that stresses instant gratification, many consumers want to obtain the product as soon as possible after making their choice, even if they have labored over that choice for weeks, months, or even years.
4. *Convenience.* Almost everybody, from a professional purchasing agent to a child buying a stick of bubble gum, wants convenience in making purchases.

FORMULATE A PROGRAM

Marketers can create the most effective communications program only with a complete understanding of the relationships among both the old and the evolving options. Perhaps even more important than the media on their own is their potential for integration into a synergistic system that uses each to its best advantage. Exhibit II shows the evolving and traditional options and their varying impact and cost per message.

Combinations are especially powerful because each medium has a different mix of benefits and economics. It is easy to envision a communications system that uses all 10 of the media and combinations listed in Exhibit II. To illustrate, media advertising gives

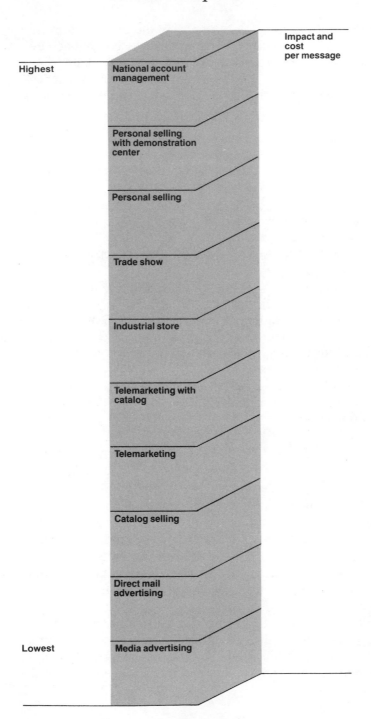

Exhibit II. Comparing the Evolving and Traditional Options

Impact and cost per message

Highest — National account management

Personal selling with demonstration center

Personal selling

Trade show

Industrial store

Telemarketing with catalog

Telemarketing

Catalog selling

Direct mail advertising

Lowest — Media advertising

broad coverage at a low cost. Direct mail can be used for a somewhat focused message to a specific group of people at a very reasonable cost. Catalog selling provides a great deal of information, particularly for a wide product assortment, to a focused audience. Telemarketing increases the cost relative to options below it but adds a two-way personalized message, convenience, speed, and the best timing.

The combination of catalogs and telemarketing mixes good economics, much information transmittal, and the advantages of the telephone. Industrial stores and trade shows offer the benefits of personal selling with the cost advantages of a stationary sales force. Of course, customer convenience suffers.

Again, personal selling provides important advantages at a high cost. The addition of a demonstration center increases the cost but provides important benefits in major sales. And, finally, national account management provides the ultimate communications medium at the highest cost.

Different approaches can be used for different customers, products, situations, and communications needs. Companies that market many products to many different types of customers will generally need a wider variety of communications modes than companies having a narrower product and customer mix. It should be no surprise that companies such as Digital Equipment and AT&T, with their many products, many types of customers, and new technologies to sell, have been at the forefront of the new approaches. They had little choice.

Time is an important dimension in the development of a synergistic communications program for three major reasons:

First, marketers must plan each communications program with regard to the events of the product's life cycle. The planned introduction of a variation in a product, for example, might require an equally carefully planned change in the communications mix—perhaps to emphasize a new use or a new set of users. Customer knowledge moves through its own life cycle. At some points in a product's life, developing brand awareness among prospects might be particularly important, while at other times the primary emphasis would be on reassuring existing customers.

Second, it takes a long time to implement communications programs. The progression from initial start-up to effective operation of a national account program, for example, can take four to five years. The same is true, but to a lesser extent, of the other media shown in Exhibit II. It can take a year to develop, test, and carefully execute a good media advertising or catalog sales program. In general, the communications methods with greater impact and higher cost per message in Exhibit II require more time to implement than those lower in the hierarchy.

Third, careful planning over time involves the raison d'être of all marketing activities—the customer. Customers remember. Thus, frequently changing communications programs is ineffective, inefficient, and confusing. Customers used to sales calls will not immediately embrace an industrial store or a telemarketing program. All communications programs must reflect a concern for the customer's memory.

The mix-and-match process of developing a program from a set of communications media alternatives has four integral dimensions: market segments, products, media, and time. A lack of concern for any of these elements weakens the whole program.

MONITOR THE TOTAL SYSTEM

In some communications-intensive companies the cost of communication can be upward of one-fourth of total sales. Obviously, such expenditures warrant careful control.

Wherever possible, managers should gather and analyze all the data related to the communications process. Executives who use industrial stores will have to think as retailers do about such things as traffic (flow of people into the store) and accessibility.

For example, they should monitor the number of visitors to an industrial store, the source of their initial communication, the percentage of "qualified" prospects, and the percentage of sales. Catalog marketers and telemarketers, of course, can monitor such factors as the average size of an order by customer type, the types of products purchased, and frequency of order.

Effectiveness and Efficiency

This article began by discussing reasons for the evolution of newer communications options which, in essence, developed because of cost pressures and the need to accomplish new tasks. The evolving options save costs in three ways.

1. *Greater Impact.* A demonstration center, for example, replaces a great deal of traditional personal selling effort. The concept that a smaller amount of high-impact media is more effective than a larger amount of low-impact media is behind a good deal of the evolving options.
2. *Time Saving.* Marketers can save time either through the use of the medium with the greatest impact (as in the demonstration center) or through less travel (as in the case of industrial stores, telemarketing, or catalogs).
3. *Greater Coordination and Closer Control.* Marketers can also eliminate waste through greater coordination, as in national account management, or through the closer control possible in industrial stores, telemarketing centers, and catalog operations than in a traditional field sales force.

In summary, then, careful cost analysis, precise needs specification, creative program formulation, and meticulous monitoring will lead to more effective and efficient communication with greater customer impact and lower costs.

Note

1. For an example of this application, see "Good Listener: At Procter & Gamble Success Is Largely Due to Heeding Customer," *The Wall Street Journal*, April 29, 1980.

2
Automation to Boost Sales and Marketing

Rowland T. Moriarty and Gordon S. Swartz

In the rush to automate, the marketing and sales function is the next frontier. As everybody knows, over the past decade information systems have been making great inroads in engineering and manufacturing. Automation has cut direct labor to a small fraction of production costs—an average of 8% to 12% in manufacturing companies. Therefore, wringing yet more cost reductions from production labor is increasingly difficult. In such technically advanced industries as computers, semiconductors, airframes, metalworking, and autos, incremental investments are now garnering diminishing returns.

On the other hand, investments in marketing and sales automation systems hold tremendous potential for productivity improvements. Marketing and sales costs average 15% to 35% of total corporate costs (not just production costs). So a focus on marketing and sales provides a welcome lever for boosting productivity. Moreover, the importance of marketing and sales services is growing. According to the U.S. trade representative and the National Association of Accountants, manufacturers' service activities account for 75% to 85% of all value added.[1] This means that the price a product can command is less a reflection of raw materials and labor than of marketing-related services like selecting appropriate product features, determining the product mix, and ensuring product availability and delivery.

In cases we have reviewed, sales increases arising from advanced marketing and sales information technology have ranged from 10% to more than 30%, and investment returns have often exceeded

100%. These returns may sound like the proverbial free lunch, but they are real.

Because of the complexity of their marketing organizations, large companies are good prospects for what we call marketing and sales productivity (MSP) systems. Tangles of national account management, direct sales, telemarketing, direct mail, literature fulfillment, advertising, customer service, dealers, and distributors all offer opportunities for efficiency improvements. But even small companies that adopt MSP systems can expect impressive results.

Marketing automation investments by a $7 billion electronics manufacturer and an $8 million custom printing company each produced a first-year return of more than 100%. The electronics concern installed a sales support system for more than 500 salespeople. Sales rose 33%, sales force productivity rose 31%, and sales force attrition dropped 40%. The reduced attrition alone produced savings in recruiting and training costs that paid for the company's $2.5 million investment in less than 12 months. At the custom printer, an $80,000 investment in a minicomputer and telemarketing software returned a 25% increase in sales and attained payback in less than 6 months.

Increasing marketing productivity even a small amount can have a great impact on the bottom line. MSP systems have a double punch because they can reduce fixed costs and variable costs. Lower fixed costs mean lower breakeven points. So a given percentage increase in sales produces a correspondingly larger increase in operating profits, as the chart on the next page shows. Meanwhile, lower variable costs mean that every sale contributes more to the bottom line. Indeed, because lower variable costs make the slope of the new contribution curve steeper, the absolute size of the financial advantage continues to grow as sales rise. (See Exhibit I.)

Despite the proven worth of this technology, few companies have automated any part of their marketing and sales functions. Even fewer appear to understand the significant strategic benefits that can accrue from marketing and sales automation; most early adopters have automated as a matter of faith rather than as part of a strategy for gaining competitive advantage. A better approach begins with an understanding of what marketing and sales automation can do, how it works, and how it can be implemented.

Exhibit I.

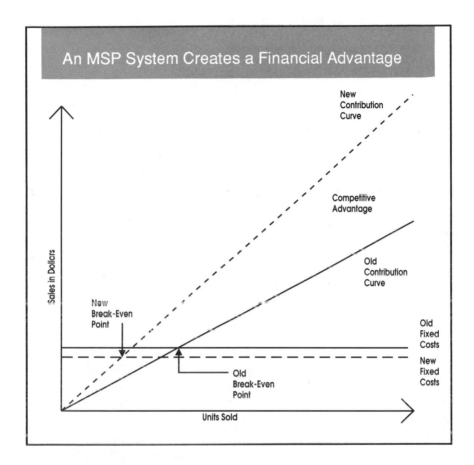

What the Systems Do

Distinct from general office automation systems, MSP networks are of course specific to marketing and sales. They support more intense product or service differentiation, improved customer service, reduced operating costs, and more streamlined operations. Here are some MSP systems and the tasks for which they are customarily used:

Salesperson Productivity Tools. Planning and reporting of sales calls, reporting of expenses, entering orders, checking inventory and order

status, managing distributors, tracking leads, and managing accounts.

Direct Mail and Fulfillment. Merging, cleaning, and maintaining
mailing lists; subsetting lists (or markets); tracking and forwarding
leads; customizing letters, envelopes, and labels; generating "picking
lists" for literature packages; and managing literature inventory.

Telemarketing. Merging, cleaning, and maintaining calling lists;
subsetting lists (or markets); tracking and forwarding leads; ranking
prospects; and prompting scripts (sales, customer service, and support).

Sales and Marketing Management. Providing automated sales management reports (sales forecasts, sales activity, forecasts versus ac-
tuals, and so on); designing and managing sales territories; and
analyzing marketing and sales programs by such criteria as market,
territory, product, customer type, price, and channel.

MSP systems can automate the work of a single salesperson, a
single marketing activity like direct mail, or a company's entire
marketing and sales operation. MSP systems also cut across every
type of information technology from single-user PCs to networks
of PCs, minicomputers, and mainframes serving thousands of
users.

A simple system meets the needs of one fast-growing $25 million
producer of data communications equipment that sells its products
through 65 distributors. To cut down on paperwork in handling
sales leads, the company adopted a PC-based MSP system. (See
Exhibit II.) Compare this with the networks supporting the more
than 5,000 direct salespeople of a major office automation vendor.
(See Exhibit III.) This vendor's system combines direct selling,
distributor relationships, telemarketing, and direct mail to: generate, qualify, rank-order, distribute, and track sales leads; fill
prospects' requests for product and price information; update customer and prospect files; provide sales and technical product support by telephone; and automate order entry and sales reporting.

While the scales of these two networks are obviously vastly
different, both of them collect, organize, and update information
about every lead generated, every sales task performed, and every
customer or prospect closed or terminated. What is less obvious,
but no less important, is the basis both systems provide for improving marketing and sales executives' decision making.

Most MSP data bases contain essential information on customers,

Exhibit II.

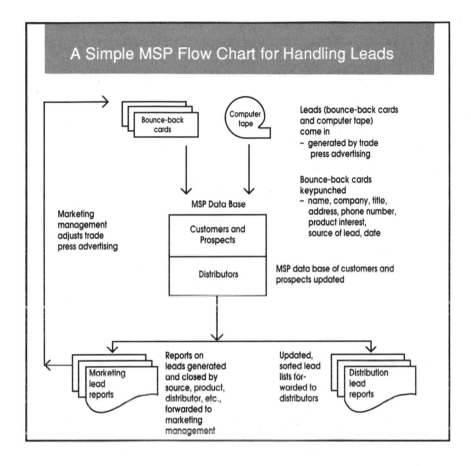

A Simple MSP Flow Chart for Handling Leads

Bounce-back cards

Computer tape

Leads (bounce-back cards and computer tape) come in
- generated by trade press advertising

Bounce-back cards keypunched
- name, company, title, address, phone number, product interest, source of lead, date

MSP Data Base

Marketing management adjusts trade press advertising

Customers and Prospects

Distributors

MSP data base of customers and prospects updated

Marketing lead reports

Reports on leads generated and closed by source, product, distributor, etc., forwarded to marketing management

Updated, sorted lead lists forwarded to distributors

Distribution lead reports

prospects, products, marketing programs, and marketing channels. Some systems supplement the essentials with industry data (growth rates, entries, exits, and regulatory trends) and data on competitors (products, pricing, sales trends, and market shares). For most businesses, the information incorporates a subtle but important shift from other data bases. Rather than focusing on products (What was the cost to produce each unit? How many units were made, sold, and shipped?), the MSP data base is customer-driven.

Whenever marketing or sales activities are performed, the data base captures information that answers questions about customers

Exhibit III.

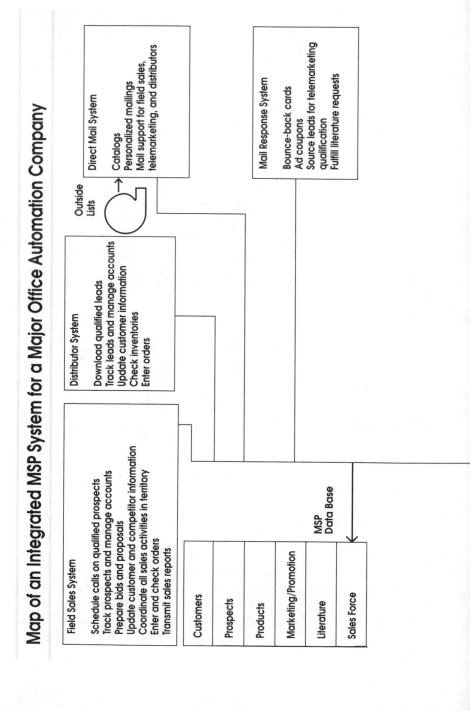

Map of an Integrated MSP System for a Major Office Automation Company

Field Sales System

Schedule calls on qualified prospects
Track prospects and manage accounts
Prepare bids and proposals
Update customer and competitor information
Coordinate all sales activities in territory
Enter and check orders
Transmit sales reports

Distributor System

Download qualified leads
Track leads and manage accounts
Update customer information
Check inventories
Enter orders

Direct Mail System

Catalogs
Personalized mailings
Mail support for field sales,
  telemarketing, and distributors

Outside
Lists

Mail Response System

Bounce-back cards
Ad coupons
Source leads for telemarketing
  qualification
Fulfill literature requests

Customers

Prospects

Products

Marketing/Promotion

Literature

Sales Force

MSP
Data Base

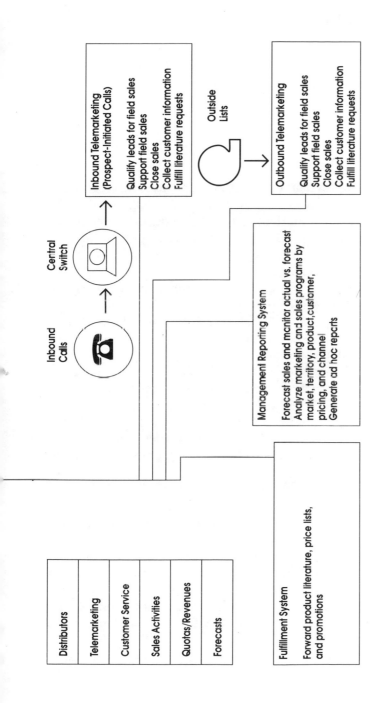

Inbound Calls

Central Switch

Inbound Telemarketing
(Prospect-Initiated Calls)

Qualify leads for field sales
Support field sales
Close sales
Collect customer information
Fulfill literature requests

Outside Lists

Outbound Telemarketing

Qualify leads for field sales
Support field sales
Close sales
Collect customer information
Fulfill literature requests

Management Reporting System

Forecast sales and monitor actual vs. forecast
Analyze marketing and sales programs by market, territory, product, customer, pricing, and channel
Generate ad hoc reports

Distributors

Telemarketing

Customer Service

Sales Activities

Quotas/Revenues

Forecasts

Fulfillment System

Forward product literature, price lists, and promotions

and their needs. Who were the prospects? What were their interests? How were these interests generated? Which sales or marketing personnel performed which tasks? When were the tasks performed? Which follow-up tasks are required and when? Did any sales result? Gradually the data base becomes a rich source of marketing and sales information, enabling management to track marketing activities and measure the results of marketing programs.

How They Aid Productivity

MSP systems improve productivity in two ways. First, automation of selling and direct marketing support tasks boosts the efficiency of the sales and marketing staff. Second, automating the collection and analysis of marketing information improves the timeliness and quality of marketing and sales executives' decision making.

These networks make direct sales and direct marketing more efficient by automating highly repetitive support tasks, like answering requests for product literature and writing letters, and by reducing the time salespeople spend on nonselling tasks, like scheduling sales calls, compiling sales reports, generating proposals and bids, and entering orders. In 1985, Xerox installed an internally developed MSP system in its southern region. Xerox credits the system with a 10% to 20% gain in sales force productivity and with trimming $3 million off the company's 1987 marketing support and overhead budget. By automating sales administration and support tasks, Xerox has given its salespeople more time to sell.[2]

MSP systems for direct marketing also hone the efficiency of customer contacts. For example, a system for the telemarketing function can schedule and dial calls based on the prospect's priority, prompt the telemarketer with a sales script, and automatically update customer files. At Aratex Services, a $500 million uniform supply company based in Encino, California, telemarketers using the company's old manual system each made 35 to 40 calls per day and about one sale per month. Working with an automated system, each telemarketer now makes 50 or 60 calls daily and lands three or four sales per month.[3]

Automated networks also elevate the impact of each sales communication. Access to the central data base gives salespeople and direct marketers information to improve the quality of the contact, whether it is by mail, by telephone, or in person. A large financial services concern uses a telemarketing system to handle account inquiries. While responding to a customer's request or query, the telemarketer is prompted by the system to update the customer's profile information and to cross-sell other financial products.

At a division of Vanity Fair that makes women's and children's apparel, salespeople use laptop PCs to access the corporate data base for up-to-date inventory and order status information on 2,000 stockkeeping units. This step has trimmed the company's order cycle from more than two weeks to just three days. It also has made ordering more accurate, resulting in greater customer satisfaction, reduced order cancellations, and a 10% increase in sales.

In companies with many channels, MSP systems upgrade efficiency by using the central data base to track and coordinate all marketing activity. Without this coordination, independent marketing groups often unwittingly pursue conflicting goals. At one multibillion-dollar office automation company, a direct salesperson had just nailed down a big order by giving a key account the "maximum" price discount. Before the deal was signed, however, the telemarketing group reached this customer and undercut the salesperson's price by 10%. Aside from the damage to its reputation, this vendor lost much of its expected margin on the sale.

This company is now installing an MSP system that will collect and organize information on all marketing programs and activities, including: (1) all customer contacts, whether by mail, phone, direct salesperson, or national account manager; (2) the status of all sales efforts; (3) the origins of all leads; (4) all leads that are being qualified internally and by whom, and all leads that have been forwarded to distributors; (5) all customers who decided to buy; (6) what and when they purchased; and (7) any incentives or promotions that helped close the deal. Coordination of information through this system is expected to prevent further embarrassments.

A Management Tool

Creation of an MSP data base is an investment in astute management. The data base chronicles every one of a company's marketing and sales activities, from advertising that generates leads to direct mail and telephone qualification of the leads to closing the first sale—all the way through the life of each account. It enables marketing and sales management to relate marketing actions with marketplace results.

At the $25 million data communications company whose lead-handling system we diagrammed, marketing managers use this system to evaluate media placements on the basis of sales closed. Before this procedure was in place, the company had no way to link information on leads to sales and evaluated media placements solely on the number of leads generated, not closed.

MSP systems also reduce marketing inertia because they streamline the implementation of marketing programs. For example, after designing an in-house system to organize and manage its customer/prospect files, one $2.5 million industrial manufacturer let 70 manufacturer's agents go and replaced them with in-house direct mail and telemarketing functions. The results? The company raised its accounts by 50% and cut marketing costs from 18% of sales to 13%.

Systems for sales force automation also drive the rapid implementation of less drastic changes in marketing programs. By using telecommunications software and laptop PCs, Du Pont's Remington Arms division has trimmed the time requirement for a national rollout of pricing and promotional programs from two weeks to less than two days.

As marketing managers become accustomed to these systems, they find new uses for them, like analyzing and modeling the buying behavior of prospects and customers. The data base at Excelan, a $39 million marketer of circuit boards and software in San Jose, California, was essential in identifying a shift in customers' buying behavior from a very technical product focus to an office automation orientation. This discovery has influenced the marketing and sales managers' decisions about hiring and training employees as well as about selecting and developing new target markets.

Account histories also improve management's ability to devise and implement account management policies based on profits. By linking orders, services delivered, and prices paid with the actual costs of lead generation, preselling, closing, distribution, and post-sale support, MSP systems furnish the tools for analyzing and adjusting the marketing mix. Grede Foundries, a Milwaukee producer of castings for original equipment manufacturers, has used the MSP system to develop a "perceived quality index" that yields a more complete and more accurate measure of customers' reactions than simply tracking returned goods. The system also provides pricing support. By tracking quoted prices and final selling prices, the system gives management a better idea of the price that will win a particular job.[4]

Moreover, automated networks coordinate and direct sales resources—including salespeople, distributors and agents, direct mailers, telemarketers, and manufacturers' representatives—toward the highest priority prospects and customers. Hewlett-Packard's Qualified Lead Tracking System (QUILTS) electronically transmits inquiries to a telemarketing center, which qualifies and ranks them and electronically returns them to H-P headquarters. The company has trimmed the turnaround time for leads from as much as 14 weeks to as little as 48 hours. "Hot" leads are handled even faster; they are telephoned to the field sales force from the telemarketing center.[5] Similarly, field salespeople in Chevron Chemical's fertilizer division in San Francisco use laptop PCs to access rank-ordered prospect lists in the company's mainframe. At any time, the salespeople have access to leads that are only 24 hours old. Before automation, new prospect lists were printed at headquarters and mailed to the field reps, which took one to two weeks.

Finally, the MSP data base is a management tool for making better use of marketing resources—that is, ensuring that they are employed to further corporate goals rather than the goals of individual marketing or sales groups. While this may sound like something management does without effort, our research shows that optimizing marketing resources is much more easily said than done. In several companies we've looked at, salespeople routinely discard hundreds or even thousands of sales leads, making little or no effort to evaluate or review them. In essence, they are dissipating the resources that generated these leads—budgets for advertising, trade shows, public relations, and other communications media.

In their defense, the salespeople complain that pursuing raw leads is a waste of time. And they are generally right. In one of these companies, salespeople who followed up the raw leads averaged only one or two sales per month, while those who followed their "instincts" averaged more than three. The cost of pursuing the raw leads was at least one lost sale per salesperson per month. To the salespeople, ignoring the leads was common sense. On the other hand, the advertising group, which was evaluated on the number of leads generated, was increasing its budgets to generate more and more leads. One company has solved this problem by implementing an MSP system that will use telemarketing to qualify leads before sending them to the salespeople. The system will also close the loop, allowing management to evaluate both the company's advertising placements and its sales efforts on the basis of their contributions to revenues and earnings.

Efficiencies gained through task automation and improved marketing management are interdependent and reinforcing. Task automation drives the collection of more complete customer and marketplace information, and more informed decision making targets marketing and sales activities where they are most effective. In this way, marketers get a bigger payoff from low-cost, low-impact selling methods, like direct mail and catalogs, as data bases customize the timing and content of mass-marketing campaigns. At the same time, high-cost, high-impact selling methods, like personal selling and national account management, become more efficient as MSP systems perform routine sales support tasks, reduce nonselling time, and synchronize the use of these resources.

When you combine low-cost, low-impact methods with high-cost, high-impact approaches to gain just the right amount of stimulus at just the right time, you can obtain hefty impact at minimum cost. Hewlett-Packard, for one, has taken advantage of this synergy and has discovered the savings made possible by orchestrating direct mail, telemarketing, and personal selling.

How to Get from Here to There

The cases we have reviewed show that companies implementing MSP systems encounter many of the same barriers they would confront adopting any new technology.[6] From our observation, the process can be streamlined by following six guiding principles.

1. *Clarify the scale of the project as well as potential additions.* An audit of the marketing and sales tasks will yield these categories: those that must be automated now, those that will or may be automated later, and those that will not be automated. This simple exercise will identify marketing and sales activities that

must be coordinated and focus the automation effort on getting measurable results without sacrificing flexibility.

It is important to view the project not from the perspective of the marketing groups but from a corporate perspective. With a corporate view, the company can build a "battleship"—a system that takes advantage of information-sharing and task-coordination synergies. Without this strategic perspective, independent marketing groups are more likely to invest in a number of incompatible and wasteful "rowboats." And even a rowboat can cause problems. At a big high-tech manufacturer, eight salespeople had their own PC-based sales force automation system installed. By raising issues of compatibility, data entry, and "file structure definitions," they delayed the start-up of a companywide, 300-salesperson MSP system for more than a year.

2. *Concentrate on tasks that can add value for the customer.* As in other corporate activities, marketers can get competitive advantage in two ways: by lowering costs and by enhancing the differentiation of the product or service offering. At the custom printer we referred to, streamlined job-costing and order-entry processes enable customers to price and place orders with one phone call. The "real-time" order-entry and order-tracking capabilities of the Vanity Fair unit's salespeople have upgraded its customer service. In both cases, customers benefit from better service, and sellers benefit from lower costs.

Other companies add value by using automation to improve the exchange of information during sales calls. The 22 salespeople in Hercules's Fragrance and Food Ingredient Group use their laptop PCs and a computer program called Flavor Briefs to consult with prospects on applications. Otherwise, Hercules salespeople would be unable to provide such detailed advice on their product line's many applications. The system saves the customer and the salesperson time and also furnishes a valuable service.

3. *In the budget process, account for hidden costs and intangible benefits.* Budgeting for an MSP system entails overcoming three principal obstacles: high perceived financial risk, poorly understood benefits, and biased capital budgeting systems.

First, automating marketing and sales is costly. A typical hardware and software outlay per salesperson ranges from $4,000 to $7,000—so automating the tasks of 100 field salespeople can cost between $400,000 and $700,000. In addition, if the MSP system must communicate with other corporate information systems, it is likely to require the development of specialized minicomputer, mainframe, or communications networking software.

Department-level telemarketing or direct mail systems range in price from $30,000 to more than $100,000. Sales or marketing management software may up the price another $30,000 to $100,000. Of course, the cost of tying all these pieces together depends on how many pieces there are, where they are located, and how they communicate. It would not be unusual for a company with 500 salespeople as well as telemarketing, fulfillment, and direct mail operations to spend between $3 million and $5 million on integrated MSP hardware and software.

But the budget process must anticipate and account for hidden costs too. In a number of cases we studied, in-house information was so scattered and communications equipment so incompatible that simply preparing a customer list required a major effort. Other hidden costs include system customization, expert consulting, and end-user training. Depending on the circumstances, these services can double or even triple the overall cost.

Because malfunctioning of an automated marketing system can threaten a business's revenue stream, it's advisable to budget for the cost of two systems—automated and manual—until the network has proved out. Naturally, all these expenses ratchet up the perceived financial risk of MSP automation.

On the other side of the equation, estimating the full financial benefit of an MSP system is extremely difficult. Tangible productivity gains, like increases in selling time and cost reductions on telephone campaigns, can be gauged fairly accurately. But intangible productivity gains, like better marketing decision making, more responsive customer service, and deeper understanding of customers, are much more difficult to track.

Still, it would be a mistake to ignore them, especially since capital budgeting processes are often biased against intangible productivity investments. Furthermore, few marketing managers and even fewer sales managers know much about their companies' capital budgeting processes—especially when huge investments in information technology are at stake. Senior executives have to take care that the process remains flexible enough to give MSP automation a reasonable evaluation.

An MSP system is a strategic investment for the whole corporation. But unlike other assets that are consumed over time, the more it is used, the more valuable it becomes. So it should be viewed as a long-term asset, not as the expense of a functional group. And, needless to say, senior management must match the scale of the company's investment to the scale of the project. Otherwise, fragmented marketing budgets will foster fragmented automation. The result, as noted above, may be many MSP rowboats with little or no coordination or compatibility.

4. *Make any tests realistic.* Because launching a full-scale network can be tremendously risky, most companies hedge their bets first by piloting automation on small portions of their marketing operations. A single function, like telemarketing or personal selling, is usually the test site. If this pilot is successful, the company adds more functions.

This ramp-up strategy, however, has serious drawbacks. It permits no insight into the complexity of coordinating multiple marketing and sales activities. Though single-function solutions may yield gratifying returns, evidence of their true worth may also stay hidden until they are combined into a system that demonstrates synergy. Consequently, estimates of financial returns based on single-function pilots may be negatively biased.

Finally, critical performance limitations may remain hidden unless the complexity and scale of the test parallel the system's actual use. One big manufacturer's telemarketing pilot ran flawlessly, providing the telemarketers with a steady stream of calls and instant access to customer profiles and scripts. But eventual integration of telemarketing with other MSP networks seriously degraded the performance of the overall system. Every time the telemarketers asked for new information during a call, they were confronted by blank computer screens for more than 40 seconds. As the business manager put it, "That's a long time to talk about baseball."

A company with a multichannel, multimethod marketing system is better off with a pilot plan that automates a multifunctional subset of the marketing organization. In this type of pilot, an integrated system, encompassing all marketing and sales functions, is installed for a single division, region, product line, or customer group. This experience is likely to be more realistic than the single-function approach.

5. *Pinpoint the roles and responsibilities of those selecting, designing, and operating the system.* Even standard MSP systems, though they may be touted as off-the-shelf products, require extensive customization. This necessity complicates the selection or design process in a number of ways.

The process requires expertise in technology (computers, data communications, and software) as well as in marketing and sales.

Naturally, a company's existing MIS systems are likely to constrain the choice (or development) of an MSP system.

Marketing professionals and MIS professionals rarely speak a common language, and they often approach marketing automation projects with different perspectives. While marketing thinks about functionality (e.g., Will the system help perform marketing and sales tasks?), MIS people often focus on technical considerations (e.g., Will the system interact with other corporate information systems? Who is responsible for ensuring the integrity of corporate data bases?).

It's senior management's job to make sure that the MIS and marketing professionals talk to each other and work together. It's not easy. An MIS group may automate its conception of marketing and sales only to discover later that the automated system does not actually work. Everybody knows of cases in which the MIS department loads the sales force down with reams of report forms to complete and return to headquarters. Of course, much of the requested information is irrelevant from the salespeople's standpoint, and the report forms end up in the same round file as the old lead cards.

During the long, complex process of designing and implementing a major MSP system, responsibilities sometimes become diffuse and project accountability gets blurred. In one case we know of, poorly defined responsibilities for MIS and marketing have caused big headaches. Bickering over cost allocations and data-base controls has made the company's $1 million MSP system useless. The MIS group will not allow marketing to access the corporation's data bases. But the marketing group's computer budget is too low to keep the marketing data base up-to-date. (Not surprisingly, headquarters viewed the entire MSP development process as a marketing expense instead of a corporate investment.)

6. *Modify the technology and the organization to support the system.* As in every instance in which management implements new technology, it must pay close attention to the attitudes of people in the organization. In successful MSP implementations that we have seen, both the organization and the MSP system have gone through an interactive process of change—altering the technology to fit the marketing and sales environment, then altering the environment to fit the technology.

To be useful, for example, the MSP data base obviously must contain accurate, up-to-date information. Because obtaining this information requires salespeople to use the system and to support the information collection process, they have to become adept at using the new technology. Problems can result, however, if the end-users lack computer skills or if they are uninterested in using the system.

Training can overcome skill problems (if enough money is budgeted and enough time set aside), but lack of interest is harder to deal with. Experience suggests that the best way to sell the sales staff on the network is to demonstrate that it can give every user something back. That is, by helping salespeople or telemarketers work more productively, MSP systems can boost not only the company's sales but also their sales and their compensation.

For many companies, postponement of automation of the marketing function may seem to be a good way of skirting a difficult decision, but this do-nothing posture condemns the organization to being a marketing laggard. It may also be a costly mistake. Early adopters of MSP systems have gained superior competitive advantage. Compared with their "manual" competitors, they perform selling tasks with greater economy and impact. They know their customers better and can tailor their sales communications to supply just the right amount of sales stimulus at just the right time. Overall, they craft and control their marketing programs more intelligently. In the long run, the competitive barriers they establish may change the nature of marketing in their industries.

In view of this impressive record, some marketers about to embark on automation may embrace unrealistically high expectations. But MSP systems cannot work miracles. They will not offset a poorly conceived or poorly executed marketing strategy. They will not compensate for an inferior sales force, and they will not sell inferior products. Complex MSP systems are difficult to implement, and the associated returns, like any other lasting accomplishment, have to be earned.

Notes

1. James Brian Quinn, Jordan J. Baruch, and Penny Cushman Paquette, "Technology in Services," *Scientific American*, December 1987, p. 50.

2. Thayer C. Taylor, "Xerox: Who Says You Can't Be Big and Fast?," *Sales & Marketing Management*, November 1987, p. 63.

3. Kate Bertrand, "Converting Leads with Computerized Telemarketing," *Business Marketing*, May 1988, p. 58.

4. Louis A. Wallis, *Computers and the Sales Effort* (New York: Conference Board, 1986).

5. Karen Blue, "Closing the Loop: Hewlett-Packard's New Lead Management System," *Business Marketing*, October 1987, p. 74.

6. Dorothy Leonard-Barton and William A. Kraus, "Implementing New Technology," *Harvard Business Review*, November–December 1985, p. 102.

3
Teamwork for Today's Selling

Frank V. Cespedes, Stephen X. Doyle, and Robert J. Freedman

Listen to this account manager, responsible for building sales and a close relationship with a key customer, describe a recent conversation with a colleague: "I called our district manager in Phoenix and explained that I was preparing an important proposal for this big account, and would he please help with the part of it having to do with an account location in his territory. He reluctantly agreed, but I haven't seen anything yet, and he hasn't returned my last two phone calls. With friends like that—"

This is how the district sales manager sees it: "I've got monthly numbers to meet with limited time and resources. And I don't get paid or recognized for helping someone else sell. So I don't."

Now let's hear from the vice president of national accounts at a major telecommunications company: "We do about $3 million a year with Zembla [a large, diversified corporation] but that's peanuts compared with the potential. A big part of Zembla's strategy is their telecommunications network, which they've sunk millions into over the past decade. Last week their information systems czar called me to complain about our salespeople in two regions. They were trying to sell a discount service to a couple of Zembla divisions, and they were succeeding. He said that this subverted his company's telecom strategy, which requires high utilization of Zembla's network to make it operate efficiently. Attempts to sell some of his people off that network were causing a lot of friction in his organization. And in ours too, I might add."

Then there's the sales representative of a company where the proverbial 80% of revenue comes from 20% of the customers. She sells equipment to some of those large accounts, while other salespeople in another sales force handle related supply items to the same accounts (among others). She says: "Many customers want to co-ordinate their purchases of equipment and supplies because of the impact they have on their production processes. But equipment sales are usually higher priced transactions than supply sales, occur much less often, and involve contact with more people from more functions in the customer's organization. So you have more sales calls and a longer selling cycle, as well as different delivery and service require-ments after the sale is made. I meet a lot with my supply brethren because, while we share all of our accounts, what's often not shared or clear are our individual goals."

A sales manager comments on his company's recent annual sales meeting: "Great resort, wonderful food, and the weather was terrific. Our senior VP of sales and marketing made his annual speech on teamwork. But that's not enough. Until teamwork becomes a daily part of operations, the occasional pitch for it is only lip service."

For many companies in the past two decades, selling has changed dramatically. Traditionally it was the vocation of a single energetic, persistent individual—"a man way out there in the blue, riding on a smile and a shoeshine," in Arthur Miller's memorable words. Now selling is often the province of a team composed of men and women who must coordinate their efforts across product lines (the products often made by different divisions and sold from different locations) to customers that require an integrated approach. Even when there is no formal sales team, moreover, it's often necessary to coordinate—as the vignettes at the start of this article show.

Mergers, acquisitions, and other changes in the business envi-ronment are forcing vendors in many industries to put greater emphasis on large customers with equally large and complex pur-chasing requirements. Conventional supermarkets, for example, accounted for about 75% of U.S. retail food sales in 1980. They will take in an estimated 25% in 1990; "super stores," "combination stores," and "warehouse stores" will account for most remaining sales. These chains possess the buying power (backed by sophis-ticated information systems) they need to insist on better service, lower prices, and a coordinated approach from their vendors, many of whom sell them multiple products through different sales forces.

Similar trends are evident in many industrial goods categories, where just-in-time inventory systems make customers aware of any discrepancies in prices, terms and conditions, delivery, or timely attention by vendors' salespeople in many buying locations. Internationally, the emergence of more multinational, even global customers places similar demands on many sales organizations—with distance, currency variations, and cultural differences in the vendor's sales force adding complications to the administration of these important shared accounts.

In these situations, selling depends on the vendor's ability to marshal its resources effectively across a range of buying locations, buying influences, product lines, and internal organizational boundaries. Coordination in these shared-account situations affects the company's expense-to-revenue ratio, ability to retain current business or develop new business at these accounts, and sales force morale and management. Yet, as the comments by salespeople indicate, coordination is not easy.

At four sellers of industrial goods we studied, only 11% of the salespeople involved in shared accounts were located in the same building, while 43% were in different sales districts and 7% in different countries. Of course, this dispersion erects time, expense, and scheduling barriers to coordination, and the problem is likely to get worse as many customers become more multinational in scope. Further, although development work on major accounts often takes years, one-quarter of the salespeople had been in their account positions less than five years. "It takes time to develop good working relationships on an account team," one sales manager explained, but account continuity is a recurring issue at these and many other companies.

In interviews, salespeople repeatedly cited more communication as the one thing that could most improve teamwork on shared accounts. In view of the distances and compensation involved, however, improving communication—especially the preferred mode, meetings—would raise these companies' marketing expense-to-revenue ratios to unacceptable levels. There is no doubt that a coordinated sales approach can be expensive. So, like any other expensive business resource, it should be employed where it will yield the highest returns.

Because the need for sales coordination depends on the complexity of the account, moreover, both large and small vendors face these issues. Large companies may enjoy scale advantages over the smaller competition, but they often have more products to sell and more layers in their sales and marketing hierarchies, making coordination among their salespeople difficult.

Smaller companies may have less bureaucracy than the big competition, but with fewer products and fewer resources they often base their marketing strategies on superior responsiveness to customers via customized marketing programs. Hence, this important source of competitive advantage for the smaller vendor raises the threshold of coordination required. Actually, our research showed that despite significant size differences among the various companies that we studied, the number of salespeople who must work together in shared accounts remained about the same at each company.

Our data and experience indicate three areas that are most important in sales coordination: compensation systems, the goal-setting process, and staffing and training issues that arise when shared accounts are an integral part of sales strategy.

Compensation Systems

In sales management, you won't get what you don't pay for. One salesperson put it this way: "Teamwork reflects many elements. However, compensation is a foundation. An individual's belief that he or she is paid fairly spurs belief in the team concept."

Many companies have three types of teamwork situations:

1. Joint efforts on behalf of certain national or international accounts, in which all team members work exclusively with these accounts.
2. Headquarters national account managers (NAMs) or account executives coordinate with field sales reps; the NAM is dedicated to one or two accounts, but these accounts are among dozens or even hundreds that field sales representatives call on.
3. District sales managers' efforts affect important accounts that cut across sales district lines, but performance evaluations are based on intradistrict results.

To encourage the kind of teamwork required, a different compensation system may be appropriate for each type of sales rep and account situation. Flexibility is the key, and this often means complexity. Yet in big-account situations, many companies design compensation plans according to "keep it simple, stupid" criteria, however complex the sales tasks are. Top management then ignores important differences tied to account assignments and often rewards selling activity that neglects coordination at the customer.

If there are many salespeople calling on key accounts and teamwork is important, then a bonus based on total account sales often makes more sense than traditional, individually oriented incentive arrangements. Interep is the nation's largest radio "rep" firm; its salespeople in major U.S. cities call on ad agencies and advertisers to sell time on the more than 3,000 radio stations it represents. To avoid bureaucracy and maintain an entrepreneurial spirit, Interep's chairman, Ralph Guild, has spread the company's sales efforts among six different sales forces.

Mergers among big advertisers and ad agencies, however, have made customers increasingly receptive to a rep firm that can act as a coordinated supplier across various radio markets for different product categories. In response, Interep uses a team approach to selling that cuts across each sales force. A prime element is the compensation system. Unlike the plans at most other rep firms, where incentives are staunchly "Lone Ranger" in design, Interep has salespeople with shared-account responsibilities participate in a bonus pool based on the particular account's sales volume. The approach has been effective: Interep's sales are growing faster than the industry's, and according to market surveys, ad agencies generally view Interep as more responsive than competitors.

Another important compensation issue is the time frame employed. Sales efforts at big accounts often take months, sometimes years, to pan out. But compensation plans usually tie incentives to quarterly or annual snapshots of performance. The usual result, as one salesperson acknowledged, is this: "Because our compensation plan is short-term oriented, I put my efforts where there are short-term benefits. Also, many short-term sales goals can be met with a minimum of teamwork; the longer term results require the hassle of working with lots of other people." Bonuses for multiple-year performance, or for qualitative objectives like building relationships with certain account decision makers, can encourage team effort.

Sharing of sales credit is a nettlesome issue. Surveys of major account sales programs show that only a minority use credit splitting to help coordinate NAMs and field sales reps.[1] In shared accounts, split credits are often better than mutually exclusive credit decisions.

But not always. One sales rep noted how a common attitude toward split credits can fuel resentment and block teamwork: "Most salespeople feel that when the split is 50/50, they're losing 50% instead of gaining 50% of the incentive pay. A lot of time and energy is wasted arguing over splits."

Actually, a company can give full credit to those involved and still not (as many managers fear) pay twice for the same sale. The key is having a good understanding of the sales tasks involved and an information system capable of tracking performance so that shared sales volume can be taken into account when setting objectives. Consider an example: two salespeople last year sold about $500,000 each to individual accounts and about $500,000 to shared accounts. Their combined sales amounted to about $1.5 million. Two approaches to goal setting and credits are possible:

> The employer sets targets and bonuses so that each person receives $25,000 for $750,000 in sales, with credit from shared account sales split 50/50. If each sells $500,000 in individual sales and $500,000 to shared accounts, each makes the $750,000 target and gets a bonus.

> The employer pays a $25,000 bonus for $1 million of sales with all shared-account volume double counted and fully credited to both people. Each salesperson must then rely on team effort for about 50% of target sales, but each also receives full credit for team sales.

A participant in the first plan may reason that an incremental $250,000 in individual sales (perhaps developed at the expense of time devoted to the more complicated joint sales effort) could reach the $750,000 target. Consequently, he or she might decide to concentrate on individually assigned accounts, encourage the colleague to continue to work hard on the team accounts, and hope to gather those half-credit sales with little or no effort. Coordination and major account penetration are likely to suffer. Under the second plan, there is at least no compensation barrier to expenditure of effort on the more labor-intensive team sales.

Compensation alone won't harness teamwork if other control systems are out of kilter. But ill-defined compensation plans can thwart teamwork even when other control systems support coordination.

Setting and Meeting Goals

Compensation means money. A less expensive way to foster teamwork is by clarifying goals—defining individual salespeople's main responsibilities and desired accomplishments (like opening new accounts, maximizing sales from existing accounts, and launching new products). When goals are unclear, selling can be frustrating because salespeople cannot know where they stand in relation to some standard. Good performance may appear then to be a random occurrence, independent of effort. This confusion can discourage effort, especially in those tasks that require working with other people.

Disseminating information about company strategy helps to clarify sales goals and the effort top management wants. Yet few companies regularly pass on information to the sales force about the company's objectives in its various market segments. Many so-called strategic plans do not make meaningful reference to the sales force's role in implementing strategy. Instead, the goals coming out of senior executive negotiations are usually kept secret because of fear that wide dissemination would unwittingly include competitors.

A strategy that does not imply certain behavior by the sales force, however, is often no strategy; it's merely an interesting idea. In the context of sales teamwork, moreover, competitive cost data are usually not what salespeople want; they need information about the company's goals in the marketplace, the nature of its potential competitive advantage, and their role in achieving those goals. Withholding this information is counterproductive. If salespeople are not selling in accordance with corporate goals, withholding information about strategy will not help; and if salespeople *are* selling in accordance with corporate goals, competitors will learn about them anyway.

One company we studied makes automatic testing equipment that is often bought to function as part of a total quality-control system at customer locations. Hence extensive customization for customers' production processes and information networks is necessary. These products are technologically dynamic and complex, demanding comprehensive product knowledge on salespeople's part. So the sales force is divided into product-oriented units.

The company holds semiannual sales meetings where the importance of integrated selling strategies is high on the agenda and where, in small groups, salespeople and senior executives talk about joint sales work and cross-selling activities on specific accounts. Top management considers these sessions as both an important input and output of strategic planning in a business where product development costs and an increasingly multinational customer base make account selection and incremental sales to major customers a key aspect of strategy.

In situations like this, where goal clarity and information about those goals are intertwined, managers might use the following checklist of questions to perform a quick audit of sales teamwork.

1. *Do the goals spelled out to salespeople fit the company's strategic objectives? The compensation plan?* One U.S. company, responding to the increasing globalization of its markets, began joint ventures with Japanese and German companies, realigned its product line and manufacturing operations at great cost, and established an ambitious "global account management" program. Quotas for the U.S. sales force, however, continued to focus on domestic accounts, and commissions were tied to domestic deliveries. Sales goals and corporate objectives were out of sync. Sometimes U.S. sales reps even tried to talk customers with foreign operations out of buying a product from one of the company's overseas operations! The frequent result: no sale at all.

2. *Does the sales force understand the goals?* Attention must be paid to "recommunicating" goals regularly—not least because the makeup of the sales force is always changing.

At IBM, account planning sessions spanning three to five days and often involving as many as 50 people have long been standard features of big-account management. The sales force discusses each account's business conditions and decision-making processes, and the staff concerned reviews all account applications, installations, and maintenance issues. The chief objective is an updated account plan for sales personnel.

Another goal is to acquaint people with the status of the account, including people in support roles. The impact on their morale and on the coordination of their efforts is an often overlooked, but crucial, aspect of sales teamwork. At one large medical equipment supplier, fast delivery is an important aspect of service to major hospital accounts. So account meetings include the truck drivers who regularly deliver to these accounts. "Knowing the warehouse," they can often make the difference in expediting a key customer's order.

3. *Are the goals measurable? Do the sales managers reinforce them?* In most busy organizations, "that which is not measured does not happen," as one sales manager sardonically noted. Some companies respond to the more protracted and more complicated nature of shared-account sales by relaxing or ignoring measures. In such cases, the field salespeople often feel "We do the work, while the major account managers play golf and get the glory." It

is precisely *because* shared-account sales demand sustained attention that measures are important. Without them, the pull in most sales organizations is toward the shorter term, individually assigned accounts.

Sales volume is only one measure of shared-account performance. Profitability, cross-selling, or new product introductions are often more appropriate measures, depending on the vendor's strategy.

Qualitative as well as quantitative measures may figure in evaluation of performance. At many investment banks, for example, a common source of data for evaluating individual performance at bonus time is input from colleagues via cross-evaluation surveys of collaborators on various deals. Account executives and product specialists may evaluate each other on certain criteria, including the other's contribution in marketing and service efforts for clients. These surveys keep account people sensitive to the coordination requirements of their jobs and keep managers aware of potential problems.[2]

Staffing and Training

"I've worked alone 14 years in this territory," one field sales rep said, "and I prefer an 'I'll call you, don't call me' relationship with team players." A revamped compensation plan and an effective goal-setting procedure may change her attitude, but the odds are against it.

Teamwork in sales, as in sports and many other endeavors, is the sum of individual efforts working cooperatively toward a common goal. And just as most ballplayers play better in some conditions than they do in others, some hitting right-handed pitchers better and some left-handers, so do different salespeople perform better in some circumstances than in others. This has implications for account staffing. The sales rep we quoted should not be required or even asked to work in team-selling situations. The "don't call me, I'll call you" attitude won't help and may hurt in these circumstances. As long as her performance is acceptable, she should continue where she is.

A team process for recruiting is helpful for spotting such loners. At many companies, including Digital Equipment, interviews with team members are a crucial part of the hiring procedure. A team process is also useful for acquainting a prospect with account characteristics and corporate goals.

A perennial question for many companies that have key-account sales programs is whether to fill vacancies internally or hire externally. Most of the companies we looked at preferred to promote from within on the ground that understanding of the organization is more important and useful than general sales experience or even industry familiarity picked up at another vendor. Why? One reason is that shared-account programs place salespeople in positions where they have little authority over others who affect their performance on accounts. In such a situation, things get done through persuasion (helped by an informal reckoning of personal debits and credits), a knowledge of how the organization sets budgets and allocates resources, and a network of relationships cultivated over time. Outsiders, however knowledgeable and competent, are at a disadvantage in these areas.

At one company, a vendor of medical supplies, the account executive is called the "quarterback" of the company's resources for an account, and managers use the metaphor of a lens to describe the account manager's job: to bring into focus for a key account the company's resources in areas ranging from R&D and product development to distribution and customer service. Effective performance in this role calls for account executives who know internal systems as well as they know their accounts' buying processes and purchase criteria.

As sales tasks change, sales training should change too. In shared-account situations, product knowledge and generic selling skills (e.g., presentation expertise and time management) remain important, but the coordination requirements make other skills necessary as well. In major-account programs, salespeople usually work across product lines, often across sales forces and, increasingly, across country sales organizations that reflect different national cultures. Furthermore, line authority in these situations is often ephemeral, since coordinators, like NAMs and account executives, often have dotted-line relationships with other sales personnel. Team building is a crucial part of sales competence in these situations.

Yet, as one sales rep (echoing many others) noted to us, "All sales training I've ever seen in my company stresses development of individual skills, not teamwork. As a result, delegating responsibility and working with and through others are seen as weaknesses, not strengths, in our sales force."

Attention to team training is particularly important in companies with multiple sales forces, especially when they speak different technical or trade languages. Exposure to the other sales force's product line in training sessions can help. Mixed sales meetings encourage idea sharing across district or product lines and, equally important, build acquaintances among individuals who can later call on one another during an account crisis or opportunity.

A barrier to such training efforts is often not the money involved but the source of the money. Sales training is a significant expenditure at most companies—and, because the numbers usually do not reflect the cost of salespeople's time out of the field, a usually underestimated expenditure. But training budgets are often set according to district results or the performance of a particular sales group. The local managers who set the budgets naturally focus training on specific sales opportunities; they have little incentive to devote training to team efforts. A task for executives at many companies is to determine whether the method they use to apportion expenditures on sales training supports a goal of better sales coordination.

Situational Teamwork

How a company thinks about improving sales coordination depends to a large extent on its products and the way it sells. Look at two organizations we studied, Company X, a supplier of automatic testing equipment, and Company Y, which sells business equipment and supplies.

While both handle large accounts where teamwork is essential, X sells technically complex and high unit-priced products, and Y sells technically simple products with lower unit prices. X has a small sales force and Y a large one. X's salespeople (mostly engineers) deal with long selling cycles and complex customer decision-making processes, while Y's salespeople (most without technical backgrounds) encounter shorter selling cycles and a more easily identifiable set of decision makers at their accounts. X's salespeople tend to place less emphasis on money (compensation systems, sales contests) and measurements (formal performance evaluation criteria) as control and coordination mechanisms than on "people issues" (relationships within the sales group and sales supervisors' skills). Y's salespeople tend to stress money and measurements as the key factors affecting teamwork.

These differences seem tied to the tasks facing salespeople at these companies and coincide with others' observations about the way task complexity affects the nature of the selling effort required.[3] The more complex the selling task, the more information must be exchanged between vendor and customer and the more information passed around among the vendor's salespeople working on a common account. Especially in technical sales situations, moreover, this information must be coordinated among people trained in certain core disciplines as well as in sales techniques. At the other extreme is the salesperson with the simple product whose mandate is a simple "go out and sell." Less information has to be transmitted between buyer and seller and among salespeople.

One inference to be drawn is that in complex sales tasks the initial selection of salespeople is more important. The technical skills required are expensive to obtain and keep honed through training; and the coordination skills necessary are more dependent on individual relationships. Where the sales task is less complex, however, requiring less information to be understood and communicated, "systems solutions" to coordination (mechanisms like compensation and measurement systems) are potentially more appropriate and respected by the sales force.

Organizations are often diligent in setting budgets, creating organization charts, and establishing other types of formal control systems. But they are often less attentive to the crucial but "softer" aspects of sales management. Sales managers in the companies we studied overwhelmingly stressed formal control systems (like compensation and quota-setting mechanisms) in their coordination efforts, while salespeople favored processes (like relationships with other salespeople and long-established company norms that aid or inhibit coordination). Sales managers are no doubt more comfortable with formal systems; they are easier to install and measure than initiatives aimed at nurturing process in the sales environment—and so easier to justify at budget-setting sessions. But in many situations, managers may be trying to address what salespeople perceive as interpersonal issues in teamwork with administrative "solutions."

While most top managers support teamwork, very few organizations actually focus on team effectiveness, and few managers get the process going on their own without the organization's support. As one sales executive commented, "Sales teamwork is ultimately a by-product of the organization and has to come from the top down. People in the trenches can be team players, but they need encouragement and incentives. Preaching teamwork won't work as long as senior managers' attitude toward the sales force remains at the carrot-and-stick level."

In seeking to make a sales organization more effective, however, it's important for management to keep aware of a key distinction: coordination doesn't necessarily mean consensus. That is, a team shouldn't approximate the dictionary definition of "two or more beasts of burden harnessed together." Years ago in *The Organization Man*, William Whyte skewered a certain pseudo teamwork that has a numbing and leveling effect on individual performance, creativity, and expression—qualities that are always vital in effective sales and marketing. But Whyte also missed the point: there are so many tasks in business that can be carried on only through groups. A sales manager with 20 years of experience put it this way: "You cannot legislate teamwork. It's an attitude that comes over the long term, and it's essential in a well-run sales organization. Despite this, there still needs to be plenty of room for individual success and achievement. Otherwise, teamwork becomes an amorphous concept that can lead a group to underachieve in harmony." Our suggestions can mean increased rewards for both the company and the individual salesperson.

Notes

1. Gary Tubridy, "How to Pay National Account Managers," *Sales & Marketing Management*, January 13, 1986, p. 52.

2. Robert G. Eccles and Dwight B. Crane, *Doing Deals: Investment Banks at Work* (Boston: Harvard Business School Press, 1988).

3. Benson P. Shapiro, "Manage the Customer, Not Just the Sales Force," *Harvard Business Review*, September–October 1974, p. 127, and Barton A. Weitz, "Effectiveness in Sales Interactions: A Contingency Framework," *Journal of Marketing*, Winter 1981, p. 85.

About Our Research: In gathering material for this article, we concentrated on four companies with sizable sales forces selling industrial goods. We administered a comprehensive questionnaire, which 835 people completed. About two-thirds were sales representatives and one-third, sales managers. About half of the group had worked in sales for more than a decade.

The perspectives in this article also reflect many conversations with sales managers, marketing managers, field sales representatives, and senior executives at these and other companies.

PART
II

Understand Your Prospects and Customers

Introduction

This section focuses on knowing, segmenting, and choosing your prospects and customers. The articles in this section argue that "knowing" the market is much more than gathering demographic statistics; it involves making a connection with the individuals responsible for purchasing decisions, and recognizing how they perceive the value of doing business with you as well as how you can best fulfill their needs competitively. Although the material in this section is especially applicable for selling in commercial and industrial marketplaces (business-to-business selling), its principles are also valuable for those who sell directly to consumers.

A great deal of market research is wasted because it is used either to confirm a chosen plan of action regardless of the findings or because it provides interesting but not implementable results. Alan Andreasen's "'Backward' Market Research" encourages marketing executives to take control of their research programs by focusing on how the research results will be implemented and by taking an active role in designing the research. Andreasen advocates turning market research "on its head"—starting where the process ends, rather than starting with the research in the hopes that something constructive will come out of the exercise.

Adopting Andreasen's straightforward approach will enable sales and marketing managers to discover basic, critical information (such as who does the purchasing in the customer organization and how they make their choices). Focused research allows managers to concentrate on how to reach the appropriate decision makers and influence their choices. Andreasen recognizes that careful and active market research design involves additional investment in time and resources, but the net result is more focused research that can be directly used to make more profitable marketing decisions. In the long run, the investment contributes to a more efficient and productive sales effort, which in turn increases value to prospects and customers.

Market segmentation is perhaps the most difficult part of market analysis, yet it holds the solution to many marketing challenges. Strong and accurate market segmentation enables marketers to better analyze their customers, select prospects for sales attention, and tailor a wide array of sales and support programs to meet the specific needs of their target groups. More specifically, segmentation is the process of grouping customers who are alike on certain dimensions and separating them from those who are dissimilar. However, it is very difficult—especially in industrial markets—to identify the dimensions along which customers are to be segmented.

In "How to Segment Industrial Markets," Benson Shapiro and Thomas Bonoma "offer a new approach that enables not only the simple grouping of customers and prospects, but also more complex grouping of purchase situations, events, and personalities." The authors establish a five-tiered hierarchy of criteria for identifying customer needs and usage patterns. Using this "nested approach" the marketer goes from the simplest, most external segmentation variables, such as demographics, to more intimate variables, such as situational factors and buyers' personal characteristics. Each level is increasingly ambiguous and requires a more detailed and costly information-gathering approach; the authors warn, however, that no level should be ignored because data are lacking.

By starting at the outermost nest and moving inward, marketers can identify the simplest set of criteria for segmenting their prospects and customers. As in "'Backward' Market Research," the authors argue that the additional cost of digging into the deeper levels will be outweighed by the benefits of more focused market segmentation, as long as the seller is aware of balancing costs with returns.

Segmentation is driven by an understanding of the ways in which purchasing decisions are made. In "Major Sales: Who *Really* Does the Buying?" Thomas Bonoma asserts: "On the one hand, companies don't buy, people do . . . On the other hand, many individuals, some of whom may be unknown to the seller, are involved in most major purchases." Purchasing is a highly complex process that involves psychological variables at least as much as economic variables. In this article, Bonoma provides a flexible means for analyzing purchasing behavior in large customers with many buying influences. This approach is based on identifying every individual who affects the purchasing decision, and then determining the authority, motivation, and perceptions of each. The article, rich in devices for analyzing the "buying center" and its members (i.e., the purchasing power structure), stresses the importance of the sales force as an information-gathering unit. Detailed, intimate knowledge gained by interacting with individuals in the buying company contributes to improved market segmentation, account selection, selling, and customer service.

The last article, Harvey Mackay's "Humanize Your Selling Strategy," stresses the value of understanding customers as human beings. In this age of sophisticated information and communications technology, it is easy to lose sight of the human side of selling. Prospects and customers respond when they sense your commitment to them: "People don't truly care how much you know until they know how much you care."

Mackay argues that profitable, satisfying relationships with customers are built over time; they require diligence, perseverance, and creativity. From his own experience as CEO, chairman, and owner of a company, Mackay argues: "My definition of a great salesperson is not someone who can get the order . . . A great sales[person] is someone who can get the order—and the reorder—from a prospect who is already doing business with someone else."

An important theme woven through all of these articles is *account selection*. Choosing prospects to pursue and accounts to emphasize is the single most important decision in the customer-seeking process because it affects:

1. the likelihood of a sale being closed and/or a longer-term relationship being developed;
2. the time and effort it will take to close the sale or develop a relationship;
3. the unit sales that will result from a successful effort;
4. the realized price of the product or service;
5. the product or service mix that will be consumed; and
6. the cost to serve the customer.

The net result is that account selection directly affects profits. Nevertheless, a great deal of selling effort is wasted on prospects who will never buy or those who will be unprofitable if they do buy.

The articles in this section provide a variety of perspectives on understanding the market. "'Backward' Market Research" argues that market research programs should focus on identifying the most profitable and strategically most important prospects and customers. "How to Segment Industrial Markets" provides a detailed approach and specific tools to visualize the characteristics and demands of each market segment. For example, it might make sense for a low-cost, no-frills producer to focus on accounts in which procurement executives have the most power and where price is the primary determinant of the vendor chosen. "Major Sales" explicitly focuses on the motivation and perception dynamics of the individuals responsible for purchasing. A careful review of these dynamics will help answer questions such as: "Can we ever close a sale at this account?" and "Can we profitably deal with this account?" Finally, "Humanize Your Selling Strategy" encourages managers to consider the interpersonal dimensions of dealing with a customer: "Are these the types of people we can and want to do business with?" "Will they meet us part way?" "Can we work together over the long haul?"

These articles also suggest that different customer-seeking approaches can be used to communicate with different market segments. For example, "How to Segment Industrial Markets" can be teamed with "New Ways to Reach Your Customers," from Part I, to identify the best approach for communicating with each prospect or customer group. Furthermore, a marketing and sales productivity (MSP) system, as advocated in "Automation to Boost Sales in Marketing," in Part I, can disseminate information on realized price and product mix by customer and relate this information to variables such as the length of the relationship with the customer or the method (e.g., direct mail, telemarketing) with which the customer was originally sourced and the sale closed.

Understanding the market requires attention to the four elements stressed throughout this volume: profits, focus, relationships, and combining art and science. Recognizing the characteristics and needs of prospects and customers is the key to selecting the most profitable ones and choosing the most efficient customer-seeking approaches. Focus allows a company to respond to the underlying needs and goals of the customer, and in so doing, plan a selling strategy that demonstrates how the seller can help the customer achieve these goals better than its competitors can. The last two articles of this section emphasize the human aspect of buyer-seller relationships. Finally, we see the integration of sophisticated market research methodology and the art of cultivating trust and commitment between seller and buyer.

Careful market analysis, segmentation, and selection set the stage for the actual engagement with the customer, leading to closing the sale and opening a satisfying and profitable long-term relationship, as discussed in Part III.

1
"Backward" Market Research

Alan R. Andreasen

An executive of an entertainment company decided that she knew too little about the consumer segments she was serving or hoped to serve. She had been practicing an obvious segmentation strategy aiming some programs at younger audiences, some at older ones, some at families, and some at singles. She needed a more sophisticated strategy, so she commissioned a research agency to analyze the company's market.

Despite high hopes, glowing promises, and the production of a glossy report heavy with statistics, the executive was disappointed in the findings. She said: "The research mostly told me things I already knew."

Her service operated in an industry whose primary consumers had already been studied more than 200 times. Each study said virtually the same thing as this one: the audience was largely female, economically upscale, well educated, urban, and mainly on either end of the age distribution scale.

"Even where the results were new," she said, "they didn't tell me what I needed to know so I could use them." The consumer profile relied on demographics as the principal segmentation variable. "Sure," the manager added, "I know that men attend less than women, but why? Do they see fewer benefits than women or are there barriers to attendance that apply to men and not to women? And what about the age differences? Does the middle-aged group drop out because we don't meet their needs or are they just into things that we can't match, like building a family?" She had learned who her customers were *not* but nothing about how to motivate them.

"When the researcher tried to explain the results, it was obvious he hadn't understood what I wanted. The results were all a bit off the mark." An example was the measurement of loyalty. The researcher assumed his client wanted a behavioral measure, so he sought information on the proportion of recent purchases that were from each competitor and on recent brand-switching patterns. But she also wanted an attitudinal measure revealing consumer intentions. She wanted to know less about their past loyalty than about their likely future loyalty.

How It Goes Wrong

We can sympathize with this executive's complaints, although clearly she must share the blame for poor study design. She neglected to make the undertaking a real collaboration with the researcher. This is a common fault. Indeed, studies of research successes and failures point again and again to close collaboration between researcher and client as the single most important factor predicting a good outcome.

The typical approach of the two parties starts with defining the problem. Then they translate the problem into a research methodology. This leads to the development of research instruments, a sampling plan, coding and interviewing instructions, and other details. The researcher takes to the field, examines the resulting data, and writes a report.

The executive then steps in to translate the researcher's submissions into action. She has of course already devoted some thought to application of the results. From my observation, however, before the research is undertaken the intended action is left vague and general. Managers tend to define the research problem as a broad area of ignorance. They say in effect: "Here are some things I don't know. When the results come in, I'll know more. And when I know more, then I can figure out what to do." In my experience, this approach makes it highly likely that the findings will be off target.

What I suggest is a procedure that turns the traditional approach to research design on its head. This procedure, a proven one, stresses close collaboration between researcher and corporate decision makers. It markedly raises the odds that the company will come up with findings that are not only "interesting" but also lead to actionable conclusions.

There are only two cases in which research is not expected to be immediately actionable. The first is when the research is intended to be basic—that is, to lay the groundwork for later investigation or action rather than have any near-term impact. The second occasion is when the research is methodological—that is, it is designed to improve the organization's ability to ask questions in the future. Except for these two instances, research should be designed to lead to a decision.

Turned on Its Head

The "backward" approach I advocate rests on the premise that the best way to design usable research is to start where the process usually ends and then work backward. So we develop each stage of the design on the basis of what comes after it, not before. The procedure is as follows:

1. Determine how the research results will be implemented (which helps to define the problem).
2. To ensure the implementation of the results, determine what the final report should contain and how it should look.
3. Specify the analyses necessary to "fill in the blanks" in the research report.
4. Determine the kind of data that must be assembled to carry out these analyses.
5. Scan the available secondary sources and/or syndicated services to see whether the specified data already exist or can be obtained quickly and cheaply from others. (While you are at it, observe how others have tried to meet data needs like your own.)
6. If no such easy way out presents itself, design instruments and a sampling plan that will yield the data to fit the analyses you have to undertake.
7. Carry out the field work, continually checking to see whether the data will meet your needs.
8. Do the analysis, write the report, and watch it have its intended effect.

As one might expect, the first step is the most important.

STEP 1.   As I mentioned before, to most managers the research "problem" is seen as a lack of important facts about their marketing environment. A manager may say, "The problem is I don't know if formula A is preferred over formula B." Or, "The problem is I don't know if my distributors are more satisfied with my organization than my competitor's distributors are with theirs, and if they aren't, what they're unhappy about."

In this way of defining the problem, the "solution" is simply a reduction in the level of ignorance. The data elicited may be very "interesting" and may give managers a great deal of satisfaction in revealing things they didn't know. But satisfaction can quickly turn to frustration and disappointment when the executive tries to use the results.

Take, for example, a life-style study done not long ago on over-the-counter drugs. Some respondents, who claimed they were always getting colds and the flu, were very pessimistic about their health. They frequently went to doctors but the doctors were never much help. They thought that OTC drugs were often very beneficial but they weren't sure why. This information, together with other details, caused the researchers to label this group "the hypochondriacs."

What to do with these results? As is usually the case with segmentation strategies, there are quantity and quality decisions to make. The company has to decide whether to pump more marketing resources into the hypochondriac group than its proportion of the population would justify. The marketing VP might first say yes because the hypochondriacs are heavy drug users.

But the picture is more complicated than that. Perhaps hypochondriacs are sophisticated buyers, set in their purchase patterns, and very loyal to favorite brands. If so, money aimed at them would have little impact on market share. Light users, on the other hand, may have fragile loyalties and throwing money at them could entice them to switch brands. Of course, just the opposite might be true: the hypochondriacs, being heavy users, might prove very impressionable and responsive to compelling ads.

On the qualitative side, life-style research could be much more helpful. Since it generates a rich profile describing each group's jobs, families, values, and preferences, this research could tell the company what to say. But the frustrated manager is likely not to know where to say these things. There is no *Hypochondriac's Journal* in which to advertise, and there may be no viewing and reading patterns that don't apply to heavy users in general—hypochondriacs or not.

A self-selection strategy could be tried wherein the company develops an ad speaking to hypochondriacs' fears and worries in the hope that they will see the message and say to themselves, "Ah, they're talking about me!" But nonhypochondriac heavy users who read the ad might say, "Well, if this product is really for those wimpy worrywarts, it certainly is not for sensible, rational me! I'll take my patronage elsewhere." In this case the research will be very interesting (fine fodder for cocktail party banter) but not actionable.

But suppose that the company had first laid out all the action alternatives it might take after the study. If the marketing VP had made it clear that his problems were (a) whether to allocate marketing dollars differently and (b) whether to develop marketing campaigns aimed at particular, newly discovered segments, he would have set the project in a more appropriate direction.

In the first case, discussions with the researcher would help the VP determine the criteria that would justify a different allocation. Naturally, before he can reach a decision the VP needs research on the likely responses of different segments to advertising and promotional money spent on them. In the second case, the manager needs to know whether there are indeed channels for best reaching these segments. Only by first thinking through the decisions to be made with the research results will the project be started with high likelihood of actionability.

STEP 2. After Step 1, management should ask itself: What should the final report look like so that we'll know exactly what moves to make when the report is in? Now the collaboration between the researcher and the manager should intensify and prove dynamic and exceedingly creative.

Scenarios are a good technique for developing ideas for the contents of the report. The initiative here lies with the researcher, who generates elements of a hypothetical report and then confronts management with tough questions like: "If I came up with this cross-tabulation with these numbers in it, what would you do?"

The first payoff from this exercise arises from improvement of the research itself. These results can take us forward by sharpening the decision alternatives and backward by indicating the best design for the questionnaire or how the analysis of the findings should be carried out. The forward effect is evident in this case.

A product manager, marketing a high-priced convenience good, is considering cancellation of a multiple-purchase discount because she thinks that most people taking advantage of it are loyal customers who are already heavy users, are upscale, and are largely price inelastic. Therefore, she speculates, the discount mainly represents lost revenue. To decide this question, one must of course predict the responses of old and new customers to the elimination of the discounts. The researcher hypothesizes tables showing various results.

Suppose the first iteration shows long-time customers to be price inelastic and new customers to be price elastic. This result suggests to the product manager the advisability of forgoing no discounts except a one-time offer to consumers who have never tried the product. In considering this alternative, the manager will realize that before she can reach a decision she needs to know whether potential new customers can be reached with the special offer in a way that will minimize (or, better, foreclose) purchases at a discount by longtime customers.

This new formulation of the decision leads to a discussion of results set out in another set of dummy tables showing responsiveness to the one-time discount by past patron behavior. Other tables would then reveal what television shows various consumer segments watch and what they read or listen to, which will indicate whether they are differentially reachable. And so goes the process of recycling between the decision context and the research design.

The recycling will reveal what research is needed. Sometimes the researcher will present contrasting tables or regression results pointing in a certain direction, only to discover that management is most likely to take the same course of action no matter what the results. This is usually a *prima facie* case for doing away with that part of the research design altogether.

Participation in the design decisions has other advantages. It serves to co-opt managers into supporting the work and deepen their understanding of many of the details of the research. That understanding permits the researcher to simplify the report immeasurably. Working with contrasting, hypothetical tables can make the manager eager for the findings and unlikely to be startled by surprising results. Participation will also help reveal to management any limitations of the study. In my experience, managers are often tempted to go far beyond research "truth" when implementing the results, especially if the reported truth supports the course of action they prefer to take anyway.

STEP 3.   The form of the report will clearly dictate the nature of the analysis. If management is leery of multivariate analysis, the researchers should design a series of step-by-step cross-tabulations. If management is comfortable with the higher reaches of statistics, the researcher can draw out some of the more advanced analytic procedures. In general, however, the analysis phase should be straightforward. If the exercise of scenario writing has gone well, the analysis should amount to little more than filling in the blanks.

STEP 4.   The backward approach is very helpful in data gathering. One large electronics manufacturer wanted to gauge young consumers' knowledge of and preferences for stereo components. Not until the researcher had prepared mock tables, showing preference data by age and sex, did the client's wishes become clear. By "young" the client meant children as young as ten. Moreover, the client believed that preteens, being a very volatile group, undergo radical changes from year to year, especially as they approach puberty.

Design plans to set a low-age cutoff for the sample at 13 and to group respondents by age category—such as 13 to 16 and 17 to 20—went out the window. If the researcher had been following the usual design approach, the client's expectations may not have surfaced until the study was well under way.

Backward design can also help determine the appropriateness of using strict probability sampling techniques. If, for example, management wants to project certain findings into some universe, the research must employ precise probability methods. On the other hand, if the client is chiefly interested in frequency counts (say, of words used by consumers to describe the company's major brands or of complaints voiced about its salespeople), sampling restrictions need not be so tight. In my experience, researchers often build either too much or too little sampling quality for the uses the company has in mind. Similarly, scenario writing will usually also reveal that management wants more breakdowns of the results, requiring larger sample sizes or more precise stratification procedures than initially planned. Through simulating the application of the findings, the final research design is much more likely to meet management's needs and permit low field costs.

STEPS 5–8.   The first four steps encompass the major advantages of the backward technique. Steps 5 through 8 revert to a traditional forward approach that applies the research decisions and judgments made earlier. If all parties have collaborated well in the early stages, the last four steps will carry through what has already been largely determined.

More Informed Decisions

What I propose here is a technique that requires marketing executives to give up their valuable time so that market research can be made more valuable. Great benefits can accrue thereby:

The organization can avoid research that will not benefit decision making.

Research results that *are* produced will be actionable.

Surprising conclusions can be anticipated and contingency plans developed.

Sample designs will be only as sophisticated as the organization's data needs warrant, and therefore more efficient.

Sample sizes will be large enough (or stratified appropriately) to allow more precise analyses of the main subgroups of interest.

Questions will be worded as management *really* wants them.

Management, being closely involved in the research design, is more likely to support the implementation phases and take quick action on the research results when they finally become available.

This procedure takes time for both managers and researchers. But determining where you want to go, then working backward to figure out how to get there, is likely to yield more valuable data leading to fruitful decisions.

2
How to Segment Industrial Markets

Benson P. Shapiro and Thomas V. Bonoma

As difficult as segmenting consumer markets is, it is much simpler and easier than segmenting industrial markets. Often the same industrial products have multiple applications; likewise, several different products can be used in the same application. Customers differ greatly and it is hard to discern which differences are important and which are trivial for developing a marketing strategy.

Little research has been done on industrial market segmentation. None of the ten articles in the *Journal of Marketing Research*'s special August 1978 section, "Market Segmentation Research," for instance, deals with industrial market segmentation in more than a passing manner. Our research indicates that most industrial marketers use segmentation as a way to explain results rather than as a way to plan.

In fact, industrial segmentation can assist companies in several areas:

Analysis of the Market. Better understanding of the total marketplace, including how and why customers buy.

Selection of Key Markets. Rational choice of market segments that best fit the company's capabilities.

Management of Marketing. The development of strategies, plans, and programs to profitably meet the needs of different market segments and to give the company a distinct competitive advantage.

In this article we integrate and build on previous schemes for segmenting industrial markets and offer a new approach that enables not only the simple grouping of customers and prospects, but also more complex grouping of purchase situations, events, and personalities. It thus serves as an important new analytical tool.

Consider the dilemma of one skilled and able industrial marketer who observed recently: "I can't see any basis on which to segment my market. We have 15% of the market for our type of plastics fabrication equipment. There are 11 competitors who serve a large and diverse set of customers, but there is no unifying theme to our customer set or to anyone else's."

His frustration is understandable, but he should not give up, for at least he knows that 15% of the market purchases one product and that knowledge, in itself, is a basis for segmentation. Segments exist, even when the only apparent basis for differentiation is brand choice.

At other times, a marketer may be baffled by a profusion of segmentation criteria. Customer groups and even individual customers within these groups may differ in demographics (including industry and company size), operating differences (production technology is an example), purchasing organization, "culture," and personal characteristics. Usually, a marketer can group customers, prospects, and purchase situations in different ways depending on the variables used to segment the market. The problem is to identify relevant segmentation bases.

We have identified five general segmentation criteria, which we have arranged as a *nested* hierarchy—like a set of boxes that fit one into the other or a set of wooden Russian dolls. Moving from the outer nest toward the inner, these criteria are: demographics, operating variables, customer purchasing approaches, situational factors, and personal characteristics of the buyers.

Exhibit I shows how the criteria relate to one another as nests. The segmentation criteria of the largest, outermost nest are demographics—general, easily observable characteristics about industries and companies; those of the smallest, inmost nest are personal characteristics—specific, subtle, hard-to-assess traits. The marketer moves from the more general, easily observable segmentation characteristics to the more specific, subtle ones. This approach will become clearer as we explain each criterion.

We should note at this point that it may not be necessary or even desirable for every industrial marketer to use every stage of the nested approach for every product. Although it is possible to skip irrelevant criteria, it is important that the marketer completely understand the approach before deciding on omissions and shortcuts.

Exhibit I. Nested Approach

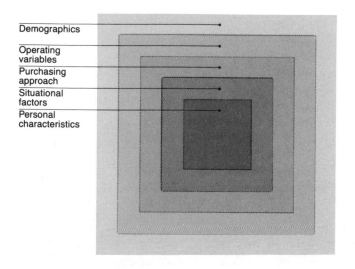

Demographics

Operating
variables

Purchasing
approach

Situational
factors

Personal
characteristics

Demographics

We begin with the outermost nest, which contains the most general segmentation criteria, demographics. These variables give a broad description of the company and relate to general customer needs and usage patterns. They can be determined without visiting the customer and include industry and company size, and customer location.

THE INDUSTRY.   Knowledge of the industry affords a broad understanding of customer needs and perceptions of purchase situations. Some companies, such as those selling paper, office equipment, business-oriented computers, and financial services, market to a wide range of industries. For these, industry is an important basis for market segmentation. Hospitals, for example, share some computer needs and yet differ markedly as a customer group from retail stores.

Marketers may wish to subdivide individual industries. For example, although financial services are in a sense a single industry, commercial banks, insurance companies, stockbrokerage houses, and savings and loan associations all differ dramatically. Their differences in terms of product and service needs, such as specialized peripherals and terminals, data handling, and software requirements make a more detailed segmentation scheme necessary to sell computers to the financial services market.

COMPANY SIZE.   The fact that large companies justify and require specialized programs affects market segmentation. It may be, for example, that a small supplier of industrial chemicals, after segmenting its prospective customers on the basis of company size, will choose not to approach large companies whose volume requirements exceed its own production capacity.

CUSTOMER LOCATION.   The third demographic factor, location, is an important variable in decisions related to deployment and organization of sales staff. A manufacturer of heavy-duty pumps for the petrochemical industry, for example, would want to provide good coverage in the Gulf Coast, where customers are concentrated, while putting little effort into New England. Customer location is especially important when proximity is a requirement for doing business, as in marketing products of low value-per-unit weight or volume (corrugated boxes or prestressed concrete), or in situations where personal service is essential, as in job shop printing.

As noted, a marketer can determine all of these demographic variables easily. Industry-oriented and general directories are useful in developing lists of customers in terms of industry, size, and location. Government statistics, reports by market research companies, and industry and trade association publications provide a great deal of demographic data.

Many companies base their industrial marketing segmentation approach on demographic data alone. But while demographics are useful and easily obtained, they do not exhaust the possibilities of segmentation. They are often only a beginning.

Operating Variables

The second segmentation nest contains a variety of segmentation criteria called "operating variables." Most of these enable more precise identification of existing and potential customers within demographic categories. Operating variables are generally stable and include technology, user-nonuser status (by product and brand), and customer capabilities (operating, technical, and financial).

COMPANY TECHNOLOGY. A company's technology, involving either its manufacturing process or its product, goes a long way toward determining its buying needs. Soda ash, for example, can be produced by two methods that require different capital equipment and supplies. The production of Japanese color televisions is highly automated and uses a few, large integrated circuits. In the United States, on the other hand, color TV production once involved many discrete components, manual assembly, and fine tuning. In Europe, production techniques made use of a hybrid of integrated circuits and discrete components. The technology used affects companies' requirements for test gear, tooling, and components and thus, a marketer's most appropriate marketing approach.

PRODUCT AND BRAND-USE STATUS. One of the easiest ways, and in some situations the only obvious way, to segment a market is by product and brand use. Users of a particular product or brand generally have some characteristics in common; at the very least, they have a common experience with a product or brand.

Manufacturers who replace metal gears with nylon gears in capital equipment probably share perceptions of risk, manufacturing process or cost structure, or marketing strategy. They probably have experienced similar sales presentations. Having used nylon gears, they share common experiences including, perhaps, similar changes in manufacturing approaches.

One supplier of nylon gears might argue that companies that have already committed themselves to replace metal gears with nylon gears are better customer prospects than those that have not yet done so, since it is usually easier to generate demand for a new brand than for a new product. But another supplier might reason that manufacturers that have not yet shifted to nylon are better prospects because they have not experienced its benefits and have not developed a working relationship with a supplier. A third marketer might choose to approach both users and nonusers with different strategies.

Current customers are a different segment from prospective customers using a similar product purchased elsewhere. Current customers are familiar with a company's product and service and company managers know something about customer needs and purchasing approaches. Some companies' marketing approaches focus on increasing sales volume from existing customers, via either customer growth or gaining a larger share of the customer's business, rather than on additional sales volume from new customers. In these cases, industrial sales managers often follow a two-step process: first, they seek to gain an initial order on trial and then, to increase the share of the customer's purchases. Banks are often more committed to raising the share of major customers' business than to generating new accounts.

Sometimes it is useful to segment customers not only on the basis of whether they buy from the company or from its competitors, but also, in the latter case, on the identity of competitors. This information can be useful in several ways. Sellers may find it easier to lure customers from competitors that are weak in certain respects. When Bethlehem Steel opened its state-of-the-art Burns Harbor plant in the Chicago area, for example, it went after the customers of one local competitor known to offer poor quality.

CUSTOMER CAPABILITIES.   Marketers might find companies with known operating, technical, or financial strengths and weaknesses to be an attractive market. For example, a company operating with tight materials inventories would greatly appreciate a supplier with a reliable delivery record. And customers unable to perform quality-control tests on incoming materials might be willing to pay for supplier quality checks. Some raw materials suppliers might choose to develop a thriving business among less sophisticated companies, for which lower-than-usual average discounts well compensate added services.

Technically weak customers in the chemical industry have traditionally depended on suppliers for formulation assistance and technical support. Some suppliers have been astute in identifying customers needing such support and in providing it in a highly effective manner.

Technical strength can also differentiate customers. Digital Equipment Corporation for many years specialized in selling its minicomputers to customers able to develop their own software, and Prime Computer sells computer systems to business users who do not need the intensive support and "hand holding" offered by IBM and other manufacturers. Both companies use segmentation for market selection.

Many operating variables are easily researched. In a quick drive around a soda ash plant, for example, a vendor might be able to identify the type of technology being used. Data on financial strength are at least partially available from credit-rating services. Customer personnel may provide other data, such as the name of current suppliers; "reverse engineering" (tearing down or disassembly) of a product may yield information on the type and even the producers of components, as may merely noting the names on delivery trucks entering the prospect's premises.

Purchasing Approaches

One of the most neglected but valuable methods of segmenting an industrial market involves consumers' purchasing approaches and company philosophy. The factors in this middle segmentation nest include the formal organization of the purchasing function, the power structure, the nature of buyer-seller relationships, the general purchasing policies, and the purchasing criteria.

PURCHASING FUNCTION ORGANIZATION. The organization of the purchasing function to some extent determines the size and operation of a company's purchasing unit. A centralized approach may merge individual purchasing units into a single group, and vendors with decentralized manufacturing operations may find it difficult to meet centralized buying patterns.[1] To meet these differing needs, some suppliers handle sales to centralized purchasers through so-called national account programs, and those to companies with a decentralized approach through field-oriented sales forces.

POWER STRUCTURES. These also vary widely among customers. The impact of influential organizational units varies and often affects purchasing approaches. The powerful financial analysis units at General Motors and Ford may, for example, have made those companies unusually price-oriented in their purchasing decisions. A company may have a powerful engineering department, for instance, that strongly influences purchases; a supplier with strong technical skills would suit such a customer. A vendor might find it useful to adapt its marketing program to customer strengths, using one approach for customers with strong engineering operations and another for customers lacking these.

BUYER-SELLER RELATIONSHIPS. A supplier probably has stronger ties with some customers than others. The link may be clearly stated. A lawyer, commercial banker, or investment banker, for example, might define as an unattractive market segment all companies having as a board member the representative of a competitor.

GENERAL PURCHASING POLICIES.   A financially strong company that offers a lease program might want to identify prospective customers who prefer to lease capital equipment or who have meticulous asset management. When AT&T could lease but not sell equipment, this was an important segmentation criterion for it. Customers may prefer to do business with long-established companies or with small independent companies, or may have particularly potent affirmative action purchasing programs (minority-owned businesses were attracted by Polaroid's widely publicized social conscience program, for example). Or they may prefer to buy systems rather than individual components.

A prospective customer's approach to the purchasing process is important. Some purchasers require an agreement based on supplier cost, particularly the auto companies, the U.S. government, and the three large general merchandise chains, Sears Roebuck, Montgomery Ward, and J.C. Penney. Other purchasers negotiate from a market-based price and some use bids. Bidding is an important method for obtaining government and quasi-government business; but because it emphasizes price, bidding tends to favor suppliers that, perhaps because of a cost advantage, prefer to compete on price. Some vendors might view purchasers that choose suppliers via bidding as desirable, while others might avoid them.

PURCHASING CRITERIA.   The power structure, the nature of buyer-seller relationships, and general purchasing policies all affect purchasing criteria. Benefit segmentation in the consumer goods market is the process of segmenting a market in terms of the reasons why customers buy. It is, in fact, the most insightful form of consumer goods segmentation because it deals directly with customer needs. In the industrial market, consideration of the criteria used to make purchases and the application for these purchases, which we consider later, approximate the benefit segmentation approach.

Situational Factors

Up to this point we have focused on the grouping of customer companies. Now we consider the role of the purchase situation, even single-line entries on the order form.

Situational factors resemble operating variables but are temporary and require a more detailed knowledge of the customer. They include the urgency of order fulfillment, product application, and the size of order.

URGENCY OF ORDER FULFILLMENT. It is worthwhile to differentiate between products to be used in routine replacement or for building a new plant and emergency replacement of existing parts. Some companies have found a degree of urgency useful for market selection and for developing a focused marketing-manufacturing approach leading to a "hot-order shop"—a factory that can supply small, urgent orders quickly.

A supplier of large-size, heavy-duty stainless steel pipe fittings, for example, defined its primary market as fast-order replacements. A chemical plant or paper mill needing to replace a fitting quickly is often willing to pay a premium price for a vendor's application engineering, for flexible manufacturing capacity, and for installation skills that would be unnecessary in the procurement of routine replacement parts.

PRODUCT APPLICATION. The requirements for a 5-horsepower motor used in intermittent service in a refinery will differ from those of a 5-horsepower motor in continuous use. Requirements for an intermittent-service motor would vary depending on whether its reliability was critical to the operation or safety of the refinery. Product application can have a major impact on the purchase process, purchase criteria, and thus on the choice of vendor.

SIZE OF ORDER. Market selection can be based at the level of individual line entries on the order form. A company with highly automated equipment might segment the market so that it can concentrate only on items with large unit volumes. A nonautomated company, on the other hand, might want only small quantity, short-run items. Ideally, these vendors would like the order split up into long-run and short-run items. In many industries, such as paper and pipe fittings, distributors break up orders in this way.

Marketers can differentiate individual orders in terms of product uses as well as users. The distinction is important as users may seek different suppliers for the same product under different circumstances. The pipe-fittings manufacturer that focused on urgent orders is a good example of a marketing approach based on these differences.

Situational factors can greatly affect purchasing approaches. General Motors, for example, makes a distinction between product purchases—that is, raw materials or components for a product being produced—and nonproduct purchases. Urgency of order fulfillment is so powerful that it can change both the purchase process and the criteria used. An urgent replacement is generally purchased on the basis of availability, not price.

The interaction between situational factors and purchasing approaches is an example of the permeability of segmentation nests. Factors in one nest affect those in other nests. Industry criteria, for instance, an outer-nest demographic description, influence but do not determine application, a middle-nest situational criterion. The nests are a useful mental construct but not a clean framework of independent units because in the complex reality of industrial markets, criteria are interrelated.

The nesting approach cannot be applied in a cookbook fashion but requires, instead, careful, intelligent judgment.

Buyers' Personal Characteristics

People, not companies, make purchase decisions, although the organizational framework in which they work and company policies and needs may constrain their choices. Marketers for industrial goods, like those for consumer products, can segment markets according to the individuals involved in a purchase in terms of buyer-seller similarity, buyer motivation, individual perceptions, and risk-management strategies.

Some buyers are risk averse, others risk receptive. The level of risk a buyer is willing to assume is related to other personality variables such as personal style, intolerance for ambiguity, and self-confidence. The amount of attention a purchasing agent will pay to cost factors depends not only on the degree of uncertainty about the consequences of the decision but also on whether credit or blame for these will accrue to him or her. Buyers who are risk averse are not good prospects for new products and concepts. Risk-averse buyers also tend to avoid untested vendors.

Some buyers are meticulous in their approach to buying—they shop around, look at a number of vendors, and then split their order to assure delivery. Others rely on old friends and past relationships, and seldom make vendor comparisons.[2] Companies can segment a market in terms of these preferences.

Data on personal characteristics are expensive and difficult to gather. It is often worthwhile to develop good, formal, sales information systems to ensure that salespeople transmit the data they gather to the marketing department for use in developing segmented marketing strategies. One chemical company attributes part of its sales success to its sales information system's routine collection of data on buyers. Such data-gathering efforts are most justified in the case of customers with large sales potential.

Reassembling the Nest

Marketers are interested in purchase decisions that depend on company variables, situational factors, and the personal characteristics of the buyers. The three outer nests, as Exhibit II shows, cover company variables, the fourth inner-middle nest, situational factors, and the inmost nest, personal characteristics.

As we move from the outer to the inner nests, the segmentation criteria change in terms of visibility, permanence, and intimacy. The data in the outer nests are generally highly visible (even to outsiders), are more or less permanent, and require little intimate knowledge of customers. But situational factors and personal characteristics are less visible, are more transient, and require extensive vendor research.

An industrial marketing executive can choose from a wide range of segmentation approaches other than the nested approach and, in fact, the myriad of possibilities often has one of the four following outcomes:

No Segmentation. "The problem is too large to approach."

After-the-Fact Segmentation. "Our market research shows that we have captured a high share of the distribution segment and low

Exhibit II.   Classification of Nests

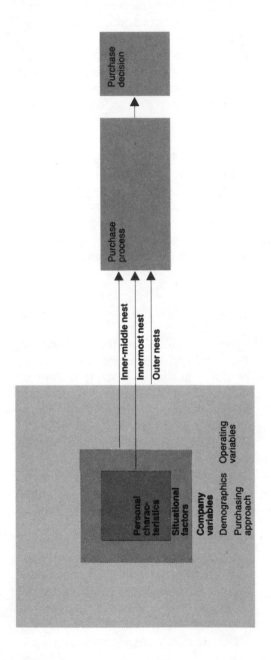

shares of the others; thus we must be doing something right for customers in high-share segments."

Superficial Segmentation. "While we know all banks are different, it's easier to organize marketing plans around banks because we can identify them and tell the salespeople whom to call on." This dangerous outcome gives a false sense of security.

Obtuse, Convoluted, and Disorganized Segmentation. "We have a 300-page report on market segmentation and customer buying patterns, but there is just too much data in there. So we have decided to focus on insurance companies and hospitals to avoid another two-day market planning meeting."

Our approach using a hierarchical structure is easy to use. Marketers can, in most cases, work systematically from the outer nests to the inner nests. They can run through the whole set of criteria and identify important factors that otherwise might be neglected. And they can balance between reliance on the easily acquired data of the outer nests and the detailed analyses of the inner nests.

We suggest that a marketer begin at the outside nest and work inward because data are more available and definitions clearer in the outer nests. On the other hand, the situational and personal variables of the inner nests are often the most useful. In our experience, managers most frequently neglect situational criteria. In situations where knowledge and analysis exist, a marketer might decide to begin at a middle nest and work inward or, less probably, outward.

After several attempts at working completely through the process, companies will discover which segmentation criteria are likely to yield greater benefits than others and which cannot be considered carefully without better data. A warning is necessary, however. A company should not decide that an approach is *not* useful because data are lacking. The segmentation process requires that assessments of analytic promise and data availability be made independently. The two steps should not be confused. When the necessary data are gathered, managers can weigh segmentation approaches.

A fine line exists between minimizing the cost and difficulty of segmentation by staying in the outer nests on the one hand and gaining the useful data of the inner nests at appreciable direct and indirect cost on the other. The outer-nest criteria are generally inadequate when used by themselves in all but the most simple or homogeneous markets because they ignore buying differences among customers. Overemphasis on the inner-nest factors, however, can be too expensive and time-consuming for small markets. We suggest achieving a sense of balance between the simplicity and low cost of the outer nests and the richness and expense of the inner ones by making the choices explicit and the process clear and disciplined.

Notes

1. See E. Raymond Corey, "Should Companies Centralize Procurement?" *Harvard Business Review*, November–December 1978, p. 102.
2. For further discussion of these, see Thomas V. Bonoma, "Major Sales: Who *Really* Does the Buying?" *Harvard Business Review*, May–June 1982, p. 111, and Benson P. Shapiro and Ronald Posner, "Making the Major Sale," *Harvard Business Review*, March–April 1976, p. 68.

3
Major Sales: Who *Really* Does the Buying?

Thomas V. Bonoma

"You don't understand: Willy was a salesman . . . . He don't put a bolt to a nut. He don't tell you the law or give you medicine. He's a man way out there in the blue, riding on a smile and a shoeshine. And when they start not smiling back—that's an earthquake."

Arthur Miller
Death of a Salesman

Many companies' selling efforts are models of marketing efficiency. Account plans are carefully drawn, key accounts receive special management attention, and substantial resources are devoted to the sales process, from prospect identification to postsale service. Even such well-planned and well-executed selling strategies often fail, though, because management has an incomplete understanding of buying psychology—the human side of selling. Consider the following two examples:

A fast-growing maker and seller of sophisticated graphics computers had trouble selling to potentially major customers. Contrary to the industry practice of quoting high list prices and giving large discounts to users who bought in quantity, this company priced 10% to 15% lower than competitors and gave smaller quantity discounts. Even though its net price was often the lowest, the company met resistance from buyers. The reason, management later learned, was that purchasing agents measured themselves and were measured by their superiors less by the net price of the sophisticated computers they bought than by the amount deducted from the price during negotiations. The discount had a significance to buyers that sound pricing logic could not predict.

Several years ago, at AT&T's Long Lines division, an account manager was competing against a vendor with possibly better technology who threatened to lure away a key account. Among the customer's executives who might make the final decision about whether to switch from Bell were a telecommunications manager who had once been a Bell employee, a vice president of data processing who was known as a "big-name system buster" in his previous job because he had replaced all the IBM computers with other vendors' machines, and an aggressive telecommunications division manager who seemed to be unreachable by the AT&T team.

AT&T's young national account manager was nearly paralyzed by the threat. His team had never seriously considered the power, motivations, or perceptions of the various executives in the customer company, which had been buying from AT&T for many years. Without such analysis, effective and coordinated action on short notice—the usual time available for response to sales threats—was impossible.

Getting at the Human Factors

How can psychology be used to improve sales effectiveness? My contention is that seller awareness of and attention to the human factors in purchasing will produce higher percentages of completed sales and fewer unpleasant surprises in the selling process.

It would be inaccurate to call the human side of selling an emerging sales concern; only the most advanced companies recognize the psychology of buying as a major factor in improving account selection and selling results. Yet in most industries, the bulk of a company's business comes from a small minority of its customers. Retaining these key accounts is getting increasingly difficult as buyers constantly look not only for the best deal but also for the vendor that best understands them and their needs. It is this understanding and the targeted selling that results from it that can most benefit marketing managers.

BUYING A CORPORATE JET

The personal aspects and their complexities become apparent when one looks closely at an example of the buying process: the purchase of a business jet, which carries a price tag in excess of $3 million. The business-jet market splits obviously into two segments: those companies that already own or operate a corporate aircraft and those that do not.

In the owner market, the purchase process may be initiated by the chief executive officer, a board member (wishing to increase efficiency or security), the company's chief pilot, or through vendor efforts like advertising or a sales visit. The CEO will be central in deciding whether to buy the jet, but he or she will be heavily influenced by the company's pilot, financial officer, and perhaps by the board itself.

Each party in the buying process has subtle roles and needs. The salesperson who tries to impress, for example, both the CEO with depreciation schedules and the chief pilot with minimum runway statistics will almost certainly not sell a plane if he overlooks the psychological and emotional components of the buying decision. "For the chief executive," observes one salesperson, "you need all the numbers for support, but if you can't find the kid inside the CEO and excite him or her with the raw beauty of the new plane, you'll never sell the equipment. If you sell the excitement, you sell the jet."

The chief pilot, as an equipment expert, often has veto power over purchase decisions and may be able to stop the purchase of one or another brand of jet by simply expressing a negative opinion about, say, the plane's bad weather capabilities. In this sense, the pilot not only influences the decision but also serves as an information "gatekeeper" by advising management on the equipment to select. Though the corporate legal staff will formulate the purchase agreement and the purchasing department will acquire the jet, these parties may have little to say about whether or how the plane will be obtained, and which type. The users of the jet—middle and upper management of the buying company, important customers, and others—may have at least an indirect role in choosing the equipment.

The involvement of many people in the purchase decision creates a group dynamic that the selling company must factor into its sales planning. Who makes up the buying group? How will the parties interact? Who will dominate and who submit? What priorities do the individuals have?

It takes about three months for those companies that already own or operate aircraft to reach a decision. Because even the most successful vendor will sell no more than 90 jets a year, every serious prospect is a key account. The nonowners, not surprisingly, represent an even more complex market, since no precedent or aviation specialists exist.

The buying process for other pieces of equipment and for services will be more or less similar, depending on the company, product, and people involved. The purchase of computer equipment, for example, parallels the jet decision, except that sales prospects are likely to include data processing and production executives and that the market is divided into small and large prospects rather than owners and nonowners. In other cases (such as upgrading the corporate communications network, making a fleet purchase, or launching a plant expansion), the buying process may be very different. Which common factors will reliably steer selling-company management toward those human considerations likely to improve selling effectiveness?

Different buying psychologies exist that make effective selling difficult. On the one hand, companies don't buy, people do. This knowledge drives the seller to analyze who the important buyers are and what they want. On the other hand, many individuals, some of whom may be unknown to the seller, are involved in most major purchases. Even if all the parties are identified, the outcome of their interaction may be unpredictable from knowledge of them as individuals. Effective selling requires usefully combining the individual and group dynamics of buying to predict what the buying "decision-making unit" will do. For this combination to be practical, the selling company must answer four key questions.

Who's in the "Buying Center"?

The set of roles, or social tasks, buyers can assume is the same regardless of the product or participants in the purchase decision. This set of roles can be thought of as a fixed set of behavioral pigeonholes into which different managers from different functions can be placed to aid understanding. Together, the buying managers who take on these roles can be thought of as a "buying center."[1]

Exhibit I shows six buying roles encountered in every selling situation. I have illustrated these roles by using the purchase or upgrading of a telecommunications system as an example. Let's consider each triangle, representing a buying role, in turn.

The **initiator** of the purchase process, whether for a jet, paper

Exhibit I. **Members of the Buying Center and Their Roles**

Initiator	Division general manager proposes to replace the company's telecommunications system
Decider	Vice president of administration selects, with influence from others, the vendor the company will deal with and the system it will buy
Influencers	Corporate telecommunications department and the vice president of data processing have important say about which system and vendor the company will deal with
Purchaser	Corporate purchasing department completes the purchase to specifications by negotiating or bidding
Gatekeeper	Corporate purchasing and corporate telecommunications departments analyze the company's needs and recommend likely matches with potential vendors
Users	All division employees who use the telecommunications equipment

towels, or communication services, recognizes that some company problem can be solved or avoided by acquiring a product or service. A company's turboprop aircraft may provide neither the speed nor the range to get top management quickly to and from scattered operations. The prospective buyer of communications equipment may want to take advantage of technological improvements or to reduce costs through owning instead of leasing.

One or more **gatekeepers** are involved in the purchase process. These individuals, who may have the title of buyer or purchasing manager, usually act as problem or product experts. They are paid to keep up on the range of vendor offerings. In the jet example, the chief pilot will ordinarily fill this role. In the telecommunications example given in Exhibit I, corporate purchasing, the corporate telecommunications staff, or increasingly, data processing experts may be consulted. By controlling (literally keeping the gate open or shut for) information and, sometimes, vendor access to corporate decision makers, the gatekeepers largely determine which vendors get the chance to sell. For some purchases the gatekeeping process is formalized through the use of an approved-vendors list, which constitutes a written statement of who can (and who, by absence, cannot) sell to the company.

Influencers are those who "have a say" in whether a purchase is made and about what is bought. The range of influencers becomes increasingly broad as major purchases are contemplated, because so many corporate resources are involved and so many people affected. In important decisions, board committees, stockholders of a public company, and even "lowly" mechanics can become influencers. One mining-machinery company encountered difficulty selling a new type of machine to its underground-mining customers. It turned out that mine maintenance personnel, who influenced the buying decision, resisted the purchase because they would have to learn to fix the new machine and maintain another stock of spare parts.

The **deciders** are those who say yes or no to the contemplated purchase. Often with major purchases, many of a company's senior managers act together to carry out the decider role. Ordinarily, however, one of these will become champion or advocate of the contemplated purchase and move it to completion. Without such a champion, many purchases would never be made. It is important to point out that deciders often do not "sign off" on purchases, nor do they make them. That is left to others. Though signers often represent themselves as deciders, such representation can be deceptive. It is possible for a vendor with a poor feel for the buying center to *never* become aware of the real movers in the buying company.

The purchase of executive computer work stations clearly illustrates both the importance of the champion and the behind-the-scenes role of the decider. A high-level executive who has become interested in using computers at his or her job after reading a magazine article or after tinkering with a home computer might decide to try out microcomputers or time-sharing terminals. The executive might then ask the company's data processing group—which is likely to be quite resistant and averse to executive meddling—to evaluate available microcomputer equipment. When trial purchases are made, the high-level executive will quietly help steer the system through the proper channels leading to acceptance and further purchases. The vendor, dealing directly with the data processing people, may never be aware that this decider exists.

The **purchaser** and the **user** are those concerned, respectively, with obtaining and consuming the product or service. The corporate purchasing department usually fills the purchaser role. Who fills the user role depends on the product or service.

Remember that I am discussing social roles, not individuals or groups of individuals. As such, the number of managers filling the buying roles varies from 1 to 35. In very trivial situations, such as a manager's purchase of a pocket calculator on a business trip, one person will fill all six roles. The triangles in Exhibit I would overlap: the manager initiates (perceives a need), gatekeeps (what brand did I forget at home?), influences himself or herself (this is more than I need, but it's only $39.95), decides, buys, and uses the equipment.

In more important buying situations, the number of managers assuming roles increases. In a study of 62 capital equipment and service acquisitions in 31 companies, Wesley J. Johnston and I quantified the buying center.[2] In the typical capital equipment purchase, an average of four departments (engineering and purchasing were always included), three levels of management hierarchy (for example, manager, regional manager, vice president), and seven different persons filled the six buying roles. For services, the corresponding numbers were four departments, two levels of management, and five managers. As might be expected, the more complex and involved the buying decision, the larger the decision unit and the more careful its decisions. For example, when packing supplies were ordered, little vendor searching or postsale evaluation was involved. When a new boiler was bought, careful vendor comparisons and postsale audits were undertaken.

Who Are the Powerful Buyers?

As useful as the buying-center concept is, it is difficult to apply because managers do not wear tags that say "decision maker" or "unimportant person."[3] The powerful are often invisible, at least to vendor representatives.

Unfortunately, power does not correlate perfectly with organizational rank. As the case of the mine maintenance personnel illustrates, those with little formal power may be able to stop a purchase or hinder its completion. A purchasing manager who will not specify a disfavored vendor or the secretary who screens one vendor's salespeople because of a real or imagined slight also can dramatically change the purchasing outcome. Sales efforts cannot be directed through a simple reading of organizational charts; the selling company must identify the powerful buying-center members.

In Exhibit II, I outline five major power bases in the corporation. In addition, I have categorized them according to whether their influence is positive (champion power) or negative (veto power).

Reward power refers to a manager's ability to encourage purchases by providing others with monetary, social, political, or psychological benefits. In one small company, for instance, the marketing vice president hoped to improve marketing decisions by equipping the sales force with small data-entry computers. Anticipating objections that the terminals were unnecessary, he felt forced to offer the sales vice president a computer of his own. The purchase was made.

Coercive power refers to a manager's ability to impose punishment on others. Of course, threatening punishment is not the same thing as having the power to impose it. Those managers who wave sticks most vigorously are sometimes the least able to deliver anything beyond a gentle breeze.

Attraction power refers to a person's ability to charm or otherwise persuade people to go along with his or her preferences. Next to the ability to reward and punish, attraction is the most potent power base in managerial life. Even CEOs find it difficult to rebut

Exhibit II. Bases of Power

Type of power	Champion	or	veto
Reward: Ability to provide monetary, social, political, or psychological rewards to others for compliance	●		
Coercive: Ability to provide monetary or other punishments for noncompliance	●		
Attraction: Ability to elicit compliance from others because they like you	●		●
Expert: Ability to elicit compliance because of technical expertise, either actual or reputed			●
Status: Compliance-gaining ability derived from a legitimate position of power in a company			●

Note:
These five power bases were originally proposed over 20 years ago by psychologists J.R.P. French, Jr. and Bertram Raven. See "The Bases of Social Power" in D. Cartwright, ed. *Studies in Social Power* (Ann Arbor: University of Michigan Press, 1959).

a key customer with whom they have flown for ten years who says, "Joe, as your friend, I'm telling you that buying this plane would be a mistake."

When a manager gets others to go along with his judgment because of real or perceived expertise in some area, *expert power* is being invoked. A telecommunications manager will find it difficult to argue with an acknowledged computer expert who contends that buying a particular telephone switching system is essential for the "office of the future"—or that not buying it now eventually will make effective communication impossible. With expert power, the skills need not be real, if by "real" we mean that the individual actually possesses what is attributed to him. It is enough that others believe that the expert has special skills or are willing to respect his opinion because of accomplishments in a totally unrelated field.

Status power comes from having a high position in the corporation. This notion of power is most akin to what is meant by the word *authority*. It refers to the kind of influence a president has over a first-line supervisor and is more restricted than the other power bases. At first glance, status power might be thought of as similar to reward or coercive power. But it differs in significant ways. First, the major influence activity of those positions of corporate authority is persuasion, not punishment or reward. We jawbone rather than dangle carrots and taunt with sticks because others in the company also have significant power which they could invoke in retaliation.

Second, the high-status manager can exercise his or her status repeatedly only because subordinates allow it. In one heavy-manufacturing division, for example, the continual specification of favored suppliers by a plant manager (often at unfavorable prices) led to a "palace revolt" among other managers whose component cost evaluations were constantly made to look poor. Third, the power base of those in authority is very circumscribed since authority only tends to work in a downward direction on the organization chart and is restricted to specific work-related requests. Status power is one of the weaker power bases.

Buying centers and individual managers usually display one dominant power base in purchasing decisions. In one small company, an important factor is whether the manager arguing a position is a member of the founding family—a kind of status power and attraction power rolled into one. In a large high-technology defense contractor, almost all decisions are made on the basis of real or reputed expertise. This is true even when the issue under consideration has nothing to do with hardware or engineering science.

The key to improved selling effectiveness is in observation and investigation to understand prospects' corporate power culture. The sales team must also learn the type of power key managers in the buying company have or aspire to. Discounts or offers of price reductions may not be especially meaningful to a young turk in the buying company who is most concerned with status power; a visit by senior selling-company management may prove much more effective for flattering the ego and making the sale. Similarly, sales management may wish to make more technical selling appeals to engineers or other buying-company staff who base their power on expertise.

The last two columns of Exhibit II show that the type of power invoked may allow the manager to support or oppose a proposal, but not always both. I believe status and expert power are more often employed by their holders to veto decisions with which they do not agree. Because others are often "sold" on the contemplated purchase, vetoing it generally requires either the ability to perceive aspects not seen by the average manager because of special expertise or the broader view that high corporate status is said to provide. Reward and coercive power are more frequently used to push through purchases and the choice of favored vendors. Attraction power seems useful and is used by both champions and vetoers. The central point here is that for many buying-center members, power tends to be unidirectional.

SIX BEHAVIORAL CLUES

Based on the preceding analysis of power centers, I have distilled six clues for identifying the powerful.

1. Though power and formal authority often go together, the correlation between the two is not perfect. The selling company must take into account other clues about where the true buying power lies.
2. One way to identify buying-center powerholders is to observe communications in the buying company. Of course, the powerful are not threatened by others, nor are they often promised rewards. Still, even the most powerful managers are likely to be influenced by others, especially by those whose power is based on attraction or expertise. Those with less power use persuasion and rational argument to try to influence the more powerful. Managers to whom others direct much attention but who receive few offers of rewards or threats of punishment usually possess substantial decision-making power.
3. Buying-center decision makers may be disliked by those with less power. Thus, when others express concern about one buying-center member's opinions along with their feelings of dislike or ambivalence, sellers have strong clues as to who the powerful buyer is.
4. High-power buyers tend to be one-way information centers, serving as focal points for information from others. The vice president who

doesn't come to meetings but who receives copies of all correspondence about a buying matter is probably a central influencer or decider.

5. The most powerful buying-center members are probably not the most easily identified or the most talkative members of their groups. Indeed, the really powerful buying group members often send others to critical negotiations becase they are confident that little of substance will be made final without their approval.

6. No correlation exists between the functional area of a manager and his or her power within a company. It is not possible to approach the data processing department blindly to find decision makers for a new computer system, as many sellers of mainframes have learned. Nor can one simply look to the CEO to find a decision maker for a corporate plane. There is no substitute for working hard to understand the dynamics of the buying company.

What Do They Want?

Diagnosing motivation accurately is one of the easiest management tasks to do poorly and one of the most difficult to do well. Most managers have lots of experience at diagnosing another's wants, but though the admission comes hard, most are just not very accurate when trying to figure out what another person wants and will do. A basic rule of motivation is as follows: all buyers (indeed, all people) act selfishly or try to be selfish but sometimes miscalculate and don't serve their own interests. Thus, buyers attempt to maximize their gains and minimize their losses from purchase situations. How do buyers choose their own self-interest? The following are insights into that decision-making process from research.

First, buyers act as if a complex product or service were decomposable into various benefits. Examples of benefits might include product features, price, reliability, and so on.

Second, buyers segment the potential benefits into various categories. The most common of these are financial, product-service, social-political, and personal. For some buyers, the financial benefits are paramount, while for others, the social-political ones—how others in the company will view the purchase—rank highest. Of course, the dimensions may be related, as when getting the lowest-cost product (financial) results in good performance evaluations and a promotion (social-political).

Exhibit III. **Dominant Motives for Buying a Telecommunications System**

	The benefits in bold type are more highly valued than the others and represent the company's "hot button"		
Benefit class			
Financial	**Product or service**	**Social or political**	**Personal**
Absolute cost savings	**Pre- and post-sales service**	Will purchase enhance the buyer's standing with the buying team or top management?	Will purchase increase others' liking or respect for the buyer?
Cheaper than competitive offerings	**Specific features**		
Will provide operating-cost reductions	**Space occupied by unit**		How does purchase fit with the buyers' self-concept?
Economics of leasing versus buying	**Availability**		

Finally, buyers ordinarily are not certain that purchasing the product will actually bring the desired benefit. For example, a control computer sold on its reliability and industrial-strength construction may or may not fulfill its promise. Because benefits have value only if they actually are delivered, the buyer must be confident that the selling company will keep its promises. Well-known vendors, like IBM or Xerox, may have some advantage over lesser-known companies in this respect.

As marketers know, not all promised benefits will be equally desired by all customers. All buyers have top-priority benefit classes, or "hot buttons." For example, a telecommunications manager weighing a choice between Bell and non-Bell equipment will find some benefits, like ownership, available only from non-Bell vendors. Other desired benefits, such as reputation for service and reliability, may be available to a much greater degree from Bell. The buyer who has financial priorities as a hot button may decide to risk possible service-reliability problems for the cost-reduction benefits available through ownership. Another manager—one primarily concerned with reducing the social-political risks as a result of service problems—may reach a different decision. Exhibit III schematically shows the four classes into which buyers divide benefits; the telecommunications example illustrates each class.

Outlining the buyer's motivation suggests several possible selling approaches. The vendor can try to focus the buyer's attention on benefits not a part of his or her thinking. A magazine sales representative, for instance, devised a questionnaire to help convince an uncertain client to buy advertising space. The questionnaire sought information about the preferred benefits—in terms of reach, audience composition, and cost per thousand readers. When the prospective buyer "played this silly game" and filled out the questionnaire, he convinced himself of the superior worth of the vendor's magazine on the very grounds he was seeking to devalue it.

Conversely, sellers can de-emphasize the buyer's desire for benefits on which the vendor's offering stacks up poorly. For example, if a competing vendor's jet offers better fuel economy, the selling company might attempt to refocus the buyer's attention toward greater speed or lower maintenance costs.

The vendor can also try to increase the buyer's confidence that promised benefits will be realized. One software company selling legal administrative systems, for example, provides a consulting service that remote users can phone if they are having problems, backup copies of its main programs in case users destroy the original, a complete set of input forms to encourage full data entry, and regular conferences to keep users current on system revisions. These services are designed to bolster the confidence of extremely conservative administrators and lawyers who are shopping for a system.

Finally, vendors often try to change what the buyer wants, or which class of benefits he or she responds to most strongly. My view of motivation suggests that such an approach is almost always unsuccessful. Selling strategy needs to work with the buyer's motivations, not around them.

How Do They Perceive Us?

How buyers perceive the selling company, its products, and its personnel is very important to efficient selling. Powerful buyers invariably have a wide range of perceptions about a vending company. One buyer will have a friend at another company who has used a similar product and claims that "it very nearly ruined us." Another may have talked to someone with a similar product who claimed that the vending company "even sent a guy out on a plane to Hawaii to fix the unit there quickly. These people really care."

One drug company representative relates the story of how the company was excluded from all the major metropolitan hospitals in one city because a single influential physician believed that one of the company's new offerings was implicated in a patient's death. This doctor not only generalized his impressions to include all the company's products but encouraged his friends to boycott the company.

A simple scheme for keeping tabs on how buyers perceive sellers is to ask sales officials to estimate how the important buyers judge the vending company and its actions. This judgment can be recorded on a continuum ranging from negative to positive. If a more detailed judgment is desired, the selling company can place its products and its people on two axes perpendicular to each other, like this:

The scarcity of marketing dollars and the effectiveness of champions in the buying process argue strongly for focusing resources where they are likely to do the most good. Marketing efforts should aim at those in the buying company who like the selling company, since they are partially presold. While there is no denying the adage, "It's important to sell everybody," those who diffuse their efforts this way often sell no one.

Gathering Psychological Intelligence

While I would like to claim that some new technique will put sound psychological analyses magically in your sales staff's hands, no such formula exists. But I have used the human-side approach in several companies to increase sales effectiveness, and there are only three guidelines needed to make it work well.

MAKE PRODUCTIVE SALES CALLS A NORM, NOT AN ODDITY

Because of concern about the rapidly rising cost of a sales call, managers are seeking alternative approaches to selling. Sales personnel often do not have a good idea of why they are going on most calls, what they hope to find out, and which questions will give them the needed answers. Sales-call planning is not only a matter of minimizing miles traveled or courtesy calls on unimportant prospects but of determining what intelligence is needed about key buyers and what questions or requests are likely to produce that information.

I recently traveled with a major account representative of a duplication equipment company, accompanying him on the five calls he made during the day. None of the visits yielded even 10% of the potential psychological or other information that the representative could use on future calls, despite the fact that prospects made such information available repeatedly.

At one company, for example, we learned from a talkative administrator that the chairman was a semirecluse who insisted on approving equipment requests himself; that one of the divisional managers had (without the agreement of the executive who was our host) brought in a competitor's equipment to test; and that a new duplicator the vendor had sold to the company was more out of service than in. The salesperson pursued none of this freely offered information, nor did he think any of it important enough to write down or pass on to the sales manager. The call was wasted because the salesperson didn't know what he was looking for or how to use what was offered him.

Exhibit IV shows a matrix that can be used to capture on a single sheet of paper essential psychological data about a customer. I gave some clues for filling in the matrix earlier in the article, but how sales representatives go about gathering the information depends

Exhibit IV. Matrix for Gathering Psychological Information

Who's in the buying center, and what is the base of their power?	Who are the powerful buyers, and what are their priorities?	What specific benefits does each important buyer want?	How do the important buyers see us?	Selling strategy

on the industry, the product, and especially the customer. In all cases, however, key selling assessments involve: (1) isolating the powerful buying-center members, (2) identifying what they want in terms of both their hot buttons and specific needs, and (3) assessing their perceptions of the situation. Additionally, gathering psychological information is more often a matter of listening carefully than of asking clever questions during the sales interview.

LISTEN TO THE SALES FORCE

Nothing discourages intelligence gathering as much as the sales force's conviction that management doesn't really want to hear what salespeople know about an account. Many companies require the sales force to file voluminous call reports and furnish other data—which vanish, never to be seen or even referred to again unless a sales representative is to be punished for one reason or another.

To counter this potentially fatal impediment, I recommend a sales audit. Evaluate all sales force control forms and call reports and discard any that have not been used by management for planning or control purposes in the last year. This approach has a marvelously uplifting effect all around; it frees the sales force from filling in forms it knows nobody uses, sales management from gathering forms it doesn't know what to do with, and data processing from processing reports no one ever requests. Instead, use a simple, clear, and accurate sales control form of the sort suggested in Exhibit IV—preferably on a single sheet of paper for a particular sales period. These recommendations may sound drastic, but where management credibility in gathering and using sales force intelligence is absent, drastic measures may be appropriate.

EMPHASIZE HOMEWORK AND DETAILS

Having techniques for acquiring sales intelligence and attending to reports is not enough. Sales management must stress that yours is a company that rewards careful fact gathering, tight analysis, and impeccable execution. This message is most meaningful when it comes from the top.

Cautionary Notes

The group that influences a purchase doesn't call itself a buying center. Nor do decision makers and influencers think of themselves in those terms. Managers must be careful not to mistake the analysis and ordering process for the buyers' actions themselves. In addition, gathering data such as I have recommended is a sensitive issue. For whatever reasons, it is considered less acceptable to make psychological estimates of buyers than economic ones. Computing the numbers without understanding the psychology, however, leads to lost sales. Finally, the notion implicit throughout this article has been that sellers must understand buying, just as buyers must understand selling. When that happens, psychology and marketing begin to come together usefully. Closed sales follow almost as an afterthought.

Notes

1. The concept of the buying center was proposed in its present form by Frederick E. Webster, Jr. and Yoram Wind in *Organizational Buying Behavior* (Englewood Cliffs, N.J.: Prentice-Hall, 1972), pp. 75–87.

2. Wesley J. Johnston and Thomas V. Bonoma, "Purchase Process for Capital Equipment and Services," *Industrial Marketing Management*, 1981, vol. 10, p. 253.

3. In the interest of saving space, I will not substantiate each reference to psychological research. Documentation for my assertions can be found in Thomas V. Bonoma and Gerald Zaltman, *Management Psychology* (Boston: Kent Publishing Company, 1981). See Chapter 8 for the power literature and Chapter 3 for material on motivation.

4
Humanize Your Selling Strategy

Harvey B. Mackay

You are sitting in a conference room with your marketing manager and sales staff, engaged in reviewing the account of a key customer. To begin her analysis, the account executive opens up the file folder and reads aloud.

"Staunch Republican"

"Midwestern value system"

"Enthusiastic booster of the Boy Scouts"

"Avid stamp collector"

"Procrastinates on major buying decisions . . . needs strong follow-through"

Of course, the report also includes data on the market position, new product lines, and plans for factory construction of the customer's company. But a sizable portion of the discussion focuses on the customer's personal chemistry and characteristics . . . and how well the salesperson understands these traits and creatively markets to them. Sound like a peculiar use of management time? For many marketers such a discussion would border on the unorthodox, but companies that ignore such vital and revealing information are at a distinct disadvantage in the marketplace.

Many companies are becoming ever more adept at using segmented marketing strategies. In mere seconds, video and print messages can establish instant rapport with a targeted customer. But in the meantime, businesses have lost sight of the need to humanize their selling strategies. Computerized purchase orders, rampant cost analysis, and sophisticated financial modeling have overwhelmed the salesperson–corporate customer relationship.

Envelopes are not a glamorous business. In fact, they are about as drab a commodity as you can imagine—in what is nearly the textbook definition of a mature industry. That means you have to be especially good at differentiating your company if you expect to gain market share. In the envelope industry, Mackay's products are constantly being assaulted by newer, sexier, more convenient ways to communicate, like telephones and computers and electronic mail. A company's margins can be paper thin.

Despite these drawbacks, in the past five years Mackay Envelope has seen its sales volume rise an average 18% a year to $35 million, and its market share rise to 2% nationally (pretty good in this fragmented industry; there are 235 envelope companies in the country). Mackay has also become one of the most profitable companies in the industry. We credit our success to one factor more than any other: salesmanship—inspired, energized, superior salesmanship.

For years it was fashionable for U.S. executives with any decent pedigree to sneer at sales, the land of Willy Loman. But today we are beginning to see a mighty redirection of the resources of the American corporation. Head counts in administration, production, and R&D are dwindling, but sales forces are on the rise. When IBM announced it would trim its staff by 12,000 by the end of 1987, it simultaneously reassigned 3,000 people to its sales force. The transformation of Campbell Soup from a gray lady to a leading business innovator is largely attributed to a new marketing strategy that has focused on targeting and selling to sharply defined customer niches. Former Porsche CEO Peter Schutz, in an interview in this publication two years ago, stressed how much time he spent in the Porsche delivery room talking with customers and learning about their motivations and idiosyncracies.[1]

At Mackay Envelope we use every means we can think of to exalt selling and salespeople. The parking place just outside the door of the main office is not reserved for the CEO. Above it is this sign.

> Reserved for
> [we fill in the name]
> Salesperson of the Month.

This is our way of declaring to our 350 employees, our visitors, and the world at large that sales are at the very heart of our business.

During speaking engagements at management seminars from Athens to New Delhi, I have talked with operators of myriad other businesses, from truffles and textiles to trucks and high technology. The problems and challenges I have heard described are extraordinarily similar, and most of them turn on a failure to manage selling fundamentals. Use of a few simple tactics and disciplines can alleviate many problems.

Know Your Customer . . . in Spades

In a one-hour lunch you can learn everything from a golf handicap to views on the federal deficit, from size of home to favorite vacation spot. "So what?" I've heard people say. "It's hard enough to remember my sales and inventory turnover from last month. Why should I clutter my brain and my files with this new version of Trivial Pursuit?" Because it establishes you as an effective listener, that's why. Effective listeners remember order dates and quality specifications. They are easier to talk with when there's a problem with a shipment. In short, effective listeners sell more customers . . . and keep them longer.

For 27 years at Mackay, we have used a device to get people to record and review this kind of data. It's a questionnaire form. People inside our company have taken to calling it the "Mackay 66" (because it has 66 questions). We complete at least one on every customer. It lists all the vital statistics we gather, such as our contact's educational background, career history, family, special interests, and life-style. It's continually updated and it's studied to death in our company. Our overriding goal is to know more about our customers than they know about themselves.

I've had people ask me, "Don't you feel like the FBI or the KGB, running dossiers on your customers?" I don't. The questionnaire is merely a system for organizing what the best executives and salespeople have done for a long time: demonstrate exceptional understanding of their customers as people.

The point here is that people don't truly care how much you know until they know how much you care. One purpose of the Mackay 66 is to empower the perceptive and empathetic salesperson with information that, channeled properly, produces a response that says "I care."

For example, question number 48 asks about the customer's vacation habits. These say a lot about people. Is he the outdoors type who loves to white-water raft on the Colorado or camp out at Yosemite? Does she like to tour Europe and Japan by bus? Is she a tennis enthusiast who plans her vacations around major professional tournaments?

How would that lover of the outdoors react to a book of photographs of Yosemite by Ansel Adams? What would the sightseeing type say on receiving an array of hard-to-get brochures of unusual and exotic tours? Imagine the reaction of that tennis buff as she reads previews of Wimbledon and the U.S. Open we sent her a few weeks before those events.

Each of these instances happened. The donor wasn't a husband, wife, friend, or neighbor but a Mackay account executive. Were these gestures perceived as insincere? They could have been, but they weren't. They represented actions taken after seller and buyer had achieved a certain level of communication and rapport. The best salespeople are "other conscious." They're sensitive people who are genuinely interested in others. They don't do things *to* people; they do things *for* people, after they've learned something about those people.

Who were the sources of information regarding the vacation habits? They could have been secretaries, receptionists, or other suppliers. They often are. In these situations, however, they were the prospective customers themselves. The information about vacations was cross-referenced to question number 51, "conversational interests." In each instance, this information was culled from the customer over breakfast or lunch (naturally, after the name of the customer's favorite restaurant was elicited from the secretary).

When the little gift came, it arrived on the prospective customer's birthday (the date is asked in question number 5), long after that introductory lunch or breakfast. Was the customer aware that the giver had an ulterior motive? Yes, in part. But what also came across was the salesperson's thoughtfulness and sincere desire to establish a solid, long-term relationship. The personal touch is so rare a commodity today, it becomes a standout. Does it always translate into new business? Not always, but often; and not always immediately, but eventually.

I learned the impact of using one's intelligence on customers when, as a young constituent, I walked into Senator Hubert Humphrey's Washington office for the first time and he amazed me by showing he knew about my goals and avocations. Although we had only a brief conversation, his genuine likability and superior information turned me into a friend, a supporter, and a loyal contributor. The intent is not to get something on somebody. The goal is to pay attention to the person across the table. Salespeople sell to people, not computer terminals. I have found that salespeople who can't understand and empathize with the goals of the people they sell to are incapable of understanding and empathizing with the goals of the broader organization they later have to serve in filling the order.

At any big social function you see effective top executives creating mental profiles on the people they meet. Leaders learn to pay attention to what's important in other people's lives. That means keeping your antennae up and noticing the details. It's not manipulation but disarmament. All of us are naturally hostile to persuasion and salesmanship. Well, everyone whose livelihood relies on making a sale had better learn to neutralize that hostility, so he or she can get on with the business of honestly selling the product. Our format simplifies the method and puts it into the hands of the little guy. With practice and a modicum of discipline, anyone can master the skill of harvesting customer awareness.

Once each year, our marketing people and our top operating people sit down and review the material on our key customers, with special emphasis on the last page the page that deals with the customer's view of the goals and issues facing that company's management, as stated to our salespeople. This analysis of common customer issues is the launching pad for our planning.

When a salesperson quits or retires, it is very difficult to sustain valuable personal relationships in business-to-business selling. But these continually updated files have allowed us to put a new client contact into position far faster than most businesses can. The greatest danger when you lose a veteran salesperson is, of course, that the client will be spirited away too. The documentation that the salesperson has built up (often over years) gives us a big edge in establishing a lasting relationship between the new Mackay account representative and the customer.

Ask the salespeople in any company, "Are you dealing with the same purchasing agent at Jones & Smith today as you were five years ago?" The answer is quite probably no. In international businesses especially, purchasing people are transferred often. Therefore, make a point of getting to know the whole department—especially the up-and-comers—and learn the company's practices on moving people. In short, dig your well before you're thirsty.

As a manager, I judge the intensity and the discipline of our 20-plus salespeople by looking at how up-to-date their customer profiles are. Scanning the profile is stage one of any account review. Sometimes a superficially completed profile or one filled with awkward hedges is a godsend of an early warning. It can signal a salesperson mismatch with an account. And *that* means a switch in account assignments before the customer decides to take a hike.

As important as the questionnaire is, it's vital not to confuse the form with the mind-set and discipline it represents. The form is just a tool to readjust people's vision. You and I have both sat across the table from too many salespeople whose eyes became glazed over with indifference, whose sighs of boredom betrayed their thought, which was: "Just sign the order, you're wasting my time"—as if you, the customer, were obligated to help boost the caller's profits. The method built around the questionnaire arms the seller with superior information and intelligence and inspires a positive attitude toward making the sale.

A salesperson never has to make a cold call. Ever. Granted you aren't likely to learn much about family background and career history until you actually have your first meeting, but there is no reason you can't become an instant expert on a prospect company in advance. If it's a public company, your broker can round up an annual report and may be able to offer valuable insights too. I own at least one share of stock in every publicly traded company that is a customer. The public library is a powerful information arsenal, with countless business periodicals and readers' guides for tracking articles down. D&B reports are readily available and highly informative, but I think their existence must be "one of the best kept secrets" in U.S. business. The prospect's own customers, its other suppliers, and even former employees all can be fertile sources.

Ask your friendly banker. "Isn't that breaching a confidence?" you ask. Not if your banker doesn't happen to be your customer's banker too. Then there's the chamber of commerce buyer's guide. (Every chamber has one.) You can even subscribe to a clipping service to monitor the local and trade press. The list of easily available background sources is nearly endless.

This research requires the same skills that went into writing a good term paper. But so few people think of applying these disciplines in a sales situation. So many people close the door on their education and training and don't even think of using in real life what they spent dozens of years learning. The best business recruits recognize that their real education doesn't begin until they enter the workplace—because then education becomes application.

I constantly remind my people that knowledge doesn't become power until it's used. That's why we use the "Mackay 66." That's why we write it all down.

In 33 years of selling, I have never called on a buyer I haven't sold. In that I'm not exceptional. The diligence and perseverance of our company's selling strategy are, however, unusual. Hardly anyone ever makes a sale on the first call. That's just as true for us as anyone else. Not every lead qualifies as a legitimate prospect. But when we decide that we want a company's envelope business, we've ultimately made the sale in virtually every case.

Years ago, as the business was building, I (as CEO) made the first call on most major prospects, and that call was invariably brief. I asked for 300 seconds of my counterpart's time, and usually the meeting lasted no more than 180 seconds. "We very much want to be your supplier," I'd say. "It means a lot to us. Here's what we can do. . . ." My comments were confined to differentiators like price, quality, service, or delivery time—whatever distinguished us from the competing supplier.

Courtship and Marriage

Many CEOs were terrific salespeople at early stages of their careers. But too often, after being installed in carpeted corner offices at headquarters, they have allowed a distance to grow between themselves and the sales arena. Then the CEO's only selling involvement takes place behind closed doors, pitching the board on a strategic plan or the executive committee on a management succession scenario.

That's a big mistake. Salespeople need to see the top people out there, mixing it up, setting the example. That's a prime reason why some of America's most visible chief executives, the Frank Perdues and Victor Kiams and Lee Iacoccas, are so effective when they get out in public to pitch their products on national television. They're not just selling products. They're also motivating their people to sell the products. Selling chickens may not be the most pleasant job in the world, but if the boss thinks it's important enough to do himself, then maybe it's important for the chicken salesperson too.

Most initial contacts are lengthy presentations with glowing claims concocted for audiences that are often too large and too highly placed. They abuse the customer's time. You don't need a

Wagnerian epic to communicate a persuasive message. After all, the Gettysburg Address has only 270 words and the Lord's Prayer, a mere 54.

The follow-up happens on the technical level. What the CEO as salesperson should be selling is not product. It is a strategic idea . . . and it is trust.

The relationship is just like a marriage: small shows of sensitivity and awareness keep the spice in it. We have one customer whose version of heaven is salmon fishing in Scotland. You can bet that at least once a year an article on salmon angling from a fine British sporting magazine shows up on his desk, together with a hand-written note. A prospective customer, whom we have pursued for a year and a half, makes a pilgrimage to New York twice a year to feast on operas and concerts. Each September this client receives, in a Mackay envelope, the Carnegie Hall and Lincoln Center season programs. The personal touch is noticeably changing his attitude toward us.

We have a customer who is a University of Michigan alumnus and a passionate Wolverine football fan. In 1986, Michigan won the Big Ten football title. My secretary found out where Rose Bowl programs were being printed, ordered a copy, and had it sent to him. He was unable to attend the game on New Year's Day, but I'm sure he sat in front of his living room TV with that program clutched in his hands.

It takes time. Strategic, humanized selling always does. It is also based on very self-evident precepts . . . astonishingly simple. As the Prussian strategist Karl von Clausewitz wrote in *On War*: "Everything in strategy is very simple, but that does not mean everything is very easy."

Care and Feeding of Salespeople

The stereotype of the huckster who cajoles his mark into resigned submission—that portrait is one for the business history books. Today's seller must understand modern communication styles and concepts. That begins with knowing when to close one's mouth and open one's ears, but it entails a whole lot more.

Before we hire a salesperson, I always socialize with the candidate and the spouse. Too many important deals are secured in a social setting, like the ballpark or the ballet, for ease in handling contacts to be ignored. It's also important to see a candidate in his or her home setting. Is what you find at all like what you were told it would be? That is, is this person a straight shooter or prone to exaggeration? You don't want to learn later that a decade-long customer has been victimized by overpromises. I make a point of having a long telephone conversation with the candidate and sprinkling it with awkward pauses just to see how he or she handles them. Given the amount of business transacted by phone these days, you had better find out if you're signing up Ted Koppel or Archie Bunker.

We send our salespeople through Dale Carnegie or Toastmasters training because these courses emphasize how important listening is to effective speaking. Any outstanding public speaker will tell you that a speech is nothing more or less than the sale of an idea. The best speakers anchor their skills by monitoring audience feedback, from body language to the cough count.

Our constant exposure to electronic media has changed the way we expect to be persuaded. Persuaders must get to the point faster, speak in a vivid and engaging way, and blend their pitches so cleverly with customized information that it never sounds like mere patter.

An entire industry, insurance, has been built on the Law of Large Numbers. There are 264 million living Americans. The insurance people can predict within one-fourth of 1% how many of us will die within the next 12 months. They can tell us where, and how, in what age bracket, and of what sex, race, and profession. The only thing they can't predict is who. The sales force must apply this same principle to its prospect lists. If the lists are long enough, there will be salespeople for Number One suppliers who retire or die, or lose their territories for a hundred other reasons.

What you can't predict is which of your competitors will succumb to the Law of Large Numbers. But fortunately, as in the insurance business, which one doesn't matter. All that matters is that your salespeople have the perseverance and patience to position your company as Number Two to enough prospects. If they're standing second in line in enough lines, sooner or later they will move up to Number One.

In our company, we recognize that the kind of dogged persistence and patience it takes to convert a Number Two position to a Number One position is very tough for the typical salesperson to master. By nature, salespeople tend to be more like racehorses than plowhorses. The instant gratification syndrome that gets a salesperson to the finish line first is an ingrained part of the salesperson's makeup. That's why we insist on the customer profiles, the follow-ups, the disciplined account review, and, most of all, the emphasis on human sensitivity. Doubtless, it is not the fanciest marketing management system, but it is uncommonly effective for managing salespeople.

Let me illustrate by passing on a conversation I had with a young salesperson named Phil (I'll call him). It was like a lot of talks I've had with my salespeople over the years. Phil came into my office looking agitated.

PHIL.   Mr. Mackay, I need your help. I've been wrestling for over a year now to get the account at International Transom, and it's just no use. I think I'd better give up.

MACKAY   *(motions him toward a chair)*. They buy from Enveloping Envelope, don't they?

PHIL   *(sits)*. Yes, for seven years, and they don't have the slightest interest in changing suppliers. I think it's time for me to write off this particular prospect and spend my time on business with greater promise.

MACKAY.   International Transom is a very attractive account, Phil. I wonder if you're not chasing the wrong goal. Accept for now that they're happy with EE. Your objective isn't to become their supplier overnight; it's to become the undisputed holder of second place. *(Phil looks skeptical, so Mackay proceeds to explain the Law of Large Numbers.)*

PHIL   *(gloomily)*. Based on what I've seen in calling on Bystrom, the purchasing agent at International Transom, it's going to be a long wait.

MACKAY.   I see you've got the customer profile there. Let me take a look. *(Phil hands him the folder. Mackay reads it.)* Aha. Just as I thought. This questionnaire reads like a dry and pretty spotty profile on someone you find intimidating, if not a little hostile. There's no vitality, no real grasp of the customer or his motivation. It's lifeless.

PHIL   *(agitated again).* But this guy is a clam, not at all outgoing.

MACKAY   *(sternly).* Did you read his desk? Were there any mementos there that told you something about him? How about plaques on the wall? What's his alma mater? If he's businesslike with you, what are his aspirations? How does he identify with company goals? You don't have in here a recent article or current analyst's report on this company. *(Arises from his desk and gesticulates as he paces to and fro.)* How well have you shown him that you know and admire his company? That you know how it fits in its industry? Do you know the strengths and weaknesses of Enveloping Envelope in terms of International Transom? Have you emphasized to Bystrom those strengths that Mackay has almost exclusively, like centralized imprinting?

PHIL.   Well, I . . . .

MACKAY.   Have you, in short, made Bystrom feel absolutely terrible about not buying from you right now? Terrible because you are so knowledgeable, aware, interested in him as a person, and representing a company that is clearly differentiated from EE in important and positive ways?

PHIL   *(looking more excited now than upset).* I see what you mean, Mr. Mackay. You're asking me to aspire to the Number Two position, if we can't be first. Instead of telling me to win, you're telling me to prepare to win.

MACKAY   *(patting Phil on the back as they move toward the office door).* Exactly, Phil. *(He beams at Phil.)* You've got the right idea.

It wasn't long before Phil's folder on his prospect sharpened and fattened considerably. In this he had a lot of help, by the way, from others at Mackay Envelope who knew International Transom, Bystrom, and Enveloping Envelope. We have a reward system that recognizes outstanding individual performers and reinforces collaborative behavior. We don't focus on just the top salesperson. Each month we also reward the best networking that leads to a sale. We recognize a salesperson whose persistence has paid off with substantial new business. We spotlight a salesperson whose customer or competitive insight produced a significant change in the way we do business.

Your Selling Strategy

My definition of a great salesperson is not someone who can get the order. Anyone can get the order if he or she is willing to make enough promises about price or delivery time or service. A great salesperson is someone who can get the order—and the reorder—from a prospect who is already doing business with someone else. No salespeople can aspire to that kind of selling unless they are prepared to think strategically and humanistically about their customers. The beauty of it is, though, that with patience and some simple tools, you don't have to be a strategic genius or a management psychologist to excel.

If, however, you are a CEO or a manager who determines the climate and attitudes in your company, then I counsel you strongly to ensure that selling and salespeople in your organization get proper leadership and the recognition they deserve. No matter how many strides you make in product quality or asset management or new design features, there is no tool more likely to harm or help your market share than your selling strategy. This is a lesson companies can learn on their own initiative . . . or, I have no doubt, they will learn at the hands of their competitors.

Note

1. David E. Gumpert, "Porsche on Nichemanship," *Harvard Business Review*, March–April 1986, p. 98.

PART
III

Close the Sale and Open the Relationship

Introduction

This section applies the book's four basic themes (profits, focus, relationships, and combining art and science) to the heart of the customer-seeking process, where sales are closed and relationships with customers are developed and nurtured. The following four articles represent a strong mixture of traditional wisdom and the latest insights on these issues. Together, these articles argue that closing the sale is only one step toward achieving profitable sales. Effective selling often involves extensive cultivation of prospects before a sale is made, and continued commitment, through service and support, to keep the customer satisfied.

"Close Encounters of the Four Kinds: Managing Customers in a Rapidly Changing Environment," by Benson Shapiro, provides a detailed framework for this section. The article analyzes the characteristics and demands of four selling approaches, ranging from simple, short-term transactions to complex, ongoing, intimate strategic-account relationships. As the author points out, strategic accounts evolved as the selling environment became more complex, and transactions could no longer satisfy all seller and buyer needs. (For instance, machines with complicated parts require post-sales training, service, and support; larger organizations require greater coordination of purchasing and selling functions across departments and geographic boundaries.) The evolution in selling approaches marks a fundamental shift in selling and purchasing philosophies: relationship selling focuses on *vendor* quality and performance rather than just on *product* price, quality, and availability. Nevertheless, complex relationship building, such as strategic accounts require, has come to complement, rather than supersede or replace, more traditional approaches to selling and buying.

This article offers a robust taxonomy for identifying the most appropriate selling approach for each customer or prospect. The primary objective is to be able to distinguish among: (1) transaction selling (discrete exchanges), (2) systems sales (requiring component integration and support), (3) major account management (involving intense service, support, and relationship development), and (4) strategic account management (establishing enduring, intimate partnerships at a high level of organizational integration). Each approach involves different goals and resource requirements, and leads to different rewards. For example, while strategic accounts can provide long-term security and competitive advantage, they are difficult to establish and sustain because of their intensity and their impact on the organizational and financial resources of the participating companies.

Choosing the right approach is essential for profitable prospect selection, selling, and account management. Applying relationship-building resources to a price-oriented transaction buyer will add seller costs that the buyer will not support. On the other hand, failing to address the needs of those willing and able to participate equitably in complex relationships will result in missed opportunities to gain a competitive edge.

In addition to illustrating the differences among these selling approaches, "Close Encounters" makes two particularly useful contributions. First, in developing criteria by which potential strategic accounts can be identified, the article reinforces the continuing attention *Seeking Customers* applies to segmenting prospects and customers. If you cannot segment your prospect and customer base, you cannot apply the right sales approach to each situation. If you are unable to segment the market, you are certain to miss sales opportunities and misallocate relationship-building resources to transactions (or underinvest in more complex relationships). Second, the article provides detailed guidelines for how to nurture complex strategic accounts, plan appropriate investments, and avoid common traps (such as attempting to develop too many relationships). Following these principles will help companies reap long-term, profitable rewards.

"Learning from Losing a Customer," by David Green, provides a concrete example of the "Close Encounters" framework in action. The article describes how a small company lost a major order because it followed a transaction orientation when the customer wanted a relationship. Despite possessing the capabilities and expertise to deliver a permanent satellite network for a major client, the supplier (VideoStar Connections) lost the sale to a competitor, primarily because it "had failed miserably at the fine art of positioning . . . Digital Equipment thought we were great for one-night stands, but not right for a long-term relationship." Reflecting on the failure led VideoStar to emphasize its long-term relationship capabilities and to recast its image as a supplier who could sustain such relationships.

In addition to reinforcing the "Close Encounters" framework, this article demonstrates the importance of the customer's perspective. The customer's needs define the nature of the selling situation—whether it is a transaction or a more complex relationship. Once these needs are recognized, it is up to the seller to determine whether the investment in meeting these needs will be profitable. Being able to recognize customers' needs, focus appropriate resources in response, and position the company competitively depend on open communications channels, as advocated in Part I.

Now we move into the life cycle of the sales and account management process. Together, *Seeking Customers* and *Keeping Customers* offer a comprehensive examination of this cycle, from adopting new ways to reach customers to establishing performance measurement systems that track customer satisfaction, retention, and profitability. Within this book alone, we see a life cycle to seeking customers. A broad description of this cycle would include the following steps:

1. Develop a customer-seeking framework.
2. Choose a set of target prospects.
3. Prepare a sales approach.
4. Sell.
5. Service and support the accounts.

While the first two parts of this book focus on steps 1 and 2, this section guides the discussion into steps 3 and 4. In particular, the next two articles are devoted to preparing and executing a workable sales approach that communicates to buyers how you, the seller, are aware of their needs, uniquely capable of meeting those needs, and committed to satisfying them.

Originally published in 1976, "Making the Major Sale," by Benson Shapiro and Ronald Posner, offers an eight-step, nuts-and-bolts framework for actively developing a major sale (whether it is a large single transaction or the opening of an ongoing relationship), "from the initial decision to pursue a prospect, through the appropriate strategy for courting an account, to the eventual close of the sale." These principles, as relevant as when they were written, offer a fine refresher for the seasoned sales manager, a powerful introduction for executives with little sales experience, or a primer for the sales rookie.

The authors argue that major sales need special handling because they are complex, their potential profit is relatively large, and they have a lasting impact on both buyer and seller. Because these relationships require significant commitment of organizational and financial resources, sellers must be aware of the meticulous detail required to make these sales profitable. The eight-step program will help ensure that sales resources are focused on appropriate prospects and are deployed efficiently throughout the sales process. In addition to offering practical guidelines for strategic selling, the authors suggest several organizational alternatives for handling major accounts, including establishment of a special sales force or a separate integrated division. In a sense, all these management techniques attempt to create the "Teamwork for Today's Selling" approach we encountered in Part I.

Clifton Reichard's "Industrial Selling: Beyond Price and Persistence" also proposes a deliberate set of steps for crafting a customer relationship. However, Reichard's emphasis is on selling the company and the salesperson before selling a specific product or service. Using the experiences of his own company, the Ball Corporation, as an example, the author encourages salespeople to focus first on nurturing a relationship of interest and trust at a broad level; this process will likely require a great deal of time, energy, and creativity long before any returns are expected. The keys to establishing a satisfying relationship lie in listening and presentation; successful relationship development depends on two-way communication between seller and buyer. Reichard argues that the heart of selling cannot be found in a formula, but in being able to appeal to the people who are making the purchasing decisions. This article's rich detail will help executives who are not familiar with the difficult and creative art of selling understand the meticulous discipline needed to prepare and execute the appropriate sales approach.

Relationship development is the natural theme that evolves in this section; however, these articles also reinforce the principles of focus and profits. The first two articles emphasize the importance of understanding the characteristics and requirements of different sales situations so that the appropriate resources can be allocated to each prospect and account. Such focus is necessary for achieving profitable results. Meanwhile, the last two articles argue that major accounts require meticulous attention to detail; sales programs must be carefully analyzed and planned at every step. In pursuing disciplined programs, however, sellers must not ignore the human factor in selling; these articles argue that the art of selling involves establishing personal bonds with individuals, whose feelings and emotions contribute to their business decisions.

1

Close Encounters of the Four Kinds: Managing Customers in a Rapidly Changing Environment*

Benson P. Shapiro

Get close to your customers and do what they want—be customer oriented!

Don't give away the store!

Selling is dead; there was respect, and courtship, and gratitude in it. Today it's all cut and dried, and there's no chance for bringing friendship to bear or personality.[1]

Customer relationships are more important than they have ever before been!

There are many different ways to think about the role of selling and customer relations in a complex world. Perhaps the truest statement about relationships between buyers and sellers appears in *Death of a Salesman* by Arthur Miller. But, it wasn't made by Willy Loman, the salesman. It was made by his devoted wife, Linda: "It's changing, Willy, I can feel it changing."[2]

The management of account relationships, particularly those between organizations such as businesses or between businesses and major institutions such as governments, *has* changed; it has grown more varied and more difficult. We need new ways to look at selling and serving customers.

The discussion begins by examining four distinct ways to sell, emphasizing the differences among them and their relative

*This article is from *Strategic Marketing Management*, Readings Selected by Robert J. Dolan (Boston: Harvard Business School, 1992).

strengths and weaknesses. The last half of the paper focuses on a new form of selling—the strategic-account relationship, a very complex approach that is replete with traps and expenses. It does not receive this attention because it is a panacea or even an appropriate choice for every vendor. It is not! The best way to understand its usefulness is to compare it with simpler, yet very serviceable approaches.

Four Approaches to Selling

For many years, indeed, back to the days of open markets and caravan traders, personal selling was a fairly simple activity, consisting of a single exchange or a series of exchanges. We can call this type of selling *transaction selling*. During the last few decades we have seen the introduction and development of three more sophisticated forms: *systems sales, major-account management,* and *strategic-account relationships*.

TRANSACTION SELLING

In transaction selling the exchange is generally quite discrete, with a product or service moving from seller to buyer and money moving in the other direction after a period of negotiation and information transfer. This approach is still useful for selling fairly simple products—ranging from office furniture to standard electronic products to raw materials—in a one-time exchange or a continuing series of exchanges. The product is usually purchased on the basis of physical attributes, availability, convenience, or price. The seller views each sales transaction as the outcome of immediately preceding efforts and as one of a series of transactions separated by "down time" for servicing the account.

SYSTEMS SALES

The advent of complex businesses required that the transaction approach be supplemented by heightened concern for customer benefits and integration of system components. A system consists of separate pieces, including capital equipment, parts, supplies, and services. Office and factory automation systems are typical examples, but petrochemical complexes and textile mills also fit the systems description. The systems sale necessitated the introduction and development of new sales techniques such as team selling, in which several departments or functional areas (applications engineering, design, field service, etc.) of the vendor are involved in the sales process.[3]

Systems sales are also used when the system is not a product but a program. In consumer packaged goods, for example, the system may be a promotional program involving several different product lines, national advertising, cooperative advertising, and in-store promotions. The system can also be a related set of services, such as a cash-management service sold to a company with many locations and bank accounts.

Thus the systems sale differs in size and complexity from the transaction sale as well as in the ratio of service time to actual selling time. Nonetheless, the heart of the activity remains the sales transaction, and there is still a tendency to view the time between sales as down time. The approach is more sophisticated but the fundamental philosophy is not.

MAJOR-ACCOUNT MANAGEMENT

The increasing size and complexity of sales and the development of purchasing approaches like national contracts and master purchasing agreements has led to more intimacy and permanence in buyer-seller relations. Instead of buying a product or service, or even a set of products and services (as in the systems purchase), the customer literally purchases a relationship with a vendor. Major-account management, or national-account management, developed because customers transcend regional sales boundaries. Major-account management, still evolving and growing in popularity, is becoming the crème de la crème of personal selling.[4] Its core is an account manager who quarterbacks the approach to the customer and employs the vendor's resources for the customer's benefit. Primary issues in national-account programs include organizational structure and the quality of support provided by functional groups other than the sales operation.[5] Its essence is an ongoing relationship with a major vendor based on intense, well-coordinated service support.

Exhibit I.   Four Selling Approaches

Transaction Orientation	Relationship Orientation
1. Transaction Selling	3. Major-Account Management
2. Systems Sales	4. Strategic-Account Relationships

Account management also signals a change in sales philosophy. Actual sales transactions "are seen as the punctuation marks of a larger relationship. Sales are 'natural fallout.'"[6] The whole concept of selling has changed. In essence, it has shifted from a transaction orientation to a relationship orientation (see Exhibit I). Whereas the systems sale is simply a more important and more complex transaction, major-account management is a fundamental change in conception. Exhibit II highlights the differences between transaction selling and relationship creation.

Account management is expensive and difficult. It can be used only for major customers. And, to be effective, it must be seen as a philosophy of customer commitment, not as a collection of advanced persuasion techniques. Its essence is superior customer responsiveness based on outstanding support systems. It goes beyond selling. Moreover, it has laid the foundation for strategic-account relationships; for, in spite of its opportunities and rewards,

Exhibit II.   Transactions and Relationships

Transaction Selling	Relationship Creation
1. Selling dominates learning.	1. Learning about the customer is intense and dominates selling.
2. Talking dominates listening.	2. Listening dominates talking.
3. Persuading the customer is product-driven and benefits-focused.	3. Teaching the customer is need-driven and problem-focused.
4. The goal is to build buyers and sales through persuasion, price, presence, and terms.	4. The goal is to build relationships through credibility, responsiveness, and trust.

Source: This exhibit is based on a chart by Thomas V. Bonoma.

as well as its significant investments and costs, even major- or national-account management cannot completely satisfy the evolving needs for closer, more permanent vendor-customer relationships. Joint product, service, and infrastructure development have led to even more intimate buyer-seller relations. Strategic-account relationships are one of several types of coalitions formed between companies that may be related as competitors, buyers and sellers, or sharers of technology or resources.[7]

STRATEGIC-ACCOUNT RELATIONSHIPS

Because strategic-account relationships are a new and specialized approach, there are few publicly documented examples. Furthermore, several are proprietary and thus beyond discussion here. It is instructive, however, to look at several examples.

The first is the Hartford Component Company, the disguised name of a manufacturer of a specialized component of measuring instruments. In the past Hartford competed directly with several companies that use the same technology and with others whose components are based on a competing technology. One of Hartford's primary customers, New Haven Instrument (N.H.I.), made measuring instruments for chemical analysis and medical diagnosis; several of its products were based on the Hartford component. After several months of negotiation—and following years of successful vendor-supplier relations—the companies agreed to a joint-development effort. Hartford management understood that to develop its technology further it needed more knowledge of product use, additional technical expertise in several related engineering disciplines, and an assured outlet for a new product whose development would require substantial investments in time and funds. N.H.I., for its part, faced intense international competition and needed a technological "leg up" to improve its market position. It lacked the ability to develop the component technology and wanted to leverage its strong customer relationships, applications knowledge, and skill in related technologies. The companies—each of which had sales of $50 million to $200 million—did not wish to merge; but each needed a more important, intimate, and permanent connection than their preferred vendor-major customer relation.

Their strategic partnership involved a joint-development project, information exchange, and a carefully developed sales agreement that gave N.H.I. a temporary exclusive right to purchase components and Hartford an assured source of sales. Despite the high costs, substantial required level of organizational cooperation and integration, and considerable loss of autonomy for each, both companies saw the arrangement as worthwhile. Because they managed the relationship well and had carefully defined expectations, both companies gained.

This example demonstrates three attributes upon which strategic-account relationships must always be based: (1) mutual importance, (2) intimacy, and (3) longevity.

Importance usually involves three forms of interdependence: financial, technological and/or design, and strategic. One company must be exceedingly important to the other financially; sometimes, as in the Hartford–New Haven case, the companies are financially important to each other. Technological and/or design cooperation is at the heart of most strategic partnerships and is the element that most clearly separates companies that will profit most from strategic-account relationships from those better suited to a traditional relationship. Strategic importance is usually based on the technological/design dependence and is supplemented by the financial importance of one firm to the other.

Intimacy and longevity flow from the nature of the joint effort, which requires sharing intimate technological, design, and operating information. Trust is a critical ingredient in the relationship because it enables intimacy to develop, while longevity protects the intimacy and allows the partners to reap the financial rewards from long-term investments with, they hope, high payouts.

Another strategic-account relationship is that between the EDS (Electronic Data Systems) division of General Motors and what was formerly the Information Systems portion of AT&T. EDS had substantial skills in integrating computers, telecommunications gear, and software to customer systems. AT&T IS sold telecommunications equipment, computers, and related equipment, but it did not have sufficient systems-integration skills to satisfy all its customers. EDS and AT&T IS signed a systems-integrator agreement under which EDS's integration skills made it considerably more important than a major distributor.

In another strategic relationship, Fujitsu Fanuc Ltd., a Japanese robot vendor, established a joint venture with General Motors. The joint venture gave Fanuc a better "window" on factory technology and robot application than it could have gained as an ordinary vendor. The joint venture, which sold robots and related factory-automation equipment to GMC and other customers, also enabled GMC to better understand and capitalize on the rapidly evolving robot technology. Moreover, GMC gained financially because it shared the returns from sales to other customers.

Comparisons and Applications

Exhibit III compares the four types of sales approaches. On the far left is the transaction approach, with systems selling, major-account management, and strategic-account relationships, each representing further evolutions in sophistication and horsepower. Most important are the differences in goal and essence. The transaction and systems approaches emphasize sales, while the major-account and strategic-relationship approaches emphasize the mutuality of a long marriage. As we move from left to right we see that the impact of the sale and the approach increase for both buyer and seller. Thus, organization level and the size of the buying and selling teams increase, as does the length of the relationship.

However, the relative amount of vendor effort also increases; integration and information flow within the vendor organization expand in response to the increased effort and because of the degree of customer responsiveness and service required. As we move from left to right on the chart, the relative amount of account work done by the sales force decreases and the amount done by supporting functional units such as manufacturing, field service, and logistics increases. More and more of the salesperson's time is spent on internal coordination and service support and less in customer persuasion. The best relationship managers have just as strong an internal focus as they do an external focus—a paradox to most traditional salespeople. Salespeople have broad account-related goals instead of narrow sales-related ones.

Because of the effort involved, a vendor can support only a few strategic-account relationships. Most customers will remain systems or transaction customers, and some will be major accounts. Since transaction selling is the easiest and cheapest, it should be used wherever possible. When products become complex and sophisticated, however, companies will need to shift to the systems approach. Many firms need go no further.

When, however, the importance of individual customers grows and they need intensive service because of their buying process

Exhibit III. The Four Types of Sales Approaches

	Transaction	Systems	Major-Account Management	Strategic-Account Relationship
Goal	Sales and satisfied customers	System sales and satisfied customers	The position as preferred supplier	An enduring, intimate relationship
Essence	Product sales because of performance, price, and effective selling	Integration benefits from good support and team selling	Intense service through account management	Company-to-company bonding with an institutional relationship leading to a shared destiny
Impact on buyer	Lowest			Highest
Impact on seller	Lowest			Highest
Organizational level and size of buying team	Lowest			Highest
Organizational level and size of selling team	Lowest			Highest

Length of relationship	Shortest			Longest
Relative amount of vendor effort	Lowest			Highest
Information needs at all levels of vendor	Lowest			Highest
Vendor management integration needs	Limited			Highest
Sales force goals	Narrow—sell products			Broad—manage the partnership
Number of customers appropriate for each approach	Most or some	Most or some	Not many	Very few

Note: In some industries such as electronics the transaction sales are called "box" or "piece part" sales to contrast them to systems sales.

and dependencies, the seller must switch to major-account management and relationship selling. The shift must be understood as a commitment to customer service and responsiveness and not merely as use of an improved selling technique. Major-account management is, indeed, a powerful tool, but it is expensive, in terms of support and integration, cost, and effort. It is an efficient weapon only when it is justified.

Finally, for the few situations in which customer importance (financial, technological and/or design, and strategic), intimacy, and longevity are high, the company should use the most potent weapon: strategic-account relationships. It is the most expensive because of support and integration demands and loss of autonomy, but it is justified where the relationship must be long and intimate and where the rewards are strategic.

Simply put, the message is: use the cheapest tool (left column, Exhibit III) wherever possible. Escalate (to the right) only when necessary and justified.

Why Get Closer?

If transaction selling is so much cheaper and easier than the three other types, why do we need systems selling, major-account management, and strategic-account relationships? When are they justified?

Systems selling evolved because of product changes and the resulting changes in customers' buying processes. Some products became more complex, with more separate parts and services. And, the pieces had to fit together. The added complexity meant that other people and departments had to become involved in the purchase. When machine tools, for example, were relatively simple, the engineer at the customer company could give a clear specification to the purchasing agent, who could negotiate for a good price. Although there might be a few conversations between the engineer and purchasing agent, the communication was generally simple and the coordination needs limited.

As machine tools were replaced by complex multipurpose machining centers, the whole buying process changed. What had been a simple stand-alone machine purchase became a complex systems purchase. Process engineers, product-design engineers, manufacturing management, logistical personnel, procurement executives, and financial specialists got involved. The machining center affected the way various departments operated: the role of inventory and product variety (bringing in product and marketing managers); the whole concept of coordinated engineering, manufacturing, and logistics; and the risks of down time. Service and support became complicated. New types of suppliers were needed.

Successful vendors developed better sales techniques to match this more complicated buying process and product configuration. Systems selling integrated these techniques into a new sales approach.

Later, additional, broader changes in the environment forced a "quantum leap" to major-account management. Mergers, acquisitions, bankruptcies, and differential growth led to a smaller, more concentrated account base in many industries. In some, such as the market for commercial jet engines and aircraft, as few as a dozen customers control the market. For the manufacturer these became do-or-die customers. Economic concentration brought added changes to the buying and selling organizations. Buying, receiving, using, producing, inventorying, shipping, and selling locations multiplied. Sales calls had to be made to more customer locations from more sales locations. And sales efforts had to be coordinated with more numerous support (manufacturing, inventorying, and so forth) locations. Communication and coordination systems could no longer confine their activities to one or a few systems or to one or a few large, complex transactions; they were embedded in a total vendor-customer relationship. And, to make matters worse, the dispersion was not simply geographical. It involved many buying and selling organizational jurisdictions; the problems of internal coordination at the vendor became as important as vendor-customer coordination.

At the same time, the impact of the vendor, not simply the product choice, increased substantially. The experiences, good and bad, of computer buyers in particular influenced views of vendor importance. Because computers of different manufacturers could not talk to one another in the 1960s, 1970s, and early 1980s, choice of a product was a long-term commitment to a vendor and to a technological approach. It was perhaps to be expected that a computer vendor, IBM, would lead in the development of major- and national-account marketing.

Individual transactions and annual vendor-to-customer sales increased dramatically in size. Bonds between vendor and customer became more intimate. Coordination became difficult; the risk of a poor choice soared; and major- and national-account management became a fad. Those who thought it was a collection of advanced sales techniques failed. Those who saw it as a new philosophy of vendor-customer cooperation and internal vendor coordination, and who were able to make it work despite organizational inertia, complexity, and jurisdictional warfare succeeded. The difference between success and failure was clear and involved many functions. Better customer relationships enabled vendor engineers, for example, to do a better job of developing new products; and the new products improved the relationship. As the better major-account marketer drew farther ahead of the disorganized, disoriented competitor, the better sales approach led to greater business success.

In some businesses, vendor-customer relationships grew even closer. Joint technological work was the cause in many but not all situations. An interesting marketing-oriented situation developed at NutraSweet, where a patented sweetener made the company a primary supplier to Coca-Cola and Pepsi-Cola. NutraSweet's "branded ingredient strategy" linked its marketing strategy inextricably to its customers, and the transactions were large and the dollar volume very great. But, more important, NutraSweet and Coke, and NutraSweet and Pepsi, developed long-term interests in promoting NutraSweet-branded diet soft drinks. In cases like these, joint marketing, operating, and/or technological dependencies can lead to strategic-account relationships.

The evolution of the four sales approaches is really the history of more complex responses to more demanding customer purchasing initiatives. Systems selling arose because of buyer demands beyond those that could be filled with the traditional transaction approach. Major-account management represented a still more powerful approach to greater customer opportunity. And, the antecedents for the strategic-account relationship approach lie in original equipment manufacturer (OEM) industrial marketing and franchised distributor arrangements. Suppliers of complex, important components to OEMs have found it necessary to undertake joint-development and engineering work, and the proprietary nature of the products and interfaces developed led to long-term relationships. A manufacturer of numerically controlled machine tools, for example, is typically locked in to a computer-control vendor for a five-year or so generation of controls.

Franchised distributors in the industrial, commercial, and consumer sphere (e.g., McDonald's and Dunkin' Donuts) have intimate, long-term relationships with the franchisor who supplies a mixture of branded marketing and advertising, technical support, capital equipment, and merchandise. The relationship of the franchisor and franchisee is a strategic-account relationship with a very specific legal definition.

Because the four different sales approaches offer such different rewards and involve such different costs, they must be applied to the right situations. Transaction selling will be ineffective where major-account management is needed, and strategic-account relationships will be wasted where major-account management will do. Thus, accounts and prospects must be segmented for different approaches.

Segmenting Accounts and Prospects

Given the differences in cost and impact among the four different sales approaches, it is appropriate to consider which accounts and prospects might be appropriate for each approach. Although much has been written about market segmentation, the approach here differs in being focused primarily on segmenting an existing customer base.[8]

SEGMENTING BY SIZE

The easiest way to segment customers is by size; typically, there are more small customers than large ones. If they are visualized as a pyramid (Exhibit IV) and are ranked by size from largest at the top to smallest at the bottom, the increasing width of the base indicates the larger number of smaller sales. This simple approach is a useful beginning.

Account volume can also be visualized in a pyramid or triangle (middle triangle, Exhibit V), but this one is upside-down with a large base at the top. That is because the few large accounts typically comprise a disproportionate amount of volume. The point at the bottom represents the many accounts that represent a small percentage of total volume.

The largest accounts also often demand and perhaps justify more service and customization per dollar or unit of volume. This is

Exhibit IV.   The Customer Pyramid

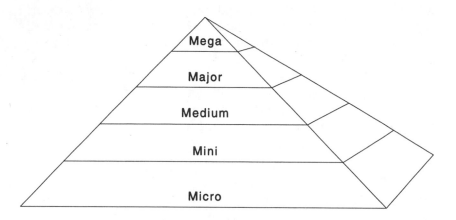

reflected in the right-hand triangle in Exhibit V, which has a wider top than the middle triangle.

A simple approach is to apply the transaction sales approach to the smallest accounts (labeled *micro* in Exhibit IV), the systems approach to the next, and so on up to the strategic-account relationship approach at the very top for the few largest mega accounts. This method is mechanistic and heavy-handed but better than a random approach. However, it neglects customer potential, account profitability, customer needs, and vendor rewards other than sales volume and profits.

Exhibit V.   Customer Potential and Customer Demands

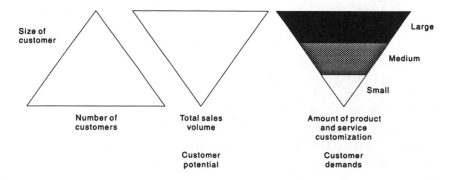

Exhibit VI.   The Customer/Order Profitability Matrix

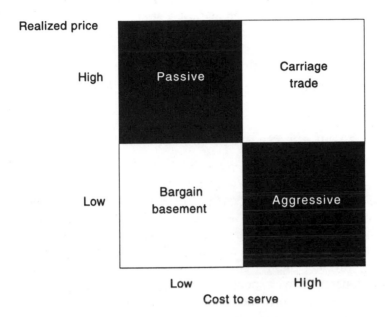

SEGMENTING BY POTENTIAL AND PROFITABILITY

Potential is easy to add to the process. The simplest way is to use the pyramids and triangles to represent realizable potential instead of current sales volume. The same general shape is likely to appear, but the approach is more future-oriented. Specifying potential requires some careful analysis of each account and is a good place to begin effective account planning.

Account profitability can be added by using the account profitability matrix (Exhibit VI), which separates accounts (and orders) by realized price and cost to serve. Passive accounts, which pay high realized prices and are inexpensive to serve, are more attractive than aggressive accounts, which pay low realized prices and are expensive to serve.[9] This approach requires an account-profitability analysis system and fairly well-developed account plans to determine which accounts will provide incremental profitable business. Such pro forma analysis is important because the cost of serving an account with the strategic-account relationship approach is much higher than with the transaction and systems sales approaches or even major-account management.

There is no reason to use a more expensive approach when customer needs and prospective vendor rewards do not justify it. Wherever possible the least expensive, easiest approach (to the left on Exhibit III) should be chosen. Only a few customers will justify the strategic-account relationship approach. And, a fairly small number of most vendors' customers, relative to the account base, will even justify major-account management.

CANDIDATES FOR RELATIONSHIP SELLING

The accounts and prospects most likely to demand advanced approaches are also usually the accounts most sensitive to vendor quality and performance as opposed to price, product quality and performance, rapid availability, and convenience. Commodity markets are characterized by buyers who emphasize price. Specialty markets are made up of buyers who want either rapid availability, convenience, product quality and performance, or vendor quality and performance.[10] Those specialty buyers who are sensitive to vendor quality and performance are most appropriate candidates for the advanced sales approaches.

Finally, some accounts have special attributes that make them appropriate for special-account relationships. An account providing an entry into a new marketplace or familiarity with new technologies or manufacturing processes may be attractive far beyond its current sales volume and profitability or future potential for volume or profitability. A good example of such an account is a mid-sized account identified for strategic-account treatment by a high-technology material supplier. The account was a consistent technological leader in the supplier's most important market and was viewed, because of this technical prowess, as the "account of the future." The materials supplier decided that being close to the technological cutting edge was more important than current volume.

Other accounts can help the vendor manage product mix in a strategic sense. Such an account might, in a strategic relationship, for example, accept "rejected" product that is not up to specification for other customers but is much better than scrap. This arrangement can have a major impact on operations and profitability.

Other attributes which make an account appropriate for development of a strategic-account relationship include industry visibility and image, and compatibility. When we confront implementation, we will give more attention to this latter consideration.

To summarize, if we define strategic accounts as those appropriate for the development of strategic-account relationships, we would look for accounts that satisfy the following criteria: (1) current sales volume, (2) future sales potential, (3) current profitability, (4) future profitability, (5) strong customer-service needs, (6) strong customer interest in vendor quality and performance, (7) entry into a new market, technology, or manufacturing process, (8) impact on product mix, (9) industry visibility and image, and (10) ability to work with, or compatibility.

Ideally, a strategic account will rank high on all criteria; but often one or even several criteria will have to be sacrificed. The list indicates the need to analyze more than current volume and even current profitability. Myopia is dangerous when planning for the long term. Perhaps only one trap is more dangerous—selecting too many strategic accounts so that none gets the attention it needs.

Special Services for the Few

The relations between the amount of special sales and service attention provided and the number of strategic accounts can be visualized as a graph (see Exhibit VII). The vertical dimension is the number or percentage of accounts receiving special effort, and the horizontal dimension is the amount of that effort. In Exhibit VIII on the upper right, a few customers get major special attention. In the lower left, many customers get little differentiation. The line between the two (lower left to upper right) can be a constant-cost line. The choice of giving a great deal of special effort to each of a few customers versus less special effort to each of a larger group is indeed strategic.

If the account base is concentrated (few customers and prospects comprise a large percentage of potential) and accounts are interested in special services, then the upper right-hand corner of intensively nurturing a few accounts with the strategic-account relationship approach will pay off. A more dispersed account and prospect potential and/or less responsiveness to special services suggests that less differentiation for a larger group of accounts would be a better strategy. Unfortunately, Exhibit VII is somewhat unidimensional and does not allow us to look at the total account

Exhibit VII. *Amount of Special Attention vs. Number of Strategic Accounts*

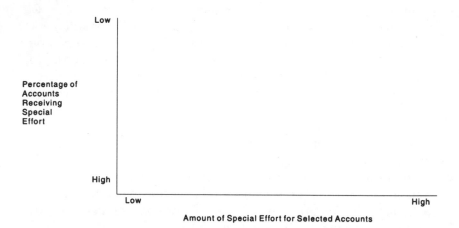

and prospect base to better determine what number of customers should get each type of sales treatment.

Having examined the four different sales approaches and seen that most vendors will use a mixture of the four, we turn to a deeper analysis of strategic-account relationships, first reiterating

Exhibit VIII. *Special Services for the Few*

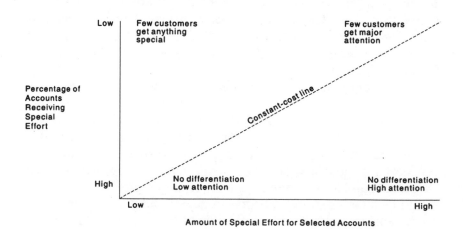

that these complex relationships are not appropriate to every vendor nor to every customer of any vendor.

WHAT DO STRATEGIC-ACCOUNT RELATIONSHIPS PROVIDE TO CUSTOMERS?

The essence of strategic-account relationships is provision of a special set of efforts by the vendor that provide the customer with a long-term competitive advantage. The customer hopes to receive some mixture of technological, operational, and strategic benefits from the approach.

Most strategic-account relationships are fostered by intense and rapid technological development. The need for technological specialization and integration has forced customers to look beyond their boundaries for the requisite skills and resources. Often the partners must integrate their technologies and design products cooperatively and, because technology needs are so pressing and the integration is so complex, the level of sharing must be high. Design and development often require a good deal of "cutting and fitting."

Many customers and prospects also seek operational rewards from the strategic-account vendor. Sometimes these result naturally from the technological integration; at other times they are the primary benefit.

Evolving approaches to manufacturing often force intimate operational coordination. Because components, equipment, and systems exchanged in a strategic partnership are often customized—with no second source and no other prospective customers—the operational integration system has fewer safety valves and alternatives for the vendor than more traditional approaches. Thus, sales forecasting and capacity planning must be jointly executed. The higher the levels of technological and design integration, the higher the need for operational integration.

The relationship between NutraSweet and its primary customers is an example of operational benefits focused on joint marketing interests. Consumer franchisor-franchisee relationships such as McDonald's and Dunkin' Donuts also demonstrate the marketing benefits of the relationship.

By their nature, strategic-account relationships work only when the relationship is strategically important to both companies. The cost and effort involved in making the partnership work can be justified only if there is a strategic need. They are not justified and will not be provided unless the need is clear to the relevant, and powerful, managers on both sides as well as to the lower-level people who must carry out the work. General Motors needed Fanuc's factory-automation skills to survive and prosper in a hostile competitive environment; Fanuc needed a large, worldwide base of leading-edge, high-volume customers, advanced applications knowledge, and factory involvement to develop its dominant position in robots. Each company needed the other to prosper.

HOW ARE STRATEGIC-ACCOUNT RELATIONSHIPS NURTURED?

We have shown that strategic-account relationships require importance, intimacy, and longevity and that intimacy sets the tone for the relationship. Technological, operational, and strategic integration lead naturally to a necessarily high level of organizational integration—a degree of integration beyond that developed in the 1970s and early 1980s as part of major-account management.

Organizational integration extends to virtually every part of the vendor's and customer's organizations: engineers talk to engineers; production people talk to one another; and, top management must get together as well. Old-fashioned arm's-length organizational relationships are not enough. In many cases, the success of people in one company is more dependent on their personal relationships in the partner organization than with anyone in their own firm. Designers, for example, must work together very closely, often merging different technologies and philosophies.

Sometimes the seller's employees must work at the customer's facilities, or even operate equipment there. In the chemical industry, some vendors have found it advantageous, even necessary, to operate leased equipment at a customer site. This raises a raft of issues about integration—everything from union contracts to cafeteria and parking privileges.

Successful organizational and personal integration can take place only between a vendor and a customer who share business values and culture. It sometimes seems that the greatest strategic and technological rewards would come from the partnership of two quite disparate companies, but the likelihood of success tends to go down in such a situation. Strong management support on both sides and unusual organizational arrangements may help, but some disparities cannot be bridged regardless of goodwill, effort, and potential reward.

Finally, there is financial integration. The strategic bond here is so great that the typical financial relationship is often too weak to reflect it. Some strategic-account relationships work on a typical "I make it, I sell it, you buy it, and you pay for it" basis. But other arrangements better reflect the closeness of the relationship. Outright acquisition is one approach; formal joint ventures, such as GM–Fanuc, are much more likely. Other approaches include development contracts, supply contracts, licensing, and very strong informal relationships. Seldom does the buyer ask for bids for a specified product. Instead, the development is joint, and the financial relationship attempts to reflect the sharing of risk, contribution, and reward.[11]

Sometimes the integration of a strategic partnership must extend beyond the two partners to the vendor's suppliers and the customer's customers. System tasks may be so complex that other levels in the supply chain or distribution channel are needed to provide strategic, technological, operational, and financial horsepower.

Finally, integration within each of the partner firms must be stronger than in a normal company. Roy Shapiro argues that the purchasing, engineering, and production functions in the customer company must themselves become more integrated in order to deal successfully with suppliers in strategic-account relationships.[12] The vendor organization must also be well integrated; everyone must sell and service the strategic partner. If the engineering and sales functions cannot operate well together, it is hard to believe that they will be able to sustain an intimate relationship with customers.

The Rewards

All this integration must be justified by substantial rewards. Strategic-account relationships offer the selling company the opportunity to leverage its skills and resources, develop long-term customers, and build strong competitive positions. Companies in a wide variety of industries have understood the rewards and opportunities. Some have realized them successfully; others have not.

Strategic-account relationships are not necessarily a way station between acquisition—in a sense the ultimate form of strategic partnership—and more arm's-length forms of buyer-seller relations. They can be very special continuing vendor-customer connections that offer rewards to both parties. At the core of many strategic-account relationships is the exchange of knowledge, "soft" management skills as well as "hard" technological capabilities. The seller learns how its product is used and develops unique applications approaches; the customer is willing to share such knowledge with an outsider because it too can gain knowledge and unique support for new activities.

If the partnership is with a distributor, a manufacturer gains commitment of the distributor's resources to its product line and to developing capabilities applicable only to the company's products. For example, a distributor's salespeople may spend substantial amounts of time learning about the benefits of the products, their competitive position, and the best ways of selling them. Distributor engineers will learn the details of how the vendor's product can interface with customers' products and systems; and the distributor's service people will develop skill in maintaining and repairing the equipment. The distributor is willing to make these commitments because of the permanence and intimacy of the relationship. In the distribution realm, the strategic-account relationship differs more in degree than in nature from a solid, close, but typical major or national distributor-vendor arrangement.

The permanency of the relationship and the knowledge exchange can produce a stronger competitive position. Sometimes, in fact, a vendor cannot afford to invest in a major new product without the long-term assurance of a customer to ensure profitability, or at least limit the financial risk.

Traps

The astute choice and efficient management of strategic-account relationships are critical determinants of success. The process of developing them, however, presents some major traps, which can be divided into four groups:

1. Attempting to develop too many strategic relationships
2. Picking unsuitable partners

3. Allocating too few resources to the relationship
4. Losing sight of the importance of cultural compatibility

Because they are so intensive and extensive, a company can adequately maintain only a few strategic-account relationships. Some companies have a very concentrated customer and prospect list; that is, they have few existing and potential accounts and even fewer with high sales potential. These companies, obviously, can develop only a few—perhaps only one—strategic-account relationships. But even companies with very extensive prospect and customer lists cannot manage more than a few such relationships, given their high demands on resources and time.

Strategic accounts almost always demand, for example, at least a degree of product and service customization, which affects the vendor's whole organization and product line. If the customization is major and the vendor has too many strategic accounts, it can be torn apart as each account pressures the company to give priority to its needs. If there are too many conflicting pulls, the vendor will be able to satisfy none of them well. Even worse, it will probably lose its internal coherence and end up with a poorly integrated product line.

If the vendor can have only a few relationships, and if the relationships are strategic, it is clear that the choice of the accounts is critical. A poor choice leads to wasted resources, but that is not its major cost. The highest cost is usually the loss of the opportunity to develop an effective strategic-account relationship with another customer. Instead, a competitor may move in and reap long-term rewards. The choice of accounts is particularly difficult when it is impossible to have strategic relationships with two accounts that compete intensively.

Therefore, the criteria for choice, and their priority, must be set out very carefully indeed. They should include the following:

A leading-edge technical and/or operational capability

A willingness to share in joint technical and/or operational development

A willingness to make the vendor an important part of the customer's business activities, including frequent meetings with a wide variety of functional units within the customer organization

Substantial sales potential

Long-term profit potential

An existing relationship as a basis for the partnership

Good cultural fit

The technical and/or operational capability and development in criteria 1 and 2 must relate to activities of clear strategic importance to the vendor. The capability may be "hard," like a scientific or engineering expertise, or "soft," like a particular operational competency (e.g., marketing, service, or manufacturing).

Some companies have attempted to develop strategic accounts without devoting enough resources to them. In some cases they have tried to develop too many account relationships, or have chosen strategic-account relationships that are not justified by other criteria. Sometimes, they have simply underestimated the cost and commitment needed. Four forms of resource starvation are particularly common:

1. Not assigning enough top management skill and power, or enough technical and functional expertise, to the relationships. Strategic accounts justify and require the best staffing and attention.
2. Using a sales-oriented approach when more engineering, production, service, and financial skills are needed. (This is not a standard sale; it is a long-term, intimate partnership.)
3. An unwillingness to customize products and services for each strategic account. The customized nature of such partnerships is one of the limiting factors of the number that can be developed. If each relationship needs a separate product line, and the base business needs to maintain its own product line, the engineering, production, service, and logistics functions must be adequate to handle the total diversity.
4. If personal relationships are to develop, people must spend time together. Travel and telephone budgets must be extensive enough to support the development of trust. And managers and experts working on the accounts must have adequate time to do their jobs. Some may have to move to the partner's location for an extended, but temporary, period. The drain of international partnerships, with their attendant travel costs—and jet lag is a real cost!—is very high indeed.

Patience is another important part of nurturing strategic-account relationships. The life cycle of the relationship dictates that, as in most situations, an investment in time must be made before rewards can be reaped. Major-account management takes a long time, and strategic-account relationship development takes even longer. Many months are needed to build a good personal relationship and even longer to build the deep institutional bonds of the relationship. Patience is particularly necessary when joint projects involve major technological development or when the customer is a mature, cyclical company. Although the down cycle is often the best time to build strategic relationships, the more visible benefits, such as sales increases, will often not accrue until the up cycle.

Another particularly good time to build strategic-account relationships is when the supplier industry is oversold and customers are in desperate need of support. Short-term optimization of profits by such maneuvers as price-gouging or allocating scarce products to new customers instead of established ones can cost dearly over the long term and make it impossible to establish the deep trust needed for this type of relationship.

Finally, some companies have failed to understand the delicate mating of cultures that leads to successful relationships. Some pairs of cultures are difficult to integrate; some are impossible. Partnerships require compromise and constant joint nurturing to succeed.

Implementation: Building Institutional Relationships

Although strategic-account relationships are fairly new, it is possible to suggest some guidelines for success. Some are similar to those for acquisitions, an even more intimate and permanent relationship. The critical issue is always the human management of the relationship, which must build something closer than the typical buyer-seller relationship but less internally integrated than an acquisition. To do this and avoid the traps, management should

1. Develop only a few strategic partnerships. In most businesses some customers will be transactional customers, some systems customers, a limited number major or national accounts, and a very small number strategic-account relationships. If the number of the latter is not countable on the fingers, the relationships will not be truly strategic.
2. Choose accounts that meet the explicit chosen criteria and share a long-term vision of the future. Only long-term relationships can really be strategic; they must last long enough to generate profits after the expensive, initial investment period. They should be seen

as long-term company-to-company relationships, not as limited to one product or technology or—worst of all—one deal.

3. Allocate adequate resources to the relationship. If the resource allocation is parsimonious, the relationship is doomed.

4. Understand that these relationships involve a substantial loss of autonomy. Decisions will be based on the needs and desires of both partners. This loss of autonomy is one of the primary costs of strategic-account relationships, and the loss will be most severe in the areas closest to the heart of the relationship—often product design and technology choice.

5. Develop a financial relationship that reflects the long-term needs and interests of both parties; that is flexible enough to adjust to changing conditions (in a long-term relationship, conditions will surely change); and that is explicit enough to avoid arguments about interpretation. It helps to identify, discuss, and clarify beforehand issues that are likely to create problems in the future. The relationship should be so intimate and pervasive that troublesome parts of it cannot be swept under the carpet in hopes that they will not be noticed. If they are, they will fester until the infection destroys the relationship. There are many financial forms the venture can take; all the relevant ones—from supply contracts to joint ventures—should be explored to find the optimum mix of flexibility and explicitness.

Finally, we turn to the management of the relationship. To succeed the partnership must be institutionalized; that is, it must supersede the relationship between any two individuals and become a relationship between organizations.

Most major-account relationships depend ultimately upon one person, an able account manager who can mobilize internal resources to support the account and call on many people at the account with confidence and competence. He or she becomes the primary node in the communications network (as shown in Exhibit IX).

A true strategic-account relationship cannot, however, operate with one primary node. There must be intense communication among many vendor and customer functions (as illustrated in Exhibit X). The obvious problem with this scheme is that the communication can easily become unmanageable, uncoordinated, and, hence, inefficient. One solution is to manage the venture through a partnership team consisting of two senior executives—one from each company—and a group of top-level functional executives. This

Exhibit IX. The Communications Network

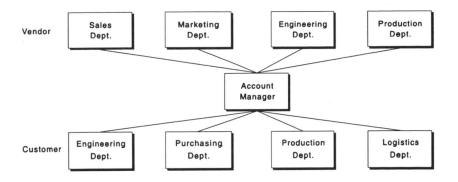

structure imitates the joint-venture board of directors in a more informal and day-to-day way.

The senior partnership team should not replace or limit other, direct communications, but manage and coordinate the relationship by nurturing cross-company integration and communication at all levels in all functions. If the engineers do not talk to one another, for example, the benefits of the partnership will not accrue, though the costs will.

National-account management has been described as a case of making and keeping promises to customers.[13] This view is appropriate in all four sales approaches, even transaction selling. It is especially relevant to the relationship-building activities that are central to major-account management and strategic-account relationships. Because of the long-term nature of the activities and results, yesterday's promises must be kept tomorrow; when they

Exhibit X. Communication Between Vendor and Customer

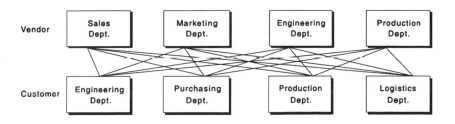

are not kept, the present relationship suffers, which can have long-term impacts. Moreover, the great upside opportunity of strategic-account relationships puts a premium on unmade promises as well, for the unmade promise is, in essence, a lost opportunity. It sacrifices long-term return, just as unkept promises hurt the present situation.

We have seen that strategic-account relationships are a response to the need to develop and manage more complex and more permanent partnerships between suppliers and customers. They are expensive and difficult, but they offer great benefits when used selectively and implemented effectively. Undoubtedly some companies will view them as a panacea. They are not. In fact, in most industries they will supplement and enhance only a small part of the company's sales and marketing efforts. They differ in intensity and degree—but not truly in nature—from major- and national-account management. They differ in fundamental nature from transaction and systems selling. There are four kinds of close encounters in selling, but one is closer than the others.

Notes

1. Arthur Miller, *Death of a Salesman* (New York: The Viking Press, 1949), p. 81 (speech by Willy Loman).
2. Ibid., p. 74.
3. Benson P. Shapiro and Ronald S. Posner, "Making the Major Sale," *Harvard Business Review*, March–April 1979.
4. Benson P. Shapiro and John Wyman, "New Ways to Reach Your Customers," *Harvard Business Review*, July–August 1981; Benson P. Shapiro and Rowland T. Moriarty, Jr., *National Account Management*, and *National Account Management: Emerging Insights* (Cambridge, Mass.: Marketing Science Institute, 1980, 1982).
5. Benson P. Shapiro and Rowland T. Moriarty, Jr., *Organizing the National Account Force*, and *Support Systems for National Account Management Programs* (Cambridge, Mass.: Marketing Science Institute, 1983).
6. Quoting from a speech by Professor Thomas V. Bonoma of the Harvard Business School.
7. For other types of coalitions, see, for example, Michael E. Porter,

Competitive Advantage (New York: Free Press, 1985), pp. 191–193, for a discussion of licensing; and Joseph L. Bower and Eric A. Rhenman, "Benevolent Cartels," *Harvard Business Review*, July–August 1985.

8. For more on commercial/industrial market segmentation, see Thomas V. Bonoma and Benson P. Shapiro, *Segmenting the Industrial Market* (Lexington, Mass.: Lexington Books, 1983); Benson P. Shapiro and Thomas V. Bonoma, "How to Segment Industrial Markets," *Harvard Business Review*, July–August 1984; and Thomas V. Bonoma and Benson P. Shapiro, "Evaluating Market Segmentation Approaches," *Industrial Marketing Management*, October 1984.

9. Benson P. Shapiro, V. Kasturi Rangan, Rowland T. Moriarty, and Elliot B. Ross, "Manage Customers for Profits (Not Just Sales)," *Harvard Business Review*, September–October 1987.

10. For more on these distinctions, see Benson P. Shapiro, "Specialties vs. Commodities: The Battle for Profit Margins," Harvard Business School Case No. 9-587-120.

11. For more on these new types of relationships, see Roy D. Shapiro, "Toward Effective Supplier Management: International Comparisons," Harvard Business School Working Paper No. 9-785-062.

12. Ibid.

13. Benson P. Shapiro and Rowland T. Moriarty, Jr., *Support for National Account Management Programs: Promises Made, Promises Kept* (Cambridge, Mass.: Marketing Science Institute, 1983).

2
Learning from Losing a Customer

David Green

This is a story of how a small, young company lost a very important order, recovered, and became much stronger and more competitive by learning about market positioning. The lessons learned proved so valuable that, when all was said and done, the company concluded that losing the big order was the best thing that had ever happened to it.

The company in question is VideoStar Connections, and since I have been its vice president of sales and marketing for the past five years, this story is also about my own experience. During that period of trial, undoubtedly the most demanding of my career, I came to realize that my job is not simply to win orders. It's also to learn everything possible from losing orders. I don't mind saying that I've learned a lot.

VideoStar was founded in 1980 to provide temporary satellite networks for delivering one-time, private television programs to corporate clients. By setting up portable satellite antennas at hotels, at civic arenas, and on company premises, VideoStar transmitted such programming as product announcements, sales meetings, and training seminars. In the booming new age of business video, our company seemed to have a promising future.

But after a few years of experience with temporary networks, our market began moving away from them. Companies that put on one or two special events saw that, for about the same cost, they could install their own antennas. These, coupled with existing in-house videotape production facilities, permitted companies to create their own permanent, private television networks. Here was a training and communication tool that was becoming not only affordable but also essential for many corporations.

For VideoStar, this development seemed to herald a new opportunity. Although the special-event business yielded high profit margins, it was extremely cyclical, having intense periods of activity followed by periods with little business, little revenue. Long-term planning was impossible since most temporary networks were ordered with very little notice.

The private-network business, on the other hand, seemed much more orderly and predictable in revenues. Besides, we had great expertise and fine facilities for handling special events, which we could apply to handling these new private networks. The writing was on the wall.

In early 1983, Hewlett-Packard, one of our earliest and best special-event customers, invited us to bid for the job of designing and installing a permanent network. We were the only bidder and won the order. We thought we were on our way.

But we didn't read the situation correctly. Shortly thereafter, a startup company, formed specifically for the private television network market, came on the scene. At first, we weren't worried; the emergence of Private Satellite Network (PSN) only confirmed our view of where the market was heading. With our strong reputation for performance and our long list of satisfied customers, we were sure we had a big advantage. But we were dead wrong. Over the next 18 months, this scrappy competitor picked off a half-dozen very important orders, including several special-event customers of ours.

The big showdown came in late 1984, when Digital Equipment, one of our prized special-event customers, issued a request for proposals for a permanent satellite network worth more than a million dollars. Digital's requirement was to communicate instantaneously with its sales and service centers across the country. It needed a private video network.

We took no chances in bidding for this all-important order. Our entire 60-employee organization, from receptionist to president, geared up for the competition. Everyone worked hard for several months preparing the presentation. Digital's order, however, went to PSN.

Stunned and bewildered, we worried about our future. After a thorough postmortem, we decided that we hadn't lost this order for lack of technical competence, customer satisfaction, or competitive pricing. In fact, Digital assured us that we would continue to get its temporary-network business. So what went wrong? The answer was simple. Digital thought we were great for one-night stands, but not right for a long-term relationship.

Honest self-appraisal is never easy, and neither is facing up to the facts. But we had no choice, and in the months following our loss of the Digital order, we took a very hard look at our business. The experience, painful as it was, proved very revealing. From it we drew three conclusions, figured out that all three were related to positioning, and then set out to reposition our company and our product for those long-term relationships we wanted to forge with our customers.

Our first conclusion had to do with perceptions: Expertise doesn't matter if the customer doesn't think you're in the business. In our case, all our expertise in special-event networking was perceived as irrelevant to the private-network business. When we argued that we were indeed in the private-network business, it looked like an add-on rather than a serious focus. Our competitor, on the other hand, was in the permanent-network business exclusively and was building an impressive list of private-network customers to prove its qualifications.

Our second conclusion dealt with the question of staying power: If the customer doesn't know much about the product, the seller with the best image of staying power will get the order. PSN enjoyed a solid financial underwriting, a well-connected board of directors, offices in New York City, and a well-publicized plan for profitability and a public offering. We were a small special-event business in Atlanta with no particular clout. As someone at Digital told us later: "Your competitor's D&B said '$10 million in the bank,' while yours read 'neat and clean premises.'" Clearly our organization didn't look like one with staying power.

Our third conclusion had to do with understanding the customer's needs: If you respond with only what the customer says he or she wants, you may not be providing what the customer needs. In its RFP, Digital asked for the installation of hardware to support its network. So, like our competitor, we responded with a proposal for hardware and the installation.

But as we would come to understand, the real product in most high-tech offerings is rarely the hardware. By responding before reflecting, we had missed an opportunity to play a role in the customer's decision making. Our proposal could have educated the customer—but it didn't.

These three conclusions drawn from the Digital experience told us that we had failed miserably at the fine art of positioning. We had not built the right image of our company and we had not changed those perceptions that stood in the way of our getting the business. Over the next several months, we set about correcting those problems by redefining and sharpening the focus of our business.

What Business Are We In?

People think they know what business they're in. But do their actions and commitment of resources support their stated business? Management needs to evaluate continually where the organization's strengths lie, match these with customer needs, and maintain its focus. When VideoStar lost the Digital order, we looked at where our people were committed, where our capital was invested, and what competitive advantages we had.

Our soul-searching yielded a disturbing reflection. Although we talked about the private-network business, our focus was clearly elsewhere. Special-event networks, sometimes yielding as much as a million dollars in revenue for a single one-day event, paid the bills and garnered the resources. To optimize our equipment investment, we provided services to broadcasters too. When the network trucks couldn't cover late-breaking stories or emergencies, our organization sprang into operation to provide satellite feeds. While tracking hurricanes up and down the Atlantic coast was exciting, it burned out our people and equipment, returned little profit, and took our eye off the ball.

In a wrenching series of decisions during the summer of 1985, we abandoned our broadcast business, reassigned some people to our private-network effort, and let others go. These were the first layoffs in our company's history, and it was a traumatic experience for those who stayed as well as for those who left. To the staff, this action signaled the gravity of the situation and underscored our determination to pursue private networks aggressively while maintaining our special-event business.

A prospective buyer often views a new product or service simply as hardware. Take personal computers. If you are the local ComputerLand franchisee, you've probably been selling hardware for the last few years to computer buffs. But as more people buy PCs and the market broadens, customer support and training have emerged as important criteria in selecting a computer vendor. People who bought PCs wanted to use them to solve problems, not just to own them. So in five years, the PC industry changed from pushing hardware to supplying a service that helps people select the right hardware while training them to use it effectively.

We at VideoStar knew we couldn't be profitable in private networks if we merely provided hardware. The competition from manufacturers such as GTE, RCA, and Scientific-Atlanta was fierce, and because clearly defined distribution relationships had not yet evolved, manufacturers often marketed directly to the end-users at or below our prices. The installation business didn't hold much profit either. There's just no way the installation cost on a $5,000 earth station can yield much margin.

If we didn't see our business clearly, our customers did. Sure, some only wanted us to provide equipment and installation. But the real business came in operational support. After we had installed its network, for example, Hewlett-Packard asked us to furnish nationwide maintenance service and satellite time and to support its network transmissions. Chrysler put in its own network, then turned to us to supply maintenance and operational support. We began to see that the business of business television is network management, not merely hardware.

With a clear definition of what our business was going to be, we needed to move out smartly to capture network management services with creative, flexible solutions. We needed to position network management as crucial to the user's success with business television and position VideoStar as a network management company—one with staying power.

Positioning depends greatly on creating an image. The natural place to begin that task is in your current strengths. How could we build on our strength in special-event networks to capture our share of the private-network business? How could we align ourselves with an important group of potential competitors—the equipment manufacturers?

And, most important, how could we also convince organizations with revenues in the billions that it was safe to establish a long-term relationship with us, even though we had revenues of but a few million?

Taking On the Competition

By the winter of 1985, almost a year after the loss of the Digital order, we had focused our business, defined our private-network product, and identified the position we wanted in the marketplace. Thanks to the steps I describe below, we were ready to take on our competitors on an equal footing.

TELLING THE STORY.   We started using slogans like "VideoStar, the Network Management Company" in our print and presentation materials. We positioned the private-network requirement as consisting of equipment, programming, and network management, and described our company's long and successful history in the industry, focusing on network management. Our message: Network management was the glue that held business television together, and VideoStar was a leader that provided network management services second to none.

IT'S ALL IN A NAME.   To take advantage of our recognized expertise in special events, we needed to communicate the relationship between the special-event and private-network businesses. But there was no name that included both. Existing terms like "videoconference" and "teleconference" were confusing and inaccurate in describing our special-event business. Worse, the private-network service we provided was called by our competitor's company name!

Sometimes the best solutions are the simple ones. We coined the term "business television" to include temporary and permanent networks. We began to use it in our presentations, proposals, ads, and other literature. We worked with consultants and the trade press to incorporate the term into the lexicon. Fortunately for us, everyone agreed that the widely used word "videoconference" was too broad and confusing when used to describe large broadcast conferences. Soon even our competitor was using "business television," and our industry adopted it. It linked VideoStar's past successful business and its targeted future.

HELP FROM FRIENDS.   Could we enhance our image through association with powerful advocates? If so, who would they be?

We recognized that our suppliers, our one private-network customer, and the investors we were courting for a capital infusion could be powerful allies. They all had good reasons for helping us. Our suppliers would benefit in more equipment sales. Our private-network customer wanted to ensure that we would be around to service its network. And investors would profit from our success.

Each group contributed. A major equipment supplier stood behind us in a critical sale. Hewlett-Packard put on demonstrations for key accounts, where we and H-P had joint marketing interests, and offered strong testimonials to prospects. Investors considering loans to and equity purchases in VideoStar asked potential customers about their interest in networks and in our company. The investors' interest implied that VideoStar had staying power.

BEEFING UP THE SALES FORCE.   Before we could convince prospective customers, we had to convince all our employees that we were in the private-network as well as the special-event segments of business television. Some of our salespeople were not right for the sort of relationship management style needed for complex, large-account selling. We replaced them with salespeople who were. We modified compensation plans to motivate the sales force, not only for the longer term sales cycle of private-network sales but also for account maintenance following the sale.

INVESTMENT IN MARKETING.   We gave more attention to market research and marketing communications. We invested in market-research programs to better identify potential customers and analyze their readiness for a network. We created professional presentation materials, private-network proposals, briefs about applications, "success stories" for placement in industry trade journals, and our own quarterly television program, all of which reflected our new positioning.

ZERO-DEFECT OPERATIONS.   Business television is live television, and there is no room for error. We had always measured our success in the special-event business on a criterion of 100% operational performance: every site operational every minute of the program. That view of success had earned VideoStar its reputation in the special-event business. We reasoned that a similar view would pay dividends in the private-network business.

Dividends for VideoStar

In the past three years we have seen our strategies pay off handsomely, most notably with our friends at Digital. Although we had lost that initial order, we continued to provide Digital with service for special-event networks while doggedly working on longer term business. We made sure our contacts at DEC knew of the changing nature and positioning of our company. They talked with our customers and evidently liked what they heard.

So, when Digital reopened the competition for an expanded network, we were ready. What Digital now needed was a plan for making a transition of network vendors that limited its risk and minimized its costs. We listened carefully to DEC executives' concerns and designed a solution that made our proposal compelling.

In the end, Digital chose us to provide all of its business television networking needs. Three years after the Big Loss and a wrenching reevaluation of our company, we were finally on our way in the permanent-network business.

In summary, here are the lessons we learned from our experience:

Positioning is critical for a small company like ours selling long-term, intangible services, particularly when customers are large, conservative companies.

In creating a positioning strategy, we first had to understand what business we were in and focus our resources on that business. The effort required some hard decisions.

The entire company had to understand what business we were in and represent that position inside and outside the company. Sales and marketing personnel had to be committed to building long-term relationships.

We had to build a strong marketing communications program that played on strengths and minimized weaknesses. While this didn't require a Madison Avenue campaign, it did require professional-appearing materials that conveyed an impressive image.

That image included technical competence and a service attitude; more important, however, to those who make the buying decision was the image of our staying power in the marketplace.

We helped ourselves by allying with customers, suppliers, and investors—all of whom stood to gain from our success.

Establishing a position is one thing; keeping it is another. As our market evolves, as customer requirements change, as technology advances, so must the positioning strategy be modified. Positioning is not a one-time effort. It is a constant pursuit.

3
Making the Major Sale

Benson P. Shapiro and Ronald S. Posner

It has become increasingly clear over the past 15 years that salesmanship has been changing, especially when one business sells industrial or consumer goods and services to another.[1] As a result, the salesperson is being called on to perform in a different way.

One major change is that, as mergers and acquisitions, sales of parts of companies, and different kinds of corporate financing have become more prevalent, the one-of-a-kind, nonrepetitive sale—such as the sale of a subsidiary or company, or a licensing arrangement—has become more important. These transactions have always existed, but they are more numerous and significant now, and are beginning to attract the attention of sales management.

Second, businesses have become larger (and at the same time more complex), and the average size of the sale has grown. In certain industries this change has been dramatic, especially with the development of system selling and large private-label contracts in consumer goods. Consider these examples:

The Industrial Chemical Division at Allied Chemical Corporation has sold sulfuric acid for many years. Its larger annual contract sales have been in the $1-million to $2-million range and have lasted for several years. Recently, the division developed a process for air-pollution control whose sales involve a total capital commitment for a utility of more than $20 million and cover many years.

Private-label contracts for consumer goods have not only grown in size but have also gone beyond the traditional general merchandise chains (Sears, Roebuck, J.C. Penney, and Montgomery Ward) to cover supermarkets, discount department stores, and regular department stores. Arrangements involving more than $10 million are not uncommon with such contracts.

Even comparatively small companies are making large sales. In the field of building cleaning and maintenance, companies with $10 million in sales often compete for million-dollar contracts.

The outcome of a few large sales can sometimes determine a company's well-being. For example, one of Lockheed's major continuing problems has been low sales of the L1011 aircraft.

In industry, the consequences of the repetitive sale are often even more profound than the initial commitment itself; for system selling, one purchase decision can involve capital, supplies, raw material, and processes. The sale of a computer system can seriously affect a corporation's procedures and policies for many years. Methods of financial reporting, inventory control, production control, marketing, and administration can all be affected.

As the complexity of the purchase and the risk involved have increased, so have the cost and intricacy of selling and servicing the account. The average industrial sales call costs more than $70, with some sales requiring years to consummate. Larger sales often require special products and services and even customer manufacture. For example, most private-label lines are designed expressly for one customer.

Because the major sale affects many functional departments of the buyer, decision making is becoming more involved and the buying criteria more sophisticated. Naturally, the buyer's personnel are concerned over such a large purchase and must carefully evaluate its impact on their operations. Thus they need continuing reassurance and, in particular, more financial data—data such as return on investment and cost/performance measurements.

In this article, we will try to develop a program of responses that marketers can use in confronting these two new situations. After explaining the basic approach, we unfold eight steps management should take to ensure a more successful and long-lasting sale. Finally we provide some organizational guidelines to help companies incorporate this approach into their overall activities.

The Basic Approach

Major sales including both one-time sales and continuing relationships, need special handling: they are more complex; their potential profit is larger; and they have a more lasting effect on both buyer and seller. A systematic approach that works for both types of selling situations is strategic selling. This is a meticulously planned, total process, requiring coordination of the buyer and seller, that identifies the customer's needs and relates the company's products to those needs.

Strategic selling is especially relevant for "big-ticket" sales because only large potential profit can justify the careful planning and large amounts of resources that are required. Although it is not a new technique, it is attracting attention because it brings to bear more people, greater resources, and more information about the customer's needs; these characteristics uniquely suit the changes that have taken place in salesmanship.

The process is particularly effective because it emphasizes the dual goals of making the sale and developing account relationships. With escalating profits and longevity of sales, this latter goal is increasingly important. In fact, for repetitive major sales the objective should be to develop long-term account relationships, not just sales. The supplier with an established account relationship has a significant competitive advantage. Because risks are high and an intimate buyer/seller relationship builds up over time, buyers are hesitant to try new suppliers and tend to remain with established ones (unless the relationship becomes unbearable or costs increase significantly).

In fact, several corporations believe that their best prospects are current customers. For example, experts in the computer industry claim IBM statistics show that each new account's purchases grow eight times in every six years—this means that the new $5,000-per-month account will be producing $40,000 per month in six years.

Since satisfactory account relationships are an advantage to a marketer, the salesperson has two responsibilities: (1) to stress the long-term benefits of the account relationship to the customer, and (2) to help develop trust and credibility in himself and his company.

There is a definite trade-off between "forcing" a customer to buy something and developing a long-term relationship with that customer. This trade-off can lead to a phenomenon called the "Pyrrhic sale," in which the sale is made at the expense of the account. In long-term relationships the customer is repeatedly in the position of being able to purchase the product. This circumstance requires the salesperson to manage the account carefully: if he (or she) forces a marginal sale, this often destroys credibility and the opportunity for future sales. But if the salesperson is willing to forego a sale that is not in the long-term interest of the account, he can build his relationship with that account.

For example, the seller of apparel who is willing to tell a customer that some items in his line do not sell well at retail, in spite of their apparent appeal, helps his customer and himself over the long run. Or picture the response a buyer would give to the pump salesperson who says, "Yes, we offer the best pumps for your needs a, b, and c, but unfortunately, our pumps are not as good for application as those offered by competitors x and y."

The one-time sale is a somewhat different situation, in that the buying company is even more careful in protecting its interest. But the seller should still want to "leave a good taste in the buyer's mouth" because the sale is visible in the business community, especially within the particular industry, and because the buyer and seller will often be involved with each other after the sale. For example, the managers of a company being acquired often become employees of the buying company. Thus they want to structure a sale that will leave all parties satisfied. This is also true of licensing arrangements and other one-time sales that create lasting relationships.

One of the intriguing aspects of the one-time sale is that both sides are usually selling to each other. For example, the acquiring company often spends a great deal of effort selling the managers of the potential acquisition on the benefits of the merger. This leads to a two-sided romance negotiation in which both parties are sellers and buyers. Thus strategic selling can be applied not only to both types of major sale but also to both sides of the one-time sale.

Step by Step

Strategic selling is an eight-part process that develops the sale from the initial decision to pursue a prospect, through the appropriate strategy for courting an account, to the eventual close of the sale. Because strategic selling is also concerned with developing account relationships, the process is not complete without a discussion of how to sustain those relationships. Let us take a look at each of these steps in turn.

1. OPENING THE SELLING PROCESS

In preparing for a sale, the salesperson should do enough homework so that he has an idea of the likelihood of a sale and the appropriate person to contact initially. Assuming he feels he has a chance to make the sale, his next step is to make the "opening," which is often done over the telephone. His object is to gain enough information from the initial contact to determine the most appropriate person or people to meet.

The best opening, particularly for one-time sales, is sometimes made through a third party; this enables the seller to gain recognition and credibility, avoid making a cold call that puts him at a disadvantage, and obtain information without announcing his intentions. Some companies have developed proven third parties into a "second sales force." Consider these examples:

> A young Los Angeles-based company that sells television production services always finds it easier and more effective for its duplication and distribution supplier to make the introduction. The latter company has been in business 30 years and has established an excellent reputation and a large, satisfied customer base.
>
> Bank of America is training its corporate loan officers to approach CPAs for an introduction to the latter's clients.

For these third-party openings and references to work over a period of time, both parties have to get something from the arrangement. Frequently, such informal relationships work out so well for each party that a more formal sales agreement results in a commission or royalty to the third party for introductions that lead to firm orders.

2. QUALIFYING THE PROSPECT

The next step is to determine whether a sale can eventually be made, or as someone has described it, to "separate the suspects from the prospects." Unfortunately, many companies appear to spend more time selling to prospects who have no intention of buying than to those who do. The old criterion of numbers—which measured selling effectiveness by the number of sales calls—is no longer valid; what matters is the *quality* of the call. The salesperson should ask himself questions like these:

Does this prospective buyer really have a need for my product?

Do the top managers recognize that need?

If they don't, is it likely that I can educate them?

Can I justify my product as a response to that need?

Can I identify influential buyers and others who may affect the decision to buy?

All of these questions boil down to two equally important issues: (1) Can my company be of service to their company? and (2) Can I bring the two companies together? It's almost impossible, for example, for a salesperson to compete with another eager seller who has a close relationship, such as a family tie, with the prospective buyer.

Psychologically, the qualification process is difficult for a salesperson to accept because he has historically been taught that the "lead" is his most valuable possession. What he must learn now is that if the lead is not likely to become a sale, he should not pursue it, and that he is going to have to make the decision about its potential for himself. Not only does he have to ask penetrating questions like those mentioned previously, but he might also have to break off a friendly relationship if it doesn't promise any business.

3. DEVELOPING THE SALES STRATEGY

In strategic selling so many activities are required, so much information has to be obtained, and so many influential people have to be attended to that it is easy to overlook important considerations.

Once he thinks the sale is possible, the salesperson needs a plan to enable him to direct his own efforts and to deploy his company's resources to make the sale and develop the account relationship. What we call the "Strategic Sales Opportunity Profile" is a simple technique to help him map out his entire strategy and organize his sales effort so that all the bases have been covered.

On one form, the salesperson can list people contacted, information obtained, his own activities, follow-up action, and results of the contact. The information he obtains will vary widely, from the practical (certain individuals need detailed cost estimates, or specific product and application data) and organizational (they will only negotiate with the seller's organizational counterpart or need reassurance about their role vis-à-vis the purchase), to the personal (they prefer concepts to details or cannot make a decision unless one of their associates confirms it).

If he completes the profile carefully, updates it regularly, and pursues each selling activity to its conclusion, he will be more likely to close the order. In addition, if he loses a sale, he will be able to make a better postmortem diagnosis.

The profile can also provide valuable information to product and market planning personnel at headquarters. By accumulating the data from the profiles nationally, planners can see trends, such as new applications for their current products, and the need for new products or services.

The salesperson's strategy should be based on the detailed information he has gathered during and after his analysis of the buyer. If he has grasped the idea of strategic selling, he will have asked the right questions: Will the person I'm going to call on make the actual decision? What kind of person is he? How does he fit into the organization? What is his background? Is it technical? Managerial? Where did he work before?

His strategy should also ensure that all of the influential buyers receive attention and the appropriate kind of attention (e.g., the traditional lunch or dinner, or financial data for the treasurer, or technical information for the engineering manager).

The key to strategic selling is calling "high and broad," something most salespeople fear or don't understand. They can talk to a purchasing agent or plant supervisor with relative impunity, but the prospect of calling on a president or an executive vice president frightens them. Although they know that high-priced sales decisions are made at very high levels, they often sell only at the lower levels, where they feel more comfortable, and let the middle-management contacts they have made there carry the story to top management.

This decision has two detrimental effects: (1) some of the strength of their sales presentation is lost in the transmittal, and (2) what is even more damaging, the salesperson often loses a chance to develop a relationship with top managers and to directly gather data on the situation as these managers perceive it. After all, top managers are the people most affected by major purchases, since they will probably have to alter corporate policies and procedures to accommodate the new product or service.

For example, the salesman for a materials handling system spent three months with the director of western warehouse operations of a large New York-based manufacturing company. All along, this contact assured the salesman that he made all the decisions for his area. Unfortunately, competition got the business for the four regional warehouses because it won over the VP of operations in New York, who had the budget approval for all new warehouse systems.

4. ORGANIZING THE JUSTIFICATION

Once the salesperson has determined whom to contact (and at a high enough level), it is time to assist the company in cost-justifying the purchase. For the company to make a decision on a multimillion dollar product or service, each top executive will have to understand exactly how the purchase will affect his operation, budget, cash flow, and personal concerns.

So, at this stage of the strategic sales process, the salesperson must meet with each top executive affected by the purchase to determine his position, unique needs, and the qualitative and financial criteria he uses to justify large purchases. This entails becoming completely conversant with the prospect's operations, gaining a detailed grasp of its finances, and understanding the effect the seller's products and services will have on those operations. In effect, the salesperson should know as much as or even more about such matters than do some of the prospect's top people.

The salesperson is more likely to succeed if he understands the few really important variables that will eventually affect the final sale. Then he can limit the data he needs to those pieces of information and the sources for that information.

Since most cost justifications will be based on certain key assumptions, it is important to get a consensus on each assumption from the decision makers. Even when the salesperson isn't sure how the purchase will affect the organization, he can solicit opinions on potential cost benefits. Answers to such questions as "Do you feel our service can increase sales by 10% over a two-year period?" or "Have you achieved a 5% decrease in labor costs with similar machinery in the past?" from several top executives can give the salesperson a way to justify the purchase, or at least to test alternative solutions to the prospect's problems. The object is to focus on what the prospect thinks is feasible and to use *his* numbers, not those the selling company believes are possible. By combining the best points made by each manager, the salesperson stands a better chance of having his reasoning accepted by the purchaser.

If he gathers data correctly, the salesperson will discover that this is his best time to sell; the decision makers are most free during this phase to say "Here's what I want" and "Here's how I want to be sold."

5. MAKING THE PRESENTATION

The presentation summarizes all of the relevant information in the form of a proposal. If the right people are in attendance, the salesperson should usually use the presentation as an opportunity to ask for the order. While there is no established pattern for the most effective sales presentation, the selling company should carefully consider these factors: elements and order of presentation; location; timing; and who will be listening.

ELEMENTS AND ORDER OF PRESENTATION. The best-selling presentations deliver no new information to the audience. The presentation should only summarize the agreements previously reached with each of the decision makers, thus reinforcing the agreed-on solutions, cost justification, and the implementation commitments. People used to working with committees will be familiar with this approach: a typical way to handle a committee is to personally sell each committee member on a proposal before the meeting, and then to gather general agreement at the meeting.

Exhibit I shows the elements that a selling company should consider for a formal presentation. Note that the presentation basically flows from action to analysis to implementation. The summary is listed first because it outlines the conclusions and recommendations of the study, and because it provides the audience with a general understanding of the direction of the proposal.

LOCATION. Marketing and sales managers often neglect the many possibilities open to them for a location—such as the prospect's facilities, a rented hotel or conference center space, the selling company's own seminar or presentation facility, an installation

Exhibit I.   Elements of a Formal Presentation

Management summary
Ties the presentation to the individuals involved in the sale, reflects mutual agreement already reached with the top decision makers, and makes note of the customer's criteria for selection.

Scope
States the objectives and nature of the problems being solved or challenges being addressed.

Advantages
Spells out the advantages in such a way that the presenting company's products or services are made exclusive (i.e., so that they cannot be duplicated by competition).

Recommended solutions
Tailors the specific products, services, and/or programs to the prospect's requirements, environment, and management objectives.

Financial analysis and cost justification (reached through mutual agreement)
Shows the economic justification to favor the seller company's method over the prospect's current means of performing the function and over possible proposals from competition.

Implementation schedule
Describes the seller's and the prospect's responsibilities, the people to be involved, and dates of completion for the main tasks.

Contract
Spells out the terms and conditions of the sale, which have already been discussed with the prospect.

---

done for another customer, or a mobile display unit mounted in a trailer or bus.

TIMING.   This is another element that will be critical to the effectiveness of a presentation. If a salesperson and the prospect haven't reached mutual agreement on major points, such as the seller's analysis, then the presentation may be premature.

ATTENDEES.   The selling company should make sure that all decision makers are at the meeting, and invite those people within its organization who can best represent it from a social as well as business point of view—i.e., the counterparts of the prospect's personnel. The total group should be small enough to remain intimate and workable. The seller should also ensure that the presentation has enough variety of speakers to be interesting but not confusing. Some team members may take active roles, some may provide supportive information, and others may be there primarily as a formality.

For several reasons, the personal involvement of top managers is justified, and frequently required, by the buying company. First, they are the only people who can make the commitments the buyer requires—i.e., adjust the selling conditions (including price, delivery, product features, and quality) and make and guarantee commitments that would sound hollow coming from lower management.

Second, they have the appropriate status to deal with top executives in the buying organization, who feel more comfortable dealing with their organizational counterparts.

Third, strategic selling involves more risk and requires greater resources—including higher powered salespeople and better developed programs and sales aids—than the more typical approach. Only top managers can provide the discipline, allocate the resources, and establish the high standards such a program needs. Moreover, they have to provide continual motivation to a sales force that can easily become discouraged by a long lead time for sales. Their interest and involvement can be demonstrated not only by attendance at the presentation, but also by account reviews with the sales representative and direct sales calls on the prospective buyer. (For the nonrepetitive sale, their involvement is perhaps more crucial—only they can abrogate standard policies and procedures to provide the attention and resources needed on a one-time basis.)

6. COORDINATING RESOURCES AND PERSONNEL

During the selling process, the salesperson is responsible for managing the resources of his company, which may include financial, operations, nonsales marketing, and general management personnel and resources. For example, a private-label sale might involve a special product configuration (product development and design personnel), production capacity (manufacturing), ware-housing and delivery requirements (distribution), and special costs, pricing, and payment schedules (finance and control). In addition, because the salesperson makes the major decisions and commitments, he should thoroughly understand his company's or-ganizational, operational, and cost structure. For example, he must know what effect the commitment to deliver a large amount of a particular product will have on the company's ability to operate profitably. He should also understand the other functional areas of his company and be able to work with the personnel.

An interesting by-product of the salesperson's introduction of other resources into the prospect company is the new lines of communication that are developed between the seller and the buyer. If they are introduced and coordinated effectively, these new resources can assist the salesperson in building the account relationship after the order is signed.

The salesperson must be given a good deal of freedom to make decisions about the sale. If a large prospective customer is inter-ested in a minor product modification, he must be able to respond quickly to that need—either positively or negatively. If the buyer gets a "run-around" such as, "Let me check with my boss so that he can check with engineering and manufacturing," the sale will be lost.

MARKETING AS A PRIMARY RESOURCE.   In the marketing depart-ment alone, the salesperson may need to call on product, pricing, and advertising support, as well as sales promotion and sales aids. Many major accounts need special products or modification of existing products (such as private labels, packaging, and product-related servicing), and their volume often makes such customiza-tion justifiable. For example, a large fastener company packages its general-line fasteners in special containers for large users. The customer can feed highly mechanized equipment automatically by using the packing container as a feed bin.

Because of their volume, major accounts often desire substantial price concessions. Although the Robinson-Patman Act puts limits on both requests and grants for special concessions, some can be cost justified. In many situations, a buyer does not contest the price itself so much as the net cost of the acquired goods and services. To the buyer, special delivery patterns, payment patterns, and other concessions are sometimes more important than the price per se.

Occasionally, major accounts are especially interested in customer-designed advertising or sales promotion programs. For example, large retailers with many stores sometimes find manufacturers who provide heavy in-store support particularly attractive. Such suppliers are often more responsive to the desires of the retailer's merchandising manager than are his own store managers. Thus the in-store support is worth more to the retailer than it costs the supplier.

However, all extra services cost money. Because they are more expensive and more unusual than in ordinary sales, the selling company must carefully analyze their cost and sales impact.

7. CLOSING THE SALE

Because of the complexity of the selling process and the length of the selling cycle, the close is the first concrete evidence that the salesperson is successful. Since the signature may occur anywhere from six months to three years after the start of the sales process, the salesperson should close on each "call"—that is, he should get an agreement from the prospect up to that point in the sales cycle. Since changes in the sales situation—such as a change in decision makers, or a shift in competitive strategy—can take place between calls, it is also a good idea to reaffirm or close again on previous agreements reached on each call.

By continually asking and getting answers to such questions as, "If we could deliver that system with an average ROI of 15% per annum, would you buy?" the salesperson knows well before the process is completed whether he has won the sale. If many decision makers give him negative responses, he can get out before too much time and money have been invested.

8. NURTURING THE ACCOUNT RELATIONSHIP

Some top marketers feel that the real selling starts after the order is signed for a major sale. For instance, a manufacturer of complex process control systems who performed a profitability analysis of each account discovered that 25% were unprofitable because of poor account management and salesmanship after the order had been signed.

If the product requires installation, training of personnel, or extended delivery schedules, the chances of the sale going sour increase unless the salesperson effectively controls the account. One way for him to do this is to develop a long-term plan for his products, services, and resources with the customer. He should also have his own account plan (like the Strategic Sales Opportunity Profile), which repeats most of the previous eight steps in qualifying, justifying, and developing strategies to expand the account. (His plan would be a more complete version of the plan he develops with his client.) For this planning process to work, he must involve the customer with the plan. In addition, the salesperson must locate inside advocates early to multiply his efforts in the account when he is not there.

The most important thing the salesperson can do is to keep selling contacts on the correctness of their buying decision, so that "buyers' blues" don't set in. He should continue as liaison between his company and his customer throughout delivery, installation, and usage. By dovetailing his product or service with his customer's operations and by making sure the product is producing the promised returns with the best utilization, the salesperson provides the extra assurance of add-on orders for his company and profitability for the customer. Post-sales service not only reinforces the customer's confidence in the seller but also tends to keep competition out, since the customer's people are too busy working with the seller.

Organizational Guidelines

Because the strategic selling process is considerably more complex than the typical sales process, it requires new organizational techniques. For a company to solve more involved selling problems, it will have to revise the makeup of its sales force, depending on the kind of sale it wants to make; it must find solutions not only for recurring and nonrecurring sales, but also for different *kinds* of recurring sales.

VARIATIONS ON A THEME

A company can handle the repetitive major sale in several ways. Where strategic selling is necessary throughout the sales organization (for example, when selling computers, heavy equipment, or private-label food packers) management can concentrate on developing that strategy alone. However, many companies do not use strategic selling alone. In that situation, management may find it useful to separate strategic selling from other types of selling and use one of the approaches that follow.

SPECIAL SALES FORCE. When a company has many major accounts and prospects, typical in the food and packaged-goods industries, it can use a special sales force of senior sales representatives to service them. Most food manufacturers and the larger food brokers assign their major salespeople to cover the buying offices of the large food chains and wholesalers, while assigning junior salespeople to the individual retail stores and independent accounts.

REGIONAL SALES MANAGEMENT. Where the seller has fewer, but scattered, major accounts, the best approach is often to assign each field sales manager to one or two accounts—an approach furniture and apparel businesses sometimes use. (However, this approach runs the risk that the sales manager will neglect managing in favor of selling.)

SMALL NATIONAL ACCOUNT GROUP. Even fewer major accounts can usually be handled by a small national structure of headquarters specialists. A large ink company, for example, uses several experienced, capable salespeople to call on the national publishers and printers that have many plants, while field salespeople call on individual plants.

There are many variations on this general approach. In some companies, especially industrial products manufacturers, market and/or product specialists fill the major account sales role. For instance, one manufacturer of complex specialized industrial materials has three selling organizations. These are: (1) the regular field sales force, which is organized geographically; (2) product managers who are responsible for each general product category, technically trained, and available to help the field sales force with technical and applications problems for major sales; and (3) marketing managers who are responsible for developing marketing programs for major industry categories (like electronics and capital equipment), who help handle major sales, and who participate in industry-oriented trade shows.

SEPARATE DIVISION.   Still others establish a separate integrated division for the large accounts so that these accounts can receive special attention from an integrated operation (i.e., manufacturing and marketing). While this is expensive and not easy to do, it ensures that large sales will not disrupt normal plant activities. This is a typical approach for companies that manufacture private-label products for large retail chains. Often these companies can reap special manufacturing savings by producing long runs and limited product lines in a separate, specially designed facility.

TOP MANAGEMENT.   Finally, top executives make the large sales in some companies. One large building cleaning and maintenance contractor, for example, has no real field sales force. Instead, customer liaison people work with existing customers. However, the real sales work is done by top headquarters executives who deal with owners and managers of large buildings.

While this arrangement provides commitment and organizational attention for the large accounts, it sometimes leads to neglect in the management of the business. The large accounts begin to demand more attention than the executives can spare.

COMPLETE INVOLVEMENT

On the other hand, nonrepetitive major sales are not handled by any established sales organization; a special sales force must be developed to handle them. The selling company has two options: (1) it can develop a task force to handle the process internally, or (2) it can contract with some form of sales agency, such as an investment banker, real estate or business broker, or private placement specialist.

If the sale is monumental (like the sale of the company), the task force must consist of people who have been removed from their other company responsibilities to as large an extent as possible. It should be put together carefully and include sales talent experienced in strategic selling and expert in finance (because of the complex nature and financial impact of such sales). In addition, people familiar with the prospective customers will be valuable to the team for their knowledge and possible personal contacts.

The nonrepetitive sales situation raises a unique training problem. Most of the learning must come through careful planning and review as the selling process is going on. However, salespeople can gain some training by working with people skilled in such sales situations (like investment bankers).

Nonrepetitive sales made by some form of facilitating sales organization, while expensive, decrease the drain on internal company resources. But even when outsiders take over much of the responsibility for the actual selling, company personnel need to be involved. Top managers don't always treat this kind of sale with the same expenditure of effort and resources as they treat other sales. They must choose the right agent—a difficult process that, to be done correctly, takes time. They must also supervise the selling process and ensure that the company's objectives are met with minimum expense. And finally, they are responsible for assisting in the actual sale, since their power and knowledge are often invaluable.

Note

1. For articles documenting this change, see "The New Supersalesman," *Business Week*, January 6, 1973, p. 441; Alton F. Doody and William G. Nickels, "Structuring Organizations for Strategic Selling," *MSU Business Topics*, Autumn 1972, p. 27; and Carl Rieser, "The Salesman Isn't Dead—He's Different," *Fortune*, November 1966, p. 124.

4

Industrial Selling: Beyond Price and Persistence

Clifton J. Reichard

Industrial selling is a mystery to many executives. A tremendous amount of effort, thought, and interpersonal strength goes into a successful sales campaign, which begins with an approach to one purchasing agent and ends with a whole company's commitment to buy. The process is so complex that it almost defies description. But creative techniques exist that move people to buy.

In this article, I give suggestions for turning industrial prospects into customers. In no way do I want to belittle maintenance selling efforts, however; keeping accounts is important for profits. Creative selling costs money, both to make calls and to gear company plants to handle new business.

Worthwhile business comes slowly. Selling effectively takes time, but if your company is working on enough potential accounts, you enhance your chances of obtaining new sales when you need them.

Before discussing the sales process, I must emphasize that I am talking here about professional buyers who make their choices after considering a variety of factors, such as quality, service, and economics. I am not referring to buyers who are only looking for the lowest price. The best buyers want value for the long term; they know that a short-term price often results in costly production problems and inefficiencies.

Inexperienced salespeople invariably start by thinking and talking price when money is the last thing they should discuss. They probably reason: "If a buyer bases decisions on quality, service, and price, how can I prove good quality and service when I'm not shipping anything? The only thing left is price."

I say to our sales force, never talk price with anyone before you've sold him on your company and yourself. The purchaser will generally guide the salesperson he or she really wants to do business with to the lower price. This leads to my first rule of selling: *people buy from whom they want to buy and make price and all other decision factors fit.*

It has not been fashionable lately to talk about relationships in business. We're told it has to be devoid of emotion. We must be cold, calculating, and impersonal.

Don't believe it. Relationships make the world go round. Businesspeople are human and social as well as interested in economics and investments, and salespeople need to appeal to both sides. Purchasers may claim to be motivated by intellect alone, but the professional salesperson knows that they run on both reason and emotions.

Selling the Company

In a planned sales approach, the seller appeals first to a buyer's rational side. How does one do this? Since it's what salespeople say that makes prospects want to buy, what are they going to say? Buyers need to be sold on the proposition that yours is the company they want to do business with. They have to be convinced that your company can and will supply them efficiently. This is a challenge because bringing in a new supplier usually creates some problems, at least initially.

Salespeople must also persuade buyers that they will handle the new company's business competently. Purchasers need to feel confident that all details will be handled as trouble-free as possible.

Communicating these things before shipments are made is difficult. Thus most salespeople believe it's sufficient to keep calling on an account and wait for a break. They think there's nothing they can do to make a break happen and, therefore, they go through the motions of keeping in touch with buyers, waiting for existing suppliers to make mistakes. This can take an awfully long time, and a company may not be able to wait.

To complicate the sales task further, sellers must win over not only their initial contacts but also, in most situations, their bosses and the manufacturing and R&D people. Salespeople should not try to go around initial contacts. They need to work through purchasing agents and eventually gain access to the other decision makers, with agents' blessings.

No one has ever claimed that the sales profession is easy. As a matter of fact, selling probably takes as much or more cerebral effort as any function in business. The reason for this is simple: businesses can choose whom they want to buy from. By contrast, if employees want to be paid, for the most part, they will do what their employer asks of them. Many executives forget that the world can get along very well without them and their businesses. Salespeople face this reality every day, and it is frightening.

This brings us to rule two of selling: *there is no business like no business.* If executives accept this, it follows that all an organization's members must commit themselves to customers and to developing new accounts. Successful companies are customer-driven, and executives should become so if they aren't already.

MAKE YOUR COMPANY INTERESTING

I call the sales process that makes things happen the planned selling approach. It calls for detailing the sales points to make on every call over the course of a year or two, which leads us to rule three: *an industrial sale results from the cumulative effort of many calls.*

No one call convinces a person to buy. A series of calls and an accumulation of respect and confidence built up over a long period of time make a sale. Calls might be made every four to six weeks, or geography might dictate calls every two to three months. In any case, calls should be frequent enough to maintain continuity, but not so often as to be aggressive.

How do salespeople decide what to say on every call over such a long period of time? I have already emphasized that buyers must be sold first on a company and that a salesperson is the right person to handle their business. Thus the first source of material for devising sales points is the selling company. My company, for example, Ball Corporation, is a packaging company with a high-technology base. Nearly three-quarters of our sales come from glass, metal cans, and barrier plastic packaging. One-quarter comes from industrial product lines and items used in space technology. Our salespeople explain this in their first call.

On subsequent calls, our sellers tell buyers about our four product groups. To build buyers' interest, the salespeople start with our Technical Products Group, which involves primarily aerospace. This helps establish our company as technologically competent and credible.

We can build a sales call around each of the following facts about the Technical Products Group:

Helps produce guidance systems for space vehicles.

Supplies antennas for space vehicles.

Produces the Ball process known as VacKote, used to lubricate moving parts in the aerospace industry.

Built and launched seven orbiting solar observatories.

Built and launched the Infra Red Astronomical Satellite (IRAS), an observatory for exploring the farthest reaches of the universe.

Built and launched from the space shuttle the Earth Radiation Budget Satellite, which will help predict long-term climate trends and improve long-term weather forecasting.

At the conclusion of a series of calls based on each of our four groups, our salespeople summarize what they talked about on each call and explain why they are recapitulating. After their presentation on the Technical Products Group, for example, they might say, "The reason I have told you all this is because we are a high-technology company in the packaging business. We have a history of making the impossible possible and turning dreams into realities."

The real reason for repeating the material, though, is for the sellers to demonstrate subtly to the buyers that they have an organized, businesslike mind. It also shows that the sellers have planned each call and proves how much they want the business. The summation is the first-time buyers will be aware that our salespeople have a plan, but by that time they are beginning to enjoy the show and becoming impressed with the caller.

Remember, you must sell a buyer on the company and on the salesperson before any sale can be made.

MOVE THE SCRIPT ALONG

For the second series of calls, Ball Corporation chooses its Metal Container Group, which is the quality, service, and productivity leader in the metal beverage container industry. Ball wasn't even in this business 15 years ago, but we dedicated our fifth new can plant in 1982. We have been successful in part because this group is run by former aerospace engineers, not traditional container manufacturers. They didn't know reasons why something couldn't be done, so they went ahead and tried it. Now we see big can companies diversifying into other product lines. Our sales force emphasizes how space technology has been applied to an old business with remarkable success.

The next series of calls focuses on the Industrial Products Group, which supplies copper-coated zinc blanks to U.S. mints for making pennies and which is developing technology for coextruded barrier plastics used in food and juice containers to help extend their shelf life. Included in this group is the largest independent metal-decorating business in the United States. Once again, our salespeople make a summation because they are selling themselves as well as their company.

By now, you are probably wondering what we are trying to sell to whom. It may come as a shock, but we are going to try to sell commercial glass containers to a food packer. Note that we haven't yet talked about glass or price, but the Glass Container Group will be the subject of the next series of calls.

How can we arouse any interest in a product like glass? The truth is that glass is, in many ways, the most exciting medium of our packaging family. Glass in its pristine state has a tensile strength three to five times stronger than steel. If you can protect a glass surface from being scratched, you can make a container that is virtually unbreakable. We have plans and patents for doing this. At present, the glass industry wastes 60% of the energy it consumes; we have plans for recouping this energy. The glass industry today is inefficient; we make one bad container for every six or seven good ones. We are working on solutions for this too, through computerized process control.

Because this industry is so inefficient, it is also very labor-intensive. Thirty-five cents of our cost dollar go to paying for labor. We are solving this through automation.

Our salespeople build an exciting series of calls around preserving glass strength, reducing container weight, using wasted energy, solving inefficiency, and reducing costs through automation. They then point out that because the raw materials needed for glass making are among the most prevalent resources on the earth's surface—sand, soda ash, and limestone—they are selling what could be the most economical packaging product on the market.

These series of calls include enough material to cover easily a year's worth of visits—each interesting, educational, concise, planned, and purposeful. The salespeople have appealed so far to the buyers' reason, and at the very least, they have convinced the buyers that Ball is a supply source worthy of consideration.

At this point, our salespeople invite prospects and their fellow decision makers to visit our research labs and corporate headquarters in Muncie. The guests also have the option of visiting a glass plant and our research and development plant for barrier plastics. Our glass prospects are very interested in plastics too, as you might guess. Remember, we are selling a company and a salesperson, and if a customer wants to think about buying plastic or metal cans from us in addition to glass, so much the better. Our glass division works closely with its competing packaging mediums. Our main goal is to get people to buy Ball.

VISIT THE HEADQUARTERS

If the salespeople have done their job well, the prospective buyers will want to visit Muncie and will encourage their colleagues to make the trip. We make it easy for them by offering the use of one of our company planes. Sometimes exploratory groups come first and, based on favorable reports, higher echelon groups come later. We treat them all the same.

Our guests arrive in time for cocktails and dinner at our corporate guest house, which is a renovated mansion built by one of the founding Ball brothers. We invite all our top corporate and group executives and their spouses to come and honor our guests. A main attraction is Edmund Ball, the retired senior officer of the corporation. Anyone from our top management who is in town attends these affairs, because we have a corporate commitment to marketing and because we want to get to know our customers and prospects well. In addition, our executives learn from the visitors' observations and reactions. Since we are truly customer-driven, this interchange is vital.

The next day we take our guests to our research and development center for a series of talks on our present and future technologies. We share with them our strategic plans and our ideas for the future.

Since some of our guests have not heard the planned sales calls, we give another sales presentation that covers the same material in a different way. For those who have heard the story, this reinforces the message. The repetition also indicates that the company speaks with one voice. We involve as many of our managers in these presentations as is appropriate.

The visit ends with a lunch in the executive dining room of our new corporate headquarters, where we discuss issues prompted by our presentations and other items of mutual interest.

The trip to headquarters not only gives us the opportunity to sell other decision makers in a company on doing business with us, it also lets us make the initial contacts look good. These are the people who recommended the visit to the others, and we don't let them down. Our program provides an enjoyable and instructive trip. We constantly change the material and refine the presentations so that people aren't bored if they come back. Our visitors are usually fascinated to find us a packaging company heavily involved in aerospace. Some follow-up visits, therefore, include a trip to Boulder, Colorado, where potential customers can see what we are doing in space technology. We tie this technology to our packaging business as much as possible.

Lift-Off?

The corporate visit concludes phase one of our planned selling approach. By this point, we have communicated all the conditions necessary to set the stage for being accepted as a supplier:

1. The salesperson demonstrated that we want the account's business so much that every call was well planned and meaningful.
2. The salesperson presented an organized and businesslike approach.
3. The salesperson also indicated that he or she can handle details by presenting the complete story of our company.
4. The sales calls introduced us as an exciting company with vast and diverse areas of expertise.
5. All the staff together has shown that we are a creative, imaginative, innovative, and solid company—desirable traits in a supplier.
6. We have communicated, through our conduct, that we are a company an account can trust—one that will do a high-quality job.

7. We have made the initial contact look good in the eyes of his or her superiors.
8. We have communicated to the original prospect that he or she needs our combined talents and skills to continue to look good in the future.
9. The prospect's purchasing people have become more involved in their company's planning process, and they can appreciate the planning we have done to secure its business.

Since we've said everything we wanted to say, all we need to do now is sit back and wait for lift-off as the orders come in. Right?

Wrong! What we might hear is, "You people are great, and if we ever need another source of supply, you'll be it." Most worthwhile accounts have good suppliers and are loyal to them. No one likes to tell an existing supplier that he's placing his business elsewhere. A prospect might want to do business with you, but he might resist breaking off with his present providers. He could do that more easily during a growth period and add suppliers without penalizing anyone. But companies need to make sales most during slow business periods. Anyone can be a super salesperson during a high-demand period. The truly super salesperson comes up with new business during oversupply periods. Despite our effective sales job, we may still have no order.

How do we move the account to buy?

The Idea Stage

Phase two of the planned selling approach begins with another series of calls. If we did our job well while we were describing our product groups, we were also gathering information about the accounts. We know, for example, how many glass molds they use, the type of corrugated carton the glass is packed in, the number of carton printings for each mold, the type and size caps used to seal the bottles and jars, and the types of equipment and number of people on the production lines.

We use this data base to come up with ideas for either increasing customers' market shares or lowering their costs.

In the glass container business it costs more to make a tall, slender jar than one that is short and squat. If an account is using a tall jar, the salesperson points out the economies in changing to a squat jar. If a prospective customer already has a shorter jar, the salesperson promotes the addition of a taller, more slender jar to appeal to today's weight-conscious consumer.

Companies make different marketing-cost decisions every day; salespeople should present all possibilities.

Here's another example: most glass container customers use glass delivered in corrugated boxes. They take the jars out of the boxes, fill and cap them, then repack them in the original cartons. Since the box makes up about 17% of our packed glass price, we gain great savings by shipping our glass in bulk to accounts. Then our money is not tied up in corrugated boxes in our warehouses while we are waiting to ship. Further, we gain 10% in warehouse space and we dispense with carton damage connected with warehousing and shipping packed cartons. We can get more glass on a truck in bulk, and thus reduce the shipping cost per container and the number of trucks we need. Shipping in bulk also eliminates concern that the carton printing a customer needs will be in our inventory.

The customer benefits by receiving more glass per delivery, and the glass arrives clean and ready for line use without much, if any, preconditioning.

Bulk glass also gives the customer the option to use a tray with a shrink-wrapped plastic cover that makes a more cost-effective, rigid unit for shipping. The supermarket saves too, because the plastic is easily removed and much easier to dispose of than a corrugated case. The crisp, newly formed tray can also be used for end-aisle displays.

The strategy in this phase is to come up with as many new ideas as possible, even though most of them will not be implemented. What's important is continuous creation of ideas and bombarding of accounts with them. You are expressing your intense desire to be their supplier and at some point they will have to give in to you.

If salespeople make up their minds they are going to sell an account, and think and work hard enough, they'll eventually succeed. Prospects can do nothing to stop them and the sales will likely come when the sellers want and need them.

Even if your company is completely sold out, your salespeople can sell and create business. They work their plan just as if they didn't have a single order. If an account decides to buy before the company can handle the business, the salespeople explain the situation as nicely as they can. Successful companies like to deal with other successful companies, and if your company has done its job right, the buyer will understand and appreciate that you are sold out. The "we can't take your order today, but we are creating capacity for tomorrow" approach invariably will lead to a decision on timing that suits both parties. Most important, the sales force must never stop selling, no matter how loaded the plants are.

Most salespeople believe that their great personality gets the order after they have used their expense accounts to gain customers' attention. But they shouldn't put the cart before the horse. They need to sell prospects first, using their brains, then use the expense account to solidify and foster good relations. Smart purchasing people don't accept entertainment unless they are doing business or expect to buy from a company. People won't buy from someone they don't like, but brains, not personality, make the sale.

The Art of Selling

What if, after all this effort, you still have no order? You have given the account every reason to buy. Now what do you do?

If this happens at Ball, we move into phase three, which involves what we call the art of selling. Selling becomes an art because people don't always act rationally. For example, how many more reasons do people need to stop smoking? The evidence that smoking is lethal one way or another is massive, yet many intelligent people continue to smoke. What generally stops them is a shock— a close friend or relative dies a painful death. The emotional experience inspires change where reason has failed.

Voters usually choose a candidate based on such intangibles as style, tone, and charisma. They have an emotional experience, then they rationalize the emotion.

Buyers sometimes do the same thing. In addition to giving prospects every reason to buy, salespeople should be prepared to move them emotionally. The art of industrial selling is very delicate and holds as much risk of failure as it does promise for success.

Let's return for a minute to the planned selling approach. How salespeople deliver a message is perhaps more important than what they say. The first goal in communicating is getting the other person to listen. If salespeople talk mechanically or deliver a canned pitch, buyers aren't going to hear them. If salespeople believe deeply in what they are saying, however, and deliver their message with feeling and conviction, buyers will listen. Don't send your sales-people out with a mechanical box loaded with visuals and a voice. Don't give them brochures to hand out to buyers. Master sales-people do their own thinking and communicating.

Sellers can learn a great deal from other professions about play-ing on people's emotions. Great trial lawyers not only research legal precedents, they practice oratory. They know that to convince a jury they must present facts persuasively and eloquently. So they dramatize them in order to move people emotionally.

I can best illustrate this point by quoting the following review of a Frank Sinatra performance many years ago: "When one speaks of great singers, one is not speaking of technique, timbre, pitch, range, or any combination thereof. It is necessary to have a nodding acquaintance with these matters, but they are, of course, only fuel. The fire must burn from within, and I never realized the intensity of that blaze within Sinatra until Thursday night. Every flicker of the eyes, every vein, every expression and passion is naked. Only then is it inescapably apparent what sets Sinatra apart from others: he lives, rejoices, and suffers every word he sings." And so it is with the best salespeople, who live, rejoice, and suffer every word of their messages.

How sellers make their presentations can excite buyers to action in ways not possible via any other means of communication. At the same time, salespeople should not be slick; a fine line lies between excitement and slickness. Not everyone has this talent. Whatever salespeople do to cause purchasers to react emotionally must be honest and sincere. Simply trying to appear honest is not good enough. Veteran buyers can spot phonies because they meet them every day.

I mentioned earlier that Edmund Ball, the corporation's patri-arch, attends the receptions and dinners for all visiting customers and prospects. A truly gentle man, Ed still plays an important role in the company even though retired. His name is on every home-canning jar and lid we manufacture, which makes him something of a celebrity. Yet he is such a modest, interesting person that people always like to meet him. Other members of the Ball family are active in our company's management, which helps perpetuate the family atmosphere that is part of our corporate style. We thus naturally include spouses in our customer visits. When we had two bachelors coming once for a visit, we worried that they might not be comfortable with this, but we decided to be ourselves and not make special arrangements. Later these men wrote to us, saying how much they enjoyed the spouses' being present, and commended us for including them. The moral of this story is that people should not try to be something they are not; including family members can rouse positive emotional responses. In the same way, people respond favorably to our respect for Ed Ball, and they admire us for it.

In case there is some misunderstanding, I am not talking about anything false or contrived. The process whereby two companies decide to do serious business together is not unlike courtship and marriage. The positive feelings each party has for the other can make great things happen. A marriage devoid of feelings holds little promise for the future.

To highlight, then, our successful industrial sales approach:

1. Plan calls.
2. Convince through facts.
3. Bombard with ideas.
4. Appeal to emotions.

Who sells the account at Ball? We all do. The salesperson is the quarterback, but doing the job right requires that the whole management team sell other management teams on doing business with us.

When does the sale occur? It can happen at any point during the sales plan implementation. Vince Lombardi once said he could send his playbook to anyone in the National Football League and his Green Bay Packers would still win, because the execution is what's most important. Attention to fundamentals and team spirit win ball games in the business world as well.

And after a company becomes a customer, we keep selling it as if it were a prospect. Selling has no ending. It is an ongoing love affair.

PART

IV

Balance Price and Value

Introduction

Nothing provokes more anxiety than the inevitable moment when the customer demands: "What's my discount?" or complains: "Your price is totally out of line—way too high!" No matter how carefully a sales program has been planned, or how amicably a pre-sale relationship has developed, there is always a natural conflict between seller and buyer over price. Each side wants a price they consider to be "fair." But what is fair to one may not be to the other. An industrial or commercial buyer, for example, wants a price *low* enough that it can keep its own costs down. The seller, on the other hand, wants a price *high* enough to cover the costs of creating, selling, and delivering a differentiated product or service. The seller wants a monopoly on the sale, while the buyer wants to have a choice among vendors.

Meanwhile, in both selling and buying companies, there is a second level to the pricing conflict. Within the selling company, pricing decisions generate disagreements between salespeople and their sales managers. The salesperson, in direct contact with the buyer, feels the heat to offer lower prices. In addition, the good salesperson is able to empathize with the customer, to understand the purchasing process from the buyer's point of view (see, for example, "Job Matching for Better Sales Performance," in Part V). At the same time sales management (particularly at higher levels) feels the pressure to satisfy company executives and shareholders with higher profits. A similar, though generally less intense, internal conflict develops in the buying organization, where different members of the "buying center" (see "Major Sales: Who *Really* Does the Buying?" in Part II) may disagree on the value of making a purchase at a given price. Nevertheless, the single-minded focus on lower prices is generally more uniformly held in the buying company, while the selling company is constantly pitting maximum sales volume against maximum price realization.

Clearly, the seller cannot seek customers profitably without addressing the pricing issue. The first article in this section, Mary Karr's "The Case of the Pricing Predicament," describes a large sale that may be lost on the basis of price. The article suggests, however, that the hypothetical selling company (Standard Machine Corporation) may be jeopardizing its sales not because of its rigid fixed-price policy alone, but because of a limited understanding of how that pricing policy figures into the larger sales process.

Having presented the case (which leaves resolution of the pricing problem to a regional Standard sales manager), Karr opens the floor to four outstanding commentators, who offer differing opinions on how to address the problem. F.G. "Buck" Rogers, formerly of IBM, emphasizes the sales-relationship perspective: "You must know your prospects and customers so well, and get into every nook and cranny of an account so deeply and continuously, that you understand the customer's business, its people, its problems, its needs, and its strategic thinking more thoroughly than any other supplier." Bruce Moore, of H.R. Krueger Machine Tool, Inc., focusing on Standard's growing foreign competition, argues that "the days of non-negotiable prices are over." Richard Lindgren, of Cross & Trecker Corporation, asserts that price may not be the critical issue; rather, "the real question is value—and that is measured not in terms of initial price but in terms of the effect that Standard's equipment will have on [the customer's] operations over the longer term." Finally, William Whitescarver, of Harris Graphics, emphasizes the problems resulting from poor communication—between seller and buyer and between salesperson and sales manager. Without a commitment to communication, a company can develop "marketplace arrogance—which typically leads to a false sense of security, lost orders, and declining market share."

While these commentators may emphasize different aspects of Standard's predicament, they do agree that the problem is one of poor selling, not high price. Standard's sales management has ignored the basic principles of effective selling, namely: profits, focus, relationships, and combining art and science. All four members of the expert panel point to Standard's inability to focus on long-term goals and to galvanize the sales force by thoroughly understanding the customer. Without committing to these principles, Standard's pricing policy is isolated from the dynamics of the selling and buying process, and is doomed to generate unprofitable sales.

"Negotiating with a Customer You Can't Afford to Lose," by Thomas Keiser, fits well with the pricing case because it provides specific tactics to use when "push comes to shove" and the salesperson and sales and marketing management must face the price-driven customer. The article presents an eight-step approach to preparation, staying cool, moving to compromise, and asserting your position. Although understanding the customer's point of view is an important element of successful negotiation, Keiser emphasizes a balanced view of customer needs and company needs. "Too much empathy can work against salespeople . . . because sales bargaining requires a dual focus—on the customer and on the best interests of one's own company. The best negotiating stance is not a single-minded emphasis on customer satisfaction but a concentration on problem solving that seeks to satisfy both parties."

Together, these articles put pricing in the broader context of the sales process, at the crossroads of costs, value creation, and profits. The increased complexity of seller-buyer interactions suggests that price is only one of many variables that contribute to the total value package that the seller can offer to the buyer. Keiser notes that "the salesperson's job is to find the specific package of products and services that most effectively increases value for the customer without sacrificing the seller's profits." When you focus on the underlying goals of the purchaser and seller, long-term rewards, and issues of mutual benefit, there are numerous creative alternatives to lowering price in order to make the sale. The astute seller will recognize ways to increase value to the customer (for instance, through quality assurance, preferred treatment, or customization) without significantly adding costs or adjusting price. Since seller and buyer value different aspects of the sales package differently, buyer value and seller profits can be enhanced at the same time. (For those who are particularly interested in the relationships among pricing, customer satisfaction, and profitability, we recommend Part VI, "Convert Customer Satisfaction into Profits," in the companion volume, *Keeping Customers*.)

1

The Case of the Pricing Predicament

Mary Karr

As soon as Scott Palmer's secretary told him that Joanne Braker from Occidental Aerospace was on the phone, he knew he was in for a long day. Inheriting the Occidental account had helped him earn top sales commissions last year, his first at Standard Machine Corporation. But a month ago, Joanne informed Scott of the purchasing department's new, more aggressive competitive bid policy, and said it would apply to the acquisition of a computerized milling machine for Occidental's new training center.

Scott nevertheless submitted his $429,000 proposal with great confidence and even boasted to his regional sales manager that the deal was "in the bag." After two weeks of unreturned phone calls, however, Scott got the feeling his confidence had been sorely misplaced.

"Hi, Joanne. Long time, no hear. What's up?"

Joanne got right to the point. "Scott, I've got a $22,000 problem you can solve."

"What do you mean?"

"You know we have to look hard at a number of different vendors on purchases of this size. And your bid is well above the competition's. Kakuchi came in under $390,000, and Akita Limited at a little over 400K."

She waited, and Scott waited back, not wanting to show his anxiousness. "The way I count it," she finally continued, "you're $22,000 too high, and I just can't sell that here."

"Well, Joanne, you get what you pay for in this world. You know that Standard's got the best machine tool equipment in the world. Not to mention our service and training. So we have to sell at sensible list prices, no more no less, if we want to keep providing the kind of products and service you expect from us."

Scott began to recount Occidental's long and fruitful relationship with Standard, and the unmatched performance of its milling, grinding, and boring machines. But Joanne interrupted. "Scott, you don't have to sell me on your equipment," she said. "And you understood what the new bidding policies meant when we announced them. We're under the gun to cut costs, so we have to look at other suppliers. I just can't budge on this till you come down to the middle someplace. That's the way it is."

Actually, Scott had always wondered just when Standard's fixed-price policy would meet strong resistance from a customer, but he had not expected complaints from Occidental. That company had maintained its manufacturing edge by investing in the sort of state-of-the-art automation Standard provided, and it had installed virtually nothing but Standard equipment for more than 20 years.

Scott told Joanne he appreciated her problem and her frankness about the other bids. But he continued to argue Standard's case. "We ship a lot more equipment than the others," he maintained, "and we ship it on time. Our prices have to reflect that. And you've seen how we train your operators and hang around after installation until everyone's up to speed."

"Akita and Kakuchi say they will too," Joanne replied firmly. "I should tell you they both provided some pretty convincing testimony from other U.S. accounts."

"I don't want to knock Akita," Scott responded. "Some of its basic equipment is decent. But how reliable will it be in a crunch? What would it have done when you bumped up against capacity last year? Installed practically overnight like we did? It would have had to train your staff in Japanese in 24 hours." He paused briefly for effect. "It's awfully far away when you're in a bind."

"It's true that none of Akita's customers have plants that are as big as ours, or that seem to be growing as fast," she conceded.

"By the way, did you take a long hard look at Kakuchi's software?" Scott bore in. "If your people can figure out how to use it, they'll get a Nobel Prize. Its training division is almost nonexistent. And I hear some of Kakuchi's European customers call their field service group, 'field circus.'"

Joanne laughed. "I've heard that too. That's why we're hoping to get you close to Akita's bid. Its A71 package looks pretty good."

"Pretty good isn't good enough, Joanne. You know that and I know that. I'm sure the rest of purchasing knows that. And do you think the guys in manufacturing want to compromise on quality to save 5% on a piece of equipment?"

"Look, Scott," she said, "we all know what we know. You know Akita's solid, and so is its equipment. And its managers know there's a lot of potential business in the two plants we're planning to build over the next four years. Everybody in the industry knows those plants are on the drawing board. So it's really a question of your attitude toward the future, not just the quoted price on one piece of equipment."

Joanne said the deadline for final bids was in two weeks. Scott explained to her that he couldn't give an inch on price unless he could convince his regional manager, Tony Della Pena.

Scott hung up, and his mind turned immediately to the office down the hall. He wondered whether a carefully worded memo to Tony might not get better results than simply walking into his office. But because he felt he was battling the clock, Scott went straight to Tony and briefed him on the conversation with Joanne, finally suggesting that Standard rebid at $407,000.

Tony held firm on the original proposal. "Scott, you've done great work in a year, really first rate. But if you'd been selling for us a little longer, you'd understand why we don't dicker with our prices, even slightly."

"But Tony, think about those two new plants. Joanne practically promised us that business for $22,000 less on this deal. It doesn't seem smart to let Occidental get experience with other equipment and suppliers now."

"I know, I know. I've seen the new products from Akita and Kakuchi. The software on the A71 looks pretty damn good. And Akita hasn't been so terrible on service in the U.S. since it built those field centers here."

"I wasn't aware of that," Scott said sheepishly.

"But there's a lot more to this business than price," Tony continued. "We don't want to mess up the industry. We aren't selling a commodity. Of course we want Occidental's long-term business, but we can't let every customer nickel-and-dime every bid. Do that, and you might as well be selling sheet steel."

"I know we want stable conditions. But it's not as if we're losing money with $407,000. And we may lose a big account just as it's about to get a lot bigger."

"Scott, you know how this company got where it is. Standard is founded on quality and reliability. We're innovators. We can't stay ahead of the curve if our prices don't support our development costs. How many man-years do you think went into building the software for our 1052? Or into upgrading it to work with new production processes? And you know what we spend on customer service. That's why we've had Occidental's business for all these years—by thorough installation, training, by rushing spare parts to them." Tony paused. "By paying our salespeople enough to know what's going on with our customers. It's not to Occidental's advantage for us to cut prices if it means it'll lose its manufacturing edge in the future."

"I hear what you're saying, Tony. But right now Occidental doesn't seem to value our service and support as much as the money it wants to save. Couldn't you at least go talk with Bob Davis about making one minor adjustment to the fixed-price policy?" Davis was corporate vice president for sales.

"I'm not going up the line to argue for an exception to a policy that's been around a lot longer than either of us have." Tony looked resolute. "This is an old company, and a successful one. You don't go running to the fourteenth floor every time you get a decision you don't like, Scott. Why don't you see what else you can do for Occidental instead of complaining to me about our pricing policies?"

Scott got the message and started toward the door, remarking as casually as he could, "Winter is coming, Tony. We could both use a week in the sun. And those new Occidental plants could bring us some pretty nice rays."

Back in his office, Scott gathered evidence for the memo he realized he should have sent Tony in the first place. Tony had chided him in the past about being too impatient to close a deal in a business where the sales cycle tended to be long. Scott thumbed through trade magazines for articles on the Asian invasion and sent his secretary to the copy machine loaded with nightmare stories about the dwindling market share of established U.S. manufacturers in industries like Standard's.

By quitting time, Scott had completed a succinct memo that outlined to Tony three possible compromises on Standard's fixed-price policy:

1. For Occidental only, Standard would rechristen the 1052 as the 1052X, change the color of the control panel from gray to blue, make a few other cosmetic changes, reduce the motor's power slightly, and offer the revised machine at $407,000.
2. Standard could rebundle the 1052 service package to justify the $407,000 price tag. This would mean eliminating the usual one

week of on-site operator training and cutting back the time trouble-shooters would remain at the facility after installation from two weeks to one. In addition, it could trim the "free" six-month service period to two months.

3. A modified combination of the first two alternatives could also cost $407,000.

As an addendum, Scott wrote a brief analysis of encroaching global competition, supporting his arguments with the articles from the trade press. He also reminded Tony about the recent Munich trade show, where other salespeople had complained of losing large accounts because of price competition, particularly from Akita. Scott thought his arguments were solid, but Tony had to decide where to go from here.

What Would You Do?

Four business leaders offer their views on this dilemma.

F.G. "BUCK" ROGERS

This is not just an argument about price. This is a multifaceted argument about a policy deeply engrained in Standard that has probably been critical to its success over the years. This situation also involves the need to sell value and a manager who has not done a good job of training his field people. Scott is obviously trying to circumvent the fixed-price policy and take the easy road to selling. He wants Occidental's business at any price and without having to do his homework.

What's going on is clear enough:

Occidental is changing its procurement policies. The company now requires multiple bidders. Joanne's in purchasing, and that's the line.

Occidental clearly likes and prefers Standard and wants Standard to get the business. Why else would Joanne tell Scott precisely how much he has to come down in price? More important, Joanne's proposed new price is still above Akita's bid of "a little over $400,000" and Kakuchi's bid of "a little under $390,000." Standard doesn't really have to be in "the middle someplace." In short,

Occidental agrees with Scott's pitch about Standard's superior package.

Scott is not solving any problems for Tony. He's creating problems. Tony won't submit Scott's proposals to headquarters. He's no dummy; he knows that headquarters will see Scott's modifications as price cuts that are not very well disguised. A proposal to Bob Davis that cavalierly undercuts the fixed-price policy would make Tony look foolish, which presumably he is not. He might talk over some alternatives or strategies with his boss, but Tony is not going to make a formal proposal or forward Scott's memo.

On the other hand, the new competition is real. A valued customer is behaving differently, and the threat posed by Japanese suppliers cannot be ignored. And the pressures are being felt by other salespeople as well. Of course, we shouldn't take the Munich trade-show complaints at face value. Just because a salesman says he lost business to a lower bid doesn't mean that's why it was lost. What else is he going to say? "I lost it because I screwed up. I was a lousy salesman. I mishandled the customer."

Finally, Scott's selling approach is all wrong. He commits the cardinal sin of selling someone else's weakness rather than the bottom-line value of doing business with Standard. Also, he tells the customer that the responsibility for getting action is out of his hands.

Let's step back from the facts of the case and consider the situation on a more general level. In today's tough and demanding marketplace, industrial customers want to negotiate, and when the deal is significant enough, you can be sure Standard will reevaluate its position. What will happen when Occidental builds its new plants? The capital budget for machinery is surely going to be several million dollars—probably tens of millions. Every supplier, including Standard, will at least consider negotiating terms on a project like that, even in an environment where price competition isn't heating up. But the negotiating will not be done by Scott or Tony alone. It will also involve Bob Davis or the president of Standard, working with their counterparts at Occidental. Scott and Tony will draw up a detailed assessment of the customer's specifications, delivery requirements, and other factors, and then higher level executives will actually do the deal.

Or consider an even more basic question: Why would any company selling big-ticket industrial items have such a rigid pricing policy in the first place? The explanation is not simply Tony's concerns about destabilizing competition and sheet steel, though that may be important. Rather, the fixed-price policy sends an unequivocal message to the sales organization: you must know your prospects and customers so well, and get into every nook and cranny of an account so deeply and continuously, that you understand the customer's business, its people, its problems, its needs, and its strategic thinking more thoroughly than any other supplier—perhaps even more thoroughly than the customer itself. This means the sales organization will be able to help customers define their needs, design their plant layouts, train their employees, support their manufacturing systems. That is, Standard will provide such a high level of service that no other supplier will win on price alone. It is a working partnership based on solution selling.

If Tony had properly inculcated his salespeople, Scott wouldn't be suggesting these phony shortcuts. Tony had many chances in his discussion of the Occidental bid to "train" Scott. He could have asked questions like: Who are the real decision makers outside of purchasing? What does Occidental's engineering department have to say? Who have you been talking with in manufacturing? How do they feel about our products, especially the ones they bought last year? What kind of calls have our service people been getting from Occidental? Any troubles? Any really good things we've done for them recently?

In short, Tony is not using the non-negotiation policy to do what it's designed to do—namely, to force the salespeople deep into the business of prospects and existing accounts, to create intricate and intimate partnerships. Scott seems to work only through Joanne. Admittedly, many companies don't want salespeople getting inside their organizations, or insist on carefully screened relationships. But with complicated, big-ticket investments they do want help from sales reps. Scott doesn't even mention what else he's doing at Occidental, and Tony doesn't ask.

Indeed, the problems with the Standard sales organization seem pretty serious. For example, this milling machine is for Occidental's "new training center." Well, shouldn't Standard try to help here? Maybe it shouldn't even sell the machine, but give it to Occidental—ostensibly for joint learning about its use and as a pilot installation for Standard's own reexamination of its training of machine operators. After a few years, Occidental could return the machine or buy it for half the original price.

Finally, Standard might consider an entirely different strategy for this particular account in this particular situation. Tony could make a pretty good case for going back to Occidental and with-drawing the bid. He could argue, in effect, the following: "We can't and won't go below $429,000. Not because of our no-discounting policy but because if we went below what we think is the right price, we'd have to cut corners on what we do for you, and we just don't think that's right. If we have to come down in price, we'd just as soon not bid. You wouldn't get what you need."

None of this is to ignore the transformation and the globalization of competition facing Standard Machine. We don't have enough information in the case to deal with that. But we do have enough to see that this is, in the first instance, not a problem of global competition, but of sales force management.

The key is to understand the customer's requirements, have broad management coverage, and put together a cost-justified so-lution that truly conveys value-added marketing.

BRUCE MOORE

Standard will lose the order from Occidental unless it modifies its pricing policy. It might also lose the chance to sell millions of dollars of machine tools for Occidental's proposed new plants. And it will have opened the gates even wider to its foreign rivals.

The scenario is rather straightforward. Occidental is willing to throw out Kakuchi's bid. But Akita Limited is producing decent equipment. Its software is good. Its service is improving. Its price is right. Without some movement by Standard, Akita will get the Occidental order. And if Akita gets its foot in Occidental's door, it will be there forever. Standard must either change its pricing policy now or change it later—and under less favorable circumstances.

The entire machine tool industry, like other U.S. manufacturing industries, faces a very different marketplace from what it faced 15 years ago. The industry must adjust its product and marketing strategies to meet the demands of an international economy. Put simply, the days of non-negotiable prices are over. But Standard's marketing executives have not convinced top management that the company is competing in a different environment.

Standard has a good opportunity with Occidental to adjust its pricing policy. The relationship between the two companies has been long and mutually rewarding. Occidental clearly prefers to do business with Standard. That's why Joanne disclosed to Scott the identities and prices of his competitors. But Scott is a young salesman trapped by inexperience. He was unprepared to deal with Occidental's new policy of soliciting multiple bids. His response was to knock the competition, always a bad idea. His arguments to Joanne in defense of Standard's marketing policies were inappropriate and fruitless. How do you quantify "sensible list prices"? After Joanne freely offered information about competing bids, Scott did not seek additional information about alternatives to the $22,000 price cut that might improve Standard's position.

The real problem at Standard is Tony, the middleman between the sales force in the field and upper management. One of Tony's jobs is to sell products to the customer. But he has another job which is just as important, if not more so. That is to sell the customer—its conditions, needs, performance requirements, attitudes—to top management. Tony is not doing this. He reiterates old company policies to Scott. He shows little concern for the possible loss of a good customer due to changing competitive conditions. He doesn't recognize that this is an important sales problem he should take to his superiors.

Standard's top managers appear to be quite competent. Their policies have produced high-quality products and excellent service support to customers. Standard has an excellent record of on-time deliveries—no small accomplishment in today's machine tool industry. With this demonstrated capability, I cannot believe they would not listen to reasonable arguments about adjusting the fixed-price policy.

One strategy Tony should consider taking to Bob Davis is a variant of what Scott proposed in his memo. Occidental is looking for greater perceived value. If Standard were to set separate prices for the components of the milling-machine package—that is, unbundle the final price—Occidental could compare relative values. And Scott could talk to Joanne about these individual prices and what really mattered to Occidental. For example, the Standard personnel who "hang around after installation until everyone's up to speed" may not be as important to Occidental as Standard thinks. There could be negotiated reductions of how long these people remain on-site. Should Occidental later need more training, it could pay extra. In all probability, these training costs would not be as much as what Standard has factored into its current price.

There are certain compromises Tony should not suggest to Davis.

For example, he should not propose shortening the free service period, since this would be considered a decrease in value by Occidental. Nor should he gimmick up the machine with paint jobs, less horsepower, and cosmetic changes like Scott suggests. Occidental is very familiar with Standard's products, would spot the changes instantly, and would perceive a decrease in value.

These and other price reduction ideas may not make the entire 5% difference. There may still be a 2% to 3% price gap. Good enough! Tony will have to sell Bob Davis on the idea that Standard's management can find the rest in cost reductions not affecting quality or performance. Surely this is not an insurmountable challenge for a machine tool company that wants to be around in the future.

RICHARD T. LINDGREN

This is a case study of a company headed for trouble—not because it won't negotiate prices, and not even because of the appearance of foreign competition. Rather, it is headed for trouble because the sales organization isn't doing what Standard's pricing policy is designed to have it do, whether that relates to domestic or foreign competition. In fact, price may not be the critical issue in this case from either Standard's or Occidental's point of view. The real question is value—and that is measured not in terms of initial price but in terms of the effect that Standard's equipment will have on Occidental's operations over the longer term.

The key for Standard is not just to make the sale, which appears to be Scott's only concern. In fact, Scott has no understanding of what the company's overall operating rationale really is. This is even more dismaying since he is able to summon clippings of the coming Japanese competition in order to undermine the rationale and price policy—when the policy may be the company's best competitive weapon to deal with foreign competition.

What the case really illustrates (more by what isn't in it than by what is) is the critical relationship between industrial suppliers and purchasers. This relationship is especially important in industries where equipment is highly complex, takes new forms, and requires a great deal of training and service. It is even more critical in industries where foreign competition is threatening to disrupt or challenge traditional ways of doing business—ways that have made sense for both supplier and customer. In those situations, which are increasingly prevalent in American industry, a close working relationship between supplier and customer is the key to sustained competitive performance for both parties. It is out of such cooperative relationships that technological improvements flow to lower parts cost, improve quality, and reduce working capital needs.

The purpose of Standard's policy on price is to force the company to pursue these kinds of relationships. It is designed to make the salespeople work closely and cooperatively with the customer so that they understand each other's needs and interests, rather than haggle over price. When the policy works, it is the best weapon that both supplier and customer have against a foreign invasion, which usually begins on the basis of price.

The tragedy of this situation is that neither Scott nor Tony appreciates the real meaning of the warning of foreign competitors, nor its relationship to and the real value of Standard's pricing policy. With sophisticated equipment like machine tools, sales is not just about sales, any more than engineering is just about engineering. Everything has to work together because, as this case shows, business is all about getting and keeping a competitive edge—and that cannot be done based on price alone.

Sure, the seller has to be reasonably price competitive. But it also has to make enough money to be able to support the kind of R&D that will constantly help keep itself and its customers competitive. In this case the customer seems to understand that; it is not asking for a low-ball bid. But the sales organization clearly isn't doing its part.

WILLIAM WHITESCARVER

Standard Machine has created for itself an opportunity to fail with a major customer. How did this unenviable situation come to pass? Let's look at how Scott and Tony have handled a major change in purchasing policies by one of Standard's most important customers.

Occidental first announced its new, competitive-bid policy a month ago, but there was virtually no reaction from Scott. He never even bothered to discuss the new policy with Tony until Joanne told him he had to come down in price. In fact, he threw Tony off base with his "it's in the bag" comment. Scott apparently did not appreciate the gravity of the competitive message being sent by Joanne. Earlier and more serious attention to the competitive-bid policy would have allowed Standard to prepare a more effective response.

Scott also stumbled by telling Joanne that only Tony could make a decision on price changes. This is a tactical error that gives Joanne an opening to go directly to Tony, the person with pricing authority.

Of course, Tony has made blunders of his own. He has information about the competition (for example, Akita's new U.S. field centers) that he has not shared with Scott. Such information might have caused Scott to be more concerned than he was about the pending Occidental order. Tony views Scott as an impatient rookie. He makes it clear that Scott does not control the Occidental business, but offers no creative help with this major account. Moreover, Tony seems insecure about his own position. Why doesn't he advise Bob Davis of the Occidental dilemma and discuss the growing strengths of the competition and possible responses?

Standard has a very high regard for its position in the industry. According to Tony, it has the best equipment, service, and training. It is an innovator and leader. Its business is founded on quality and reliability, so it can command a premium for its product. All of this may be true, or may have been true, but it also has the ring of marketplace arrogance—which typically leads to a false sense of security, lost orders, and declining market share.

Despite his shaky start, Scott has come up with some workable alternatives for handling the Occidental bid.

Equipment changes, alterations to the service and training package, and/or reduction of the warranty would likely be acceptable to a customer completely familiar with Standard's equipment. This would also protect Standard's fixed-price policy. Joanne has clearly opened the door for a price above $407,000. She seems willing to work with Scott to develop a mutually acceptable plan.

One final point. Scott, Tony, and Bob Davis need to coordinate their efforts and educate senior management that Standard is facing the same competitive pressures as Occidental. It is time for Standard to install cost-reduction programs of its own. These programs should in turn be reflected in product pricing. Standard should prepare sales tactics and selling strategies that will develop continuous business, not just look at customers order by order. If done well, the long-established, fixed-price policy can remain a major positive selling tool for Scott and his colleagues at Standard Machine.

Note

At the time of this article's publication F.G. "Buck" Rogers was a retired vice president of marketing for IBM. Bruce Moore was former president and CEO of H.R. Krueger Machine Tool, Inc. and director of the National Machine Tool Builders Association. Richard T. Lindgren was president and CEO of Cross & Trecker Corporation, the largest producer of machine tools in the United States. William Whitescarver was president of the Bindery & Forms Press Division of Harris Graphics, a subsidiary of AM International.

2
Negotiating with a Customer You Can't Afford to Lose

Thomas C. Keiser

"I like your product, but your price is way out of line. We're used to paying half that much!"

"Acme's going to throw in the service contract for nothing. If you can't match that, you're not even in the running."

"Frankly, I think we've worked out a pretty good deal here, but now you've got to meet my boss. If you thought I was tough."

"Tell you what: If you can drop the price by 20%, I'll give you the business. Once you're in our division, you know, you'll have a lock on the whole company. The volume will be huge!"

"I can't even talk to you about payment schedule. Company policy is ironclad on that point."

"Look here, at that price, you're just wasting my time! I thought this was a serious bid! Who do you think you're talking to, some green kid?"

This wasn't supposed to happen. You've invested a lot of time earning a customer's trust and goodwill. You've done needs-satisfaction selling, relationship selling, consultative selling, customer-oriented selling; you've been persuasive and good-humored. But as you approach the close, your good friend the customer suddenly turns into Attila the Hun, demanding a better deal, eager to plunder your company's margin and ride away with the profits. You're left with a lousy choice: do the business unprofitably or don't do the business at all.

This kind of dilemma is nothing new, of course. Deals fall through every day. But businesses that depend on long-term customer relationships have a particular need to avoid win-lose situations, since backing out of a bad deal can cost a lot of future deals as well. Some buyers resort to hardball tactics even when the salesperson has done a consummate job of selling. The premise is that it costs nothing to ask for a concession. Sellers can always say no. They will still do the deal. But many sellers—especially inexperienced ones—say yes to even the most outrageous customer demands. Shrewd buyers can lure even seasoned salespeople into deals based on emotion rather than on solid business sense. So how do you protect your own interests, save the sale, and preserve the relationship when the customer is trying to eat your lunch?

Joining battle is not the solution unless you're the only source of whatever the customer needs. (And in that case you'd better be sure you never lose your monopoly.) Leaving the field is an even worse tactic, however tempting it is to walk away from a really unreasonable customer.

Surprisingly, accommodation and compromise are not the answers either. Often a 10% price discount will make a trivial difference in the commission, so the salesperson quickly concedes it. But besides reducing your company's margin significantly, this kind of easy accommodation encourages the customer to expect something for nothing in future negotiations.

Compromise—splitting the difference, meeting the customer halfway—may save time, but because it fails to meet the needs of either party fully it is not the proverbial win-win solution. A competitor who finds a creative way to satisfy both parties can steal the business.

The best response to aggressive but important customers is a kind of assertive pacifism. Refuse to fight, but refuse to let the customer take advantage of you. Don't cave in, just don't counter-attack. Duck, dodge, parry, but hold your ground. Never close a door; keep opening new ones. Try to draw the customer into a creative partnership where the two of you work together for inventive solutions that never occurred to any of your competitors.

There are eight key strategies for moving a customer out of a hardball mentality and into a more productive frame of mind.

1. *Prepare by knowing your walkaway and by building the number of variables you can work with during the negotiation.* Everyone agrees about the walkaway. Whether you're negotiating an arms deal with the Russians, a labor agreement with the UAW, or a contract you can't afford to lose, you need to have a walkaway: a

combination of price, terms, and deliverables that represents the least you will accept. Without one, you have no negotiating road map.

Increasing the number of variables is even more important. The more variables you have to work with, the more options you have to offer; the greater your options, the better your chances of closing the deal. With an important customer, your first priority is to avoid take-it-or-leave-it situations and keep the negotiation going long enough to find a workable deal. Too many salespeople think their only variable is price, but such narrow thinking can be the kiss of death. After all, price is one area where the customer's and the supplier's interests are bound to be at odds. Focusing on price can only increase animosity, reduce margin, or both.

Instead, focus on variables where the customer's interests and your own have more in common. For example, a salesperson for a consumer-goods manufacturer might talk to the retailer about more effective ways to use advertising dollars—the retailer's as well as the manufacturer's—to promote the product. By including marketing programs in the discussion, the salesperson helps to build value into the price, which will come up later in the negotiation.

The salesperson's job is to find the specific package of products and services that most effectively increases value for the customer without sacrificing the seller's profit. For example, an automotive parts supplier built up its research and development capacity, giving customers the choice of doing their own R&D in-house or farming it out to the parts supplier. Having this option enabled the supplier to redirect negotiations away from price and toward creation of value in the product-development process. Its revenues and margins improved significantly.

Even with undifferentiated products, you can increase variables by focusing on services. A commodity chemicals salesperson, for example, routinely considered payment options, quantity discounts, bundling with other purchases, even the relative costs and benefits of using the supplier's tank cars or the customer's. Regardless of industry, the more variables you have, the greater your chances of success.

2. *When under attack, listen.* Collect as much information as possible from the customer. Once customers have locked into a position, it is difficult to move them with arguments, however brilliant. Under these circumstances, persuasion is more a function of listening.

Here's an example from my own company. During a protracted negotiation for a large training and development contract, the customer kept trying to drive down the per diem price of our professional seminar leaders. He pleaded poverty, cheaper competition, and company policy. The contract was a big one, but we were already operating at near capacity, so we had little incentive to shave the per diem even slightly. However, we were also selling books to each seminar participant, and that business was at least as important to us as the services. The customer was not asking for concessions on books. He was only thinking of the per diem, and he was beginning to dig in his heels.

At this point our salesperson stopped talking, except to ask questions, and began listening. She learned a great deal—and uncovered an issue more important to the customer than price.

The customer was director of T&D for a large corporation and a man with career ambitions. To get the promotion he wanted, he needed visibility with his superiors. He was afraid that our professionals would develop their own relationships with his company's top management, leaving him out of the loop. Our salesperson decided to give him the control he wanted. Normally we would have hired free-lancers to fill the gap between our own available staff and the customer's needs. But in this case she told him he could hire the free-lancers himself, subject to our training and direction. The people we already employed would be billed at their full per diem. He would save money on the free-lancers he paid directly, without our margin. We would still make our profit on the books and the professional services we did provide. He would maintain control.

Moreover, we were confident that the customer was underestimating the difficulty of hiring, training, and managing free-lancers. We took the risk that somewhere down the road the customer would value this service and be willing to pay for it. Our judgment turned out to be accurate. Within a year we had obtained the entire professional services contract without sacrificing margin.

It was a solution no competitor could match because no competitor had listened carefully enough to the customer's underlying agenda. Even more important, the buyer's wary gamesmanship turned to trust, and that trust shaped all our subsequent negotiations.

When under attack, most people's natural response is to defend themselves or to counterattack. For a salesperson in a negotiation, either of these will fuel an upward spiral of heated disagreement. The best response, however counterintuitive, is to keep the customer talking, and for three good reasons. First, new information can increase the room for movement and the number of variables. Second, listening without defending helps to defuse any anger. Third, if you're listening, you're not making concessions.

3. *Keep track of the issues requiring discussion.* Negotiations can get confusing. Customers often get frustrated by an apparent lack of progress; they occasionally go back on agreements already made; they sometimes raise new issues at the last moment. One good way to avoid these problems is to summarize what's already been accomplished and sketch out what still needs to be discussed. Brief but frequent recaps actually help maintain momentum, and they reassure customers that you're listening to their arguments.

The best negotiators can neutralize even the most outspoken opposition by converting objections into issues that need to be addressed. The trick is to keep your cool, pay attention to the customer's words and tone, and wait patiently for a calm moment to summarize your progress.

4. *Assert your company's needs.* Effective salespeople always focus on their customers' interests—not their own. They learn to take on a customer perspective so completely that they project an uncanny understanding of the buyer's needs and wants. Too much empathy can work against salespeople, however, because sales bargaining requires a dual focus—on the customer and on the best interests of one's own company. The best negotiating stance is not a single-minded emphasis on customer satisfaction but a concentration on problem solving that seeks to satisfy both parties. Salespeople who fail to assert the needs of their own company are too likely to make unnecessary concessions.

The style of assertion is also extremely important. It must be nonprovocative. "You use our service center 50% more than our average customer. We've got to be paid for that . . ." will probably spark a defensive reaction from a combative customer. Instead, the salesperson should build common ground by emphasizing shared interests, avoiding inflammatory language, and encouraging discussion of disputed issues. This is a better approach: "It's clear that the service center is a critical piece of the overall package. Right now you're using it 50% more than our average customer, and that's driving up our costs and your price. Let's find a different way of working together to keep service costs down and still keep service quality high. To begin with, let's figure out what's behind these high service demands."

5. *Commit to a solution only after it's certain to work for both parties.* If a competitive customer senses that the salesperson is digging into a position, the chances of successfully closing the deal are dramatically reduced. A better approach is to suggest hypothetical solutions. Compare these two approaches in selling a commercial loan.

"I'll tell you what. If you give us all of the currency exchange business for your European branches, we'll cap this loan at prime plus one."

"You mentioned the currency exchange activity that comes out of your European branches. Suppose you placed that entirely with us. We may be able to give you a break in the pricing of the new loan."

The first is likely to draw a counterproposal from a competitive customer. It keeps the two of you on opposite sides of the negotiating table. The second invites the customer to help shape the proposal. Customers who participate in the search for solutions are much more likely to wind up with a deal they like.

Some salespeople make the mistake of agreeing definitively to an issue without making sure the overall deal still makes sense. This plays into the hands of an aggressive customer trying to get the whole loaf one slice at a time. It's difficult to take back a concession. Instead, wrap up issues tentatively. "We agree to do X, provided we can come up with a suitable agreement on Y and Z."

6. *Save the hardest issues for last.* When you have a lot of points to negotiate, don't start with the toughest, even though it may seem logical to begin with the deal killers. After all, why spend time on side issues without knowing whether the thorniest questions can be resolved?

There are two reasons. First, resolving relatively easy issues creates momentum. Suppose you're working with a customer who's bound and determined to skin you alive when it comes to the main event. By starting with lesser contests and finding inventive solutions, you may get the customer to see the value of exploring new approaches. Second, discussing easier issues may uncover additional variables. These will be helpful when you finally get down to the heart of the negotiation.

7. *Start high and concede slowly.* Competitive customers want to see a return on their negotiation investment. When you know

that a customer wants to barter, start off with something you can afford to lose. Obviously, game playing has its price. Not only do you train your customers to ask for concessions, you also teach them never to relax their guard on money matters. Still, when the customer really wants to wheel and deal, you have little choice.

The customer too can pay a price for playing games. A classic case involves a customer who always bragged about his poker winnings, presumably to intimidate salespeople before negotiations got started. "I always leave the table a winner," he seemed to be saying. "Say your prayers." What salespeople actually did was raise their prices 10% to 15% before sitting down to negotiate. They'd let him win a few dollars, praise his skill, then walk away with the order at a reasonable margin.

A number of studies have shown that high expectations produce the best negotiating results and low expectations the poorest. This is why salespeople must not let themselves be intimidated by the customer who always bargains every point. Once they lower their expectations, they have made the first concession in their own minds before the negotiation gets under way. The customer then gets to take these premature concessions along with the normal allotment to follow.

A man I used to know—the CEO of a company selling software to pharmacies—always insisted on absolute candor in all customer dealings. He'd begin negotiations by showing customers his price list and saying, "Here's our standard price list. But since you're a big chain, we'll give you a discount." He broke the ice with a concession no one had asked for and got his clock cleaned nearly every time.

The key is always to get something in return for concessions and to know their economic value. Remember that any concession is likely to have a different value for buyer and seller, so begin by giving things that the customer values highly but that have little incremental cost for your company: control of the process, assurance of quality, convenience, preferred treatment in times of product scarcity, information on new technology (for example, sharing R&D), credit, timing of delivery, customization, and service.

There's an old saying, "He who concedes first, loses." This may be true in a hardball negotiation where the customer has no other potential source of supply. But in most competitive sales situations, the salesperson has to make the first concession in order to keep the deal alive. Concede in small increments, get something in return, and know the concession's value to both sides. Taking time may seem crazy to salespeople who have learned that time is money. But in a negotiation, not taking time is money.

8. *Don't be trapped by emotional blackmail.* Buyers sometimes use emotion—usually anger—to rattle salespeople into making concessions they wouldn't otherwise make. Some use anger as a premeditated tactic; others are really angry. It doesn't matter whether the emotion is genuine or counterfeit. What does matter is how salespeople react. How do you deal with a customer's rage and manage your own emotions at the same time?

Here are three different techniques that salespeople find useful in handling a customer who uses anger—wittingly or unwittingly—as a manipulative tactic.

Withdraw. Ask for a recess, consult with the boss, or reschedule the meeting. A change in time and place can change the entire landscape of a negotiation.

Listen silently while the customer rants and raves. Don't nod your head or say "uh-huh." Maintain eye contact and a neutral expression, but do not reinforce the customer's behavior. When the tirade is over, suggest a constructive agenda.

React openly to the customer's anger, say that you find it unproductive, and suggest focusing on a specific, nonemotional issue. There are two keys to this technique. The first is timing: don't rush the process or you risk backing the customer into a corner from which there is no graceful escape. The second is to insist that the use of manipulative tactics is unacceptable and then to suggest a constructive agenda. Don't be timid. The only way to pull this off is to be strong and assertive.

For example, imagine this response to a customer throwing a fit: "This attack is not constructive. [Strong eye contact, assertive tone.] We've spent three hours working the issues and trying to arrive at a fair and reasonable solution. Now I suggest that we go back to the question of payment terms and see if we can finalize those."

Of course, there is substantial risk in using any of these techniques. If you withdraw, you may not get a second chance. If you listen silently or react ineffectively, you may alienate the customer further. These are techniques to resort to only when the discussion is in danger of going off the deep end, but at such moments they have saved many a negotiation that looked hopeless.

The essence of negotiating effectively with aggressive customers is to sidestep their attacks and convince them that a common effort at problem solving will be more profitable and productive. Your toughest customers will stop throwing punches if they never connect. Your most difficult buyer will brighten if you can make the process interesting and rewarding. The old toe-to-toe scuffle had its points, no doubt. Trading blow for blow was a fine test of stamina and guts. But it was no test at all of imagination. In dealing with tough customers, creativity is a better way of doing business.

PART

V

Energize the Selling Effort

Introduction

To this point, we have considered the elements of a successful customer-seeking effort, including prospect and account selection, closing the sale, and managing price. Now, we shift to the issue of managing the sales force to ensure that the desired activities actually take place. Clearly, sales management is a broad topic, worthy of entire books. Here our goal is merely to emphasize the critical aspects of sales management within the context of the larger customer-seeking process. Like the other elements of this process, effective sales force management involves commitment to the four basic themes of selling: profits, focus, building relationships, and combining art and science.

Throughout this book we have stressed that effective selling is a multifunctional process that requires companywide input and co-ordination. Nevertheless, the sales force is most directly responsible for identifying prospects and accounts, interacting with customers, and to a great extent, pricing. Naturally, different companies assign pricing policy in different proportions to the finance, marketing, and sales functions. However, it is typically the sales force that informs customers of prices or price changes; has to convince customers that higher prices reflect greater value; and serves as the messenger when customers express dissatisfaction over prices. As a conduit of pricing information, the sales force makes a significant impact on pricing decisions, helping to set prices that will ensure profitable sales.

The sales force is also a large cost component in many companies. As we saw in "Automation to Boost Sales and Marketing" (Part I), marketing and sales costs average 15% to 35% of total corporate costs. Thus, efficiency is an important issue. A well-run sales force employs measures such as expense-to-revenue ratios, sales dollars generated per call, and the success, or "hit," ratio (the percentage of calls that leads to sales) to gauge sales efficiency.

Inefficient sales force management will have a direct negative effect on company profits. Consider, for example, the issue of turnover. High sales force turnover rates tend to reduce efficiency and effectiveness in several ways. New salespeople are invariably less able to select prospects and demonstrate value to customers; they also generally produce fewer revenue dollars per expense dollar (including compensation), and demand disproportionate amounts of training and management time. When unsuccessful rookie salespeople leave, they take the training and development they received with them. Then the sales manager and related executives have to spend time and resources recruiting replacements instead of focusing on prospects, accounts, and long-term salespeople. This chain of inefficiencies can significantly increase company costs per dollar of revenue, thereby cutting into profits. Effective sales management focuses on creating an environment that minimizes turnover and maximizes commitment to profitable selling.

As we have argued throughout this book, profitability depends upon focus. At a strategic level, focus means targeting the appropriate prospects and customers, selling the right products and services, and providing high value-added support to keep customers satisfied. These themes are developed in earlier sections of this book as well as in the companion volume, *Keeping Customers* (see, for example, Part VI, "Convert Customer Satisfaction into Profits"). However, there is also a tactical dimension to focus, which involves getting every salesperson to implement these strategies. Task clarity—establishing a positive and direct relationship between a salesperson's efforts and the reported results—gives salespeople the motivation to focus on the most profitable activities.

The first two articles in this section, "What Counts Most in Motivating Your Sales Force?" by Stephen Doyle and Benson Shapiro, and their follow-up, "Make the Sales Task Clear," emphasize the power of task clarity. Through extensive primary research, the authors identified and ranked four variables affecting sales force motivation and performance. The authors discovered that task clarity is the strongest motivating factor, followed by personality (the need to achieve), compensation design, and quality of management. The authors suggest that sales managers adopt a multifunctional approach that integrates all these factors, giving priority to task clarity. "To design such a plan, managers should assess the current level of each variable, how much each variable would have to be modified to bring it up to maximum realizable goals, and the costs associated with that degree of modification of each factor."

In "Make the Sales Task Clear" the authors propose a framework to help managers implement this type of program. In this article they further develop the role of task clarity, suggesting four areas by which managers can enhance it: (1) *deployment* (specifying account coverage), (2) *account management* (determining attainable goals for each account), (3) *information systems* (ensuring the timeliness and accuracy of feedback), and (4) *field sales management* (active responsibility for deployment, account planning, goal setting, feedback, coaching, and performance appraisal on a regular basis).

Together, these two articles emphasize a systemic view of motivation in which information and reporting systems and criteria for determining rewards and recognition are fully integrated:

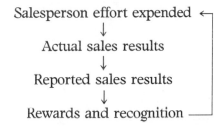

The information systems advocated in "Automation to Boost Sales and Marketing" (Part I) can be employed to enhance and promote task clarity, creating a powerful management structure that measures and rewards focused selling behavior.

The sales force lives on relationships. In previous sections we have discussed relationships between the selling company and its customers, and between the sales force and other parts of the company, such as the marketing and support functions. Our look at task clarity emphasizes the importance of the relationships *within the sales function*—between sales managers and their salespeople. These relationships are increasingly being enhanced by disciplined quantitative tools, such as automation systems and the results of behavioral research. Nevertheless, sales force management still relies heavily on the judgment and insight that develop from experience.

At a broad level, sales managers possess several tools to implement the activities that emanate from the company's marketing strategy and business plan: (1) organization, (2) recruitment, (3) training, (4) field sales management, and (5) compensation, evaluation, and motivational programs. Together, these tools can create a strong sales force committed to promoting the company's sales goals.

At the organizational level, there is no perfect sales organization. Although managers attempt to create the ideal organizational structure, each configuration has both advantages and disadvantages. For example, a geographically organized sales force, in which each salesperson is responsible for all accounts and prospects within a given territory, promotes efficiency by minimizing travel time and expenses. However, this approach forces each salesperson to sell all the organization's products and services, handle all types of accounts, and perform all sales functions. These expectations can reduce effectiveness, particularly if prospects and customers differ greatly by size (e.g., national accounts versus small, local accounts) or industry (e.g., banks versus restaurants). If various products and services require special knowledge or in-depth experience, the geographical approach can diminish the authority of the salesperson in the eyes of the customer.

Specialization of the sales force by product or service, or by account type, solves some problems but creates others. For example, the product-specialized sales force may be inefficient because of significant travel demands or because several company salespeople may call on the same prospects and accounts, resulting in duplicated efforts and confused customers. In addition, product or service specialization prevents the salesperson from leveraging a customer relationship in introducing new products or services.

Because different prospects and customers have divergent needs, a sales force can be specialized by customer industry and/or size (as described in "How to Segment Industrial Markets," in Part II). The industry focus helps the salesperson understand prospect and customer needs at a detailed level. However, industry specialization, like product specialization, can lead to inefficient travel costs; furthermore, intimate knowledge of an industry does not necessarily translate into in-depth product knowledge. Salespeople may end up knowing more about their customers than they do about their own company's capabilities.

Account specialization, which is a natural outgrowth of industry specialization, leads to major and national account management. But as we saw in "Teamwork for Today's Selling" (Part I), it is difficult to foster account-oriented teamwork from salespeople dispersed across geography and product lines. However, when there is a strong opportunity for cross-selling and an intense need for relationship building—as described in "Close Encounters" (Part III)—major or national account organizations are often chosen.

Finally, because opening an account can be very different from maintaining it, there is sometimes good reason to divide these two functions: after the sale is made a specialized account opener will hand off the account to an account manager, who will service the account over the long term. This approach tends to be used when the nature of the seller-customer relationship is heavily weighted toward post-sales service provision.

Determining the appropriate dimension of specialization is a function of the selling company's marketing and business goals as well as the needs and nature of the prospect and account base. Implementing the desired organization is a function of attracting the best salespeople and ensuring their commitment to the company's goals. In other words, the company must have rigorous, disciplined recruitment programs.

In "Job Matching for Better Sales Performance," Herbert and Jeanne Greenberg offer guidelines for more effective recruitment, improving the hiring company's ability to attract productive salespeople with a lower turnover rate. Having studied 360,000 individuals in a wide variety of industries, the Greenbergs debunk the common myth of the "ideal" salesperson as a young, white, married, experienced, and college-educated male—these variables were not found to be statistically correlated with superior sales performance or low turnover rates. Instead, the Greenbergs argue that sales success depends upon "whether the candidate has been matched with the particular position—that is, whether the person's characteristics agree with the functional requirements of the job."

The Greenbergs suggest that in designing recruitment programs companies should focus first on the underlying aspects and demands of the job (e.g., whether the sales task needs close supervision; whether teamwork is the norm; or whether a high degree of conceptual ability is necessary). In evaluating the applicant's ability to meet these demands, the company should focus on underlying characteristics such as:

Ego Drive—"a strong need to persuade and convince."

Empathy—"the ability to tune in on a prospect or a subordinate and to accept feedback from that person."

Ego Strength—"the ability to rise above the rejection that often comes in sales situations."

This attention to personal characteristics, rather than external characteristics (such as age, gender, or education), supports Doyle and Shapiro's argument that personality is a strong motivating factor. The results of the Greenbergs' research suggest that investments in well-planned recruitment programs will pay off with a highly motivated, focused, and committed sales force.

After the initial hire, however, the sales force must continually be encouraged to perform efficiently and effectively. We have already discussed some of the elements of sales force motivation, particularly with respect to task clarity. At a broader level, the entire sales management program must also include training, field sales management, and compensation packages. Although we do not have space in this book to consider training and field sales management with individual articles, they are nevertheless essential elements of effective sales development, and deserve some specific attention here.

The best single rule for both training and field sales management is to key off the sales task. If the task is clearly defined and measured, it will enable sales executives to tailor training and field management to the needs of the task and of the individuals responsible for its implementation. Training must consider the functions of the sales task (e.g., generating leads, opening the account), specific information on the products and services being sold, knowledge of customers and prospects, and a solid understanding of the company's goals, policies, and procedures. If the salesperson lacks the mechanics of entering an order or has not been trained to listen to the customer, he or she is unlikely to succeed even if they are the right person for the job.

Field management, which we have discussed briefly in the context of task clarity, helps the salesperson to make the connections between centralized programs and policies (including compensation schemes and training courses) and their own needs, as well as those of their accounts, prospects, and territories. The field sales management team—particularly the first-level manager—should provide the day-to-day evaluation, training, motivation, and support needed to succeed in a highly competitive environment, where, for example, if four salespeople compete for each piece of business, each will, on average, succeed only one-quarter of the time.

Finally, we turn to the issue of compensation, which has long been among the primary means of providing incentive and motivation to the sales force. "How to Pay Your Sales Force," by John Steinbrink, is an outstanding summary article based upon extensive field research. Originally published in 1978, this article continues a long and distinguished tradition of compensation analysis in the *Harvard Business Review*, beginning with the seminal work of Harry Tosdal in the early 1950s. Although the article does not consider such motivational factors as task clarity (as developed in the later research by Doyle and Shapiro), it provides a comprehensive and rigorous framework for evaluating the full range of compensation packages (from straight salary to salary plus commission plus bonus) as well as related areas, such as expense practices, additional personal and psychological incentives, financial incentives (such as contests), nonfinancial compensation (such as publicity and commendation), and fringe benefits.

To achieve effective sales force management, compensation must be part of a fully integrated evaluation-and-motivation system, where all elements work harmoniously to support a clearly defined sales task. In an increasingly demanding sales environment, sales force management must be carefully planned and focused. As in the other elements of the customer-seeking process—knowing the market, targeting customers, developing relationships, and setting prices—achieving this high level of integration and coordination requires sophisticated information and automation systems as well as a healthy dose of instinct and good judgment.

1
What Counts Most in Motivating Your Sales Force?

Stephen X. Doyle and Benson P. Shapiro

For decades the difficulty of motivating salespeople has been frustrating sales and marketing managers. To the most effective ones, two things are clear: one, the job is difficult; two, there is no one simple solution. Believing that "good salespeople are born, not made," many managers recognize that recruiting is important. Others holding that "if you pay for performance, you'll get it" believe that incentive compensation produces motivation. The more successful sales executives recognize that motivation is largely a result of a combination of effective recruiting practices, sensible pay plans, and good management. What else may be involved has been an open question.

Previous studies on employee motivation clearly demonstrate that a variety of factors (rewards, supervision, goals, and so forth) shape and guide how well people work.[1] From a sales manager's point of view, then, two questions are paramount:

1. Which factors have the most influence on motivation of salespeople?
2. What are the implications for management action and decision making?

To answer the first question, we recently conducted a study to determine how much a person's personality and incentive pay determine level of motivation. Then, because we believed from prior experience that task clarity, another variable, has a pronounced effect on salesperson motivation, we included it in our study as well. Finally, we looked at the impact of good management. (We describe the methodology in the Appendix.)

Exhibit I.   The Four Motivating Factors in Order of Importance*

Motivating factor	Description	Percent variation explained by the factor
Task	Design of the sales job itself	33.6%
Personality	Strength of the salesperson's need for achievement	21.2
Compensation	Design of the program by which salespeople are paid	11.6
Quality of management	Method of field sales supervision	—

*The ability to motivate is expressed by the percent variation explained by each factor.
Note: Data in all exhibits represent averages.

In our research, we conducted in-depth interviews with salespeople and their managers, analyzed a questionnaire filled out by more than 200 salespeople in four different organizations, and observed some actual sales calls.

The four participating companies provide a broad sampling of current sales management practices. Two of the companies sell business products and two sell transportation services; all four are industry leaders. Of the business products companies, one manufactures and sells minicomputers; the other, office equipment. The transportation companies specialize in air freight serving domestic and international markets. One transportation services company and one business products company pay salespeople a straight salary. The other two companies use incentive plans.

Our results are clear. The most important determinants of motivation are: (1) the nature of the task, (2) the personality, particularly the strength of the salesperson's need for achievement, and (3) the type of compensation plan. Unfortunately, our measurement of the fourth determinant, the quality of management, is not precise enough for us to say any more than that field supervision is important. We believe, however, that if a company's management is not far outside the normal range in quality, its effect on motivation is below that of task clarity and salesperson personality. Exhibit I shows the four factors ranked in order of their importance. (The ranking is a result of a statistical analysis that measured independently each factor's ability to motivate salespeople.)[2]

Before discussing in more detail the impact each variable has on motivation and performance, we'd like to describe more fully exactly why motivating salespeople is such an enormous problem. Understanding the salesperson's role is key.

Salespeople vary greatly in what they do as well as what they are expected to do.[3] Some, alone and unsupervised, sell simple products such as books and magazines door to door. Others, working as a team, sell complex technical products such as power plants and aircraft. For some salespeople the eventual purchase of their product is far removed from their "sale." For example, when detail people who do missionary selling of pharmaceutical drugs leave the physician's office, it is difficult for anyone, perhaps even the physician, to know if a sale was made. Only through a postaudit of prescriptions is it possible to identify the outcome.

The salespeople we are concerned with here are full-time professionals who generally sell to business and industry, not to consumers. We believe, however, that our findings are generally applicable even to part-time salespeople selling door to door.

The salesperson we are interested in:

Meets rejection by influential executives many times a week. (If four companies are vying for a particular order, three salespeople will be turned down and, in a sense, personally rejected.)

Works independently, away from direct supervision, for long periods.

Works alone, away from the community of people.

Functions at a high energy level all day, every day.

Makes quick, accurate assessments of many new business situations and people on a regular basis.

Appreciates and is constantly sensitive to the personal and organizational needs of others.

Seems "bigger than life" in order to sell to the customer and make a positive, lasting impression.

Balances the needs of a demanding customer with the sometimes unresponsive abilities and nature of the company. (At times it is difficult for the salesperson to identify the "antagonist." Sometimes it is a purchasing agent or an executive in the buying company, and sometimes it seems to be the shipping manager in the salesperson's own company.)

Exhibit II.   Task Clarity of Sales Job in Four Companies

Condition determining task clarity	Business products organizations	Transportation services organizations
Time span of performance feedback	Short—one day to one week	Long—one to three months
Degree that individual results can be accurately measured	High	Low to moderate
Task clarity	High	Low

It is no wonder that salespeople are difficult to motivate. Now let's take a closer look at the four factors necessary for a motivated sales system, and then we'll explore the implications for action.

A Clear Sales Task

Obviously, the nature of selling differs from one company to another. For example, a pharmaceutical detail person calling on physicians has a very different job from an account executive selling apparel or an account manager selling materials-handling systems. We can categorize what people do in vastly different sales jobs according to how clear their tasks are. Task clarity is the degree to which there is a clear and positive relationship between exerting effort and attaining results. In sales, this characteristic varies from one selling job to another, depending on two major conditions: (1) the time span of performance feedback and (2) the degree that one can accurately determine the individual results of salespeople.

Our research shows that these components of task clarity can be accurately determined. In the participating companies, the selling jobs displayed strong differences, which are outlined in Exhibit II.

We determined the conditions of the sales tasks in the four companies from the comments of managers and our own assessments, which correspond, furthermore, to the individual assessments of the salespeople. For example, a salesperson in a business products company with a clear task comments:

"It is quite easy to describe our job. We go by the numbers; in fact, we have numbers for everything. Our performance goals are very clear. Also on Friday afternoon we get a printout that gives feedback on our results. It is very easy to see the relationship between my effort and results. My territory stays the same for a year; I get frequent updates about new orders and reorders. In fact, I just told some trainees that attaining sales goals is not difficult as long as they plan and are willing to exert some effort."

A transportation services salesperson with an unclear task describes her job much differently: "Sure we get credited sales reports, but they are only 50% to 60% accurate. The accounting office has admitted that they have trouble crediting revenue to the person who produced it. Even though I understand their problem, it makes it tough on us in terms of accurately pinpointing what we produce. The truth is that our objective measures, such as shipment counts, are not accurate at the district level. I guess you could say no one really knows how well his or her territory is doing at any given time."

This salesperson's district sales manager supported her comments. He stated that field sales reports are inaccurate because of the difficulty in crediting the revenue from millions of shipments, averaging less than $50 per shipment, to the salesperson involved in the sale. For example, each week a large manufacturer of microprocessors located in the Santa Clara Valley of California ships and receives hundreds of air freight parcels to customers all over the United States. The sale—the manufacturer's decision to use air freight as well as a specific air transportation company—may have been made in the Santa Clara Valley or in various destination cities. The individual salesperson, therefore, has no way of knowing whether the revenue increases in his or her territory were caused by a colleague in a distant city.

As a result regional and district revenue reports do not reflect individuals' efforts. Also, because of the nature of the sales task, fewer than 7% of the sales calls generate new business. The most tangible evidence of new business is an oral or written commitment on the part of the shipper to use the services of the company at some future time.

Our study shows that the clarity of the sales task is strongly related to on-the-job performance and effort. Motivation and effort in the clear sales task of the two business products organizations are substantially greater than in the relatively unclear sales task of

*Exhibit III.   Relation of Effort to Task Clarity
and Personality**

	Hours spent in selling or in sales-related activities per week
A. Task clarity	
Clear—business products	58
Unclear—transportation services	42
B. Personality	
Higher need to achieve	53
Lower need to achieve	47

*See Appendix for an explanation of the variable used.

the transportation services companies (see A in Exhibit III). If a sales task is unclear, selling can be frustrating. In such a situation, the salesperson will not know where he or she stands and will not be able to pinpoint the results of his or her own efforts. Good performance seems to be a random occurrence in no way related to effort. This lack of connection is discouraging and dampens the pride that might otherwise come from accomplishment.

People Who Need to Achieve

Managers know intuitively that personality differences are an important determinant of on-the-job performance, and a number of studies confirm their feelings.[4] Our study was aimed at finding out how differences in need for achievement, as described by David McClelland, influence the motivation of sales representatives.[5] McClelland has characterized the person with a high need to achieve as one who likes to take responsibility for solving problems, sets moderate achievement goals, takes calculated risks, desires feedback on performance, and is likely to find selling rewarding and challenging.

We found that the degree of a person's need for achievement is directly related to sales force motivation (see B in Exhibit III). As need for achievement increases, so do effort and motivation. In fact, as a group, the motivation of those with higher achievement needs is 13% greater than those with lower needs.

The total group of 204 salespeople scored relatively high on need for achievement. There are two probable explanations for this. First, as McClelland states, people who have a high need for achievement tend to gravitate toward sales jobs. Second, the participating companies' selection and hiring processes use multiple interviews and emphasize a record of past accomplishments that could show a high need to achieve. (Implicitly, all the companies were trying to recruit people with a high need to achieve.) A regional sales manager in one of the business products companies comments:

"Our motivational plan is built around goals, evaluation, and hiring the right people. It is not unusual for an applicant to visit our office six or seven times before a hiring decision is made. I want to get to know each person as thoroughly as possible before I make a commitment. During these interviews I look for a strong record of accomplishment [in school, business, or social settings] and indications that the applicant is very results oriented."

Compensation Plan Design

In 1953, Harry Tosdal wrote that "a large portion of sales managers seem dissatisfied with their present compensation plans. Unfortunately, there is no nice or easy solution."[6] The problem of designing effective sales compensation programs has not been solved since Tosdal's observation. A recent Research Institute of America (RIA) study indicates that 24% of all responding companies had redesigned their sales pay plans during the past 2 years—the same percentage of change as had been reported in its 1971 survey.[7] The 1975 RIA study comments that "companies do considerable milling about and searching for the combination that will give them the best results."

Designing an effective sales compensation program, however, is a complex management assignment. All the sales executives we talked to expressed concern about whether plans would increase immediate sales and, if so, whether they would sacrifice the development of long-term accounts. Other areas of concern were equitable pay, how a plan should be communicated, and what percent of total take-home pay should be a fixed base. They also worried about whether incentive plans would interfere with the introduction of new product lines and strategy changes and, finally, whether money or status is the real motivator.

We couldn't attempt to answer all these pragmatic and challenging questions and focused only on identifying whether incentive compensation would be a more effective motivator for salespeople than straight salary. Straight salary is a fixed, agreed-on amount of gross pay that does not vary from week to week during a definite period of time. With an incentive compensation plan all or a certain percentage of a salesperson's income varies in relation to that individual's performance.

Much has been written about the design of sales pay programs.[8] According to Tosdal, the two most widely used compensation designs—straight salary and commission—both offer definite advantages.[9] Straight salary provides security and reduces employees' worries about fluctuations in take-home pay. It is also simple in design and administration and avoids questions of parity in pay across different functions in the same company. On the other hand, commissions provide a powerful incentive. Studies conducted in 1953 by Tosdal and in 1975 by RIA show that most managers favor some form of incentive compensation:

Type of Plan	Tosdal (1,254 companies)	RIA (9,000 companies)
Straight salary	20%	24%
Straight commission	24%	20%
Combination of both	56%	56%

Although sales managers make strikingly similar choices of plans, they continue to search for the "right" compensation plan just as they did in the early 1950s. A senior vice president of one company participating in our study comments:

"The board of directors asked me to develop a financial package for the managers of a recently acquired subsidiary. Our consultants showed us a number of complex incentive plans, but the basic question I have is whether the extra dollars invested in incentive pay will result in return on investment in terms of motivation. If not, we should forget about all the incentive pay plans and use

Exhibit IV. *How Design of Compensation Plan as well as Incentive Plan, Combined with Tasks of Different Clarity, Relate to Effort*

	Hours spent selling or in sales-related activities per week
A. Plan	
Incentive compensation	51
Straight salary	48
B. Incentive plan and task	
Clear task (business products) with incentive compensation	62
Unclear task (transportation services) with incentive compensation	43

straight salary. But the interesting question is on what basis do we decide to go straight salary or incentive."

Our findings demonstrate:

In general, incentive pay is a more effective motivator than straight salary.

The ability of incentive pay to act as a motivator is very much influenced by the nature of the selling task.

Exhibit IV shows that sales representatives in the business products and transportation services companies that paid on incentive had only slightly higher levels of motivation than sales representatives in the other two companies studied that paid on straight salary.

The true power of incentive pay surfaces when we take into account the nature of the sales task.

In the business products organization where the sales task is clear, incentive pay has a much larger motivational impact than the incentive program in the transportation services company where the sales task is unclear.

Sales representatives' comments support our analysis. A salesperson in the transportation company with the incentive plan states: "None of us, including the manager, believes in the commission. It's more of a game than a science. All of us like the extra dollars, but in terms of motivation, the bonus has little impact."

The comments of a salesperson paid on incentive in the business equipment industry are different: "There is no doubt in my mind that our company's incentive and recognition systems have a big influence on motivation. I used to earn about $15,000; this year I will hit $25,000 to $30,000. I feel proud about this, and I like being able to have a chance to make a good dollar. I am in control of my own destiny."

Compare this statement with the comments of another sales representative who is paid a straight salary in the other business equipment company: "Our management needs to rethink its philosophy of sales compensation. It really bothers me that I don't get paid for results. In my territory, sales are up 64% over last year. The sales manager says I am doing a good job, but it's not reflected in my take-home pay. Maybe it's one of the reasons that in this office the people don't make too many sales calls."

Two implications stem from these findings. First, the design and implementation of a sales incentive system is time consuming and costly. If the sales task is unclear, the ability of an incentive to motivate is significantly diminished, which suggests that a straight salary would be more practical and less problematic. Second, sales pay must not be seen as an isolated variable but as part of a system. In this system, on-the-job performance is influenced not only by the design of the pay plan but also by characteristics of the sales task and the personality of the salespeople.

How these factors in combination influence the ability of pay to serve as a source of motivation is shown in Exhibit V. Our overall findings and comparative rankings are shown in Exhibit VI.

Quality of Management

In recruiting and training their sales representatives, managers spend a lot of money—a good deal of which is often wasted due to ineffective sales supervision. Furthermore, because the salesperson's role can be especially frustrating, the first-line sales supervisor's role has additional importance. But little is known about what constitutes effective supervision in a sales setting.[10] In fact, most contemporary articles on sales management merely describe current fads and trends.

Exhibit V. How Incentive Plan, in Combination with Personality and Task Clarity, Affects Effort

Motivating factor	Hours spent selling or in sales-related activities per week
Straight salary (two companies)	48
Incentive (two companies)	51
Incentive plan + clear task	62
Incentive plan + clear task + high need to achieve	65

Because of this lack, we aimed a segment of our study at identifying what sales supervisors can do to contribute to the good performance of their subordinates. We identified the following skills as contributing toward effective leadership. Although the list is tentative, we include it because of the importance of first-line supervision and the "systems" nature of our findings:

Goal Setting. Sets high but attainable performance standards for subordinates and other groups. Gives responsibility and challenging assignments.

Exhibit VI. Overall Findings for Task Clarity, Personality, and Compensation in Relation to Effort

Motivating factor	Hours spent selling or in sales-related activities per week
Task	
Clear	58
Unclear	42
Personality	
High need to achieve	53
Low need to achieve	47
Compensation	
Incentive	51
Straight salary	48

Evaluation. Provides timely and frequent feedback to subordinates on their progress toward established goals.

Coaching. Assists the sales representative to identify training needs and areas for improvement, particularly in regard to personal selling skills and time management. Structures opportunities for the application of newly learned skills. Rewards improvements.

Empathize. Shows personal concern and sensitivity to others. Develops constructive working relationships with subordinates. Knows when to withdraw and let the salespeople try it on their own.

Know-How. Demonstrates a thorough knowledge of personal selling and marketing. Keeps abreast of events both inside and outside the organization that may affect the success of subordinates.

A Sales Management System

With our results in mind, we suggest managers adopt a multi-functional approach to achieve the greatest possible improvement in sales performance.[11] Managers need to stress the positive effects of task design, personality, and compensation—in that order. To design such a plan, managers should assess the current level of each variable, how much each variable would have to be modified to bring it up to the maximum realizable goals, and the costs associated with that degree of modification of each factor.

John Roche, manager of marketing training and development at Emery Air Freight, applied such a framework in 1976. Before then each Emery salesperson was assigned a territory with hundreds of accounts. The process of selecting accounts for sales calls was understandably vague and difficult. As a result, many calls resulted in dead ends with a comparable high ratio of failure to success.

The clouds hanging over the sales representatives' success were compounded by two problems with measurement:

1. Because it took from three to five months for feedback on sales to reach them, salespeople—who need to know how they are doing from day to day—could not get a psychologically meaningful picture of their performance.
2. Even when they did, it was often impossible to determine whether they or the salespeople on the other end should get credit for the sale.

A senior vice president and general manager of Emery described it this way: "Every day we move thousands of shipments to customers all over the world. We don't really know which sales representative closed the sale. For example, a city like New York . . . there are hundreds of shipments in and out of there every day which the New York sales force may have had nothing to do with. Perhaps it was our sales rep or a truck driver in Kansas City who is generating business into New York. We have come to the conclusion that we cannot equitably measure a salesperson in terms of revenue or shipment counts because no one really knows who is responsible for closing the sale on 50% of the shipments that move across our docks."

The high risk of failure, large account load, and imprecise feedback considerably decreased the scope in which a salesperson could take effective individual action—the key feature of the selling task. On a scale of 1 to 10 (with 10 high and 1 low) salespeople rated their individual control over their sales results at just above 3.

In applying its systems approach, Emery management first authorized a redesign of the sales task in three offices and an evaluation of the impact on sales performance. The design included:

Target Accounts. Salespeople were instructed to sell to a smaller group of customers. Each selected account, however, had a large potential for increased business.

Feedback and Measurement. A computer-based information system was designed to provide timely updates to salespeople on their weekly performance in relation to their targets.

Planning. The salespeople were taught how to determine potential value from their accounts and how to plan their time and calls to maximize sales results.

This design improved the marketing capability of the sales force and also allowed the achievement-oriented salespeople to function at greater potential. In other words, the job was structured toward a higher probability that the salespeople would be able to measure and control their own success or failure.

The results of the job redesign in the three offices of Emery are impressive, in terms of both the salespeoples' sense of successful control over their task and their improved sales. The salespeoples' rating of their individual control over results climbed from an initial low of 3.2 to a consistent 8.9. In terms of shipments, the

Exhibit VII.   **Percent Increase in Number of Shipments in Three Emery Offices During the Previous Year***

Control offices	Test sites	Difference
6.24%	One 9.23%	47.9%
6.35	Two 8.41	32.4
6.35	Three 7.86	23.8
6.31 (increase)	8.50 (increase)	34.7 (average difference in sales increases)

*Shipments were used instead of revenues to control for inflation. Also there were no significant pricing or service changes in the test sites.

three offices moved to among the top producers in their respective regions, increasing shipments an average of 34.7% from 1978 to 1979 (see Exhibit VII).

The initial results and the sales force's acceptance of the job redesign led James J. Brown, senior vice president and general manager, to redesign the sales task throughout the company. Brown said that: "In addition to increasing the motivation and productivity of the sales force, we find a positive by-product is the availability to management of timely and accurate information. It helps us forecast, staff, respond to customers' needs and competitors' actions, and direct the sales force toward specific prospects in profitable, growing industries."

Success: A Sum of the Parts

Although we have identified four factors that both individually and in combination have a large impact on salesperson motivation, it is not clear why they work together the way they do. We believe, however, that task clarity, personality, compensation plan, and quality of management are important because of the relationships expressed in the following chart:

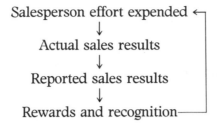

Salesperson effort expended ←
↓
Actual sales results
↓
Reported sales results
↓
Rewards and recognition

1. *Clear tasks* ensure that the linkage between the effort expended and the actual sales results is good and tight. Task clarity also makes it easier to measure and report sales results accurately and makes a good measurement system possible.
2. *Need for achievement* makes good salespeople. They thrive in a system in which the effort they expend clearly relates to results.
3. *Incentive compensation* makes a strong link between reward (and often recognition) and expended effort (through reported actual sales results).
4. *Good management* ensures accurate reporting of actual sales results, equitable rewards for reported sales results, and valuable recognition of these results.

Rewards and recognition motivate the salesperson to increase the effort expended. Willingness to do the work is only part of generating good sales results, however; salespeople must also be able to do the work. Thus good training, both in a center and in the field, is necessary to enable salespeople to accomplish their goals. Such a comprehensive sales system will generate a capable, motivated, and successful sales force—with rewards for both the individual salesperson and the company.

Appendix

METHODOLOGY

In our research of the motivating factors, we used multiple measures such as structural questionnaires, open-ended interviews, and field visits with sales representatives. These were designed to gather information on the relationships among the independent variables—design of the sales pay plan, quality of supervision, nature of the selling task—and the dependent variables, motivation and performance.

We used four measures to assess motivation and performance. The first was actual hours per week spent selling and in sales-related activities. The second was hours spent in the evening or on weekends in job-related activities. The third was the percent increase or decrease in units sold and revenues compared to the same period the previous year. The fourth and last measure was the strength of the sales representative's expectations.*

This article uses the first measure (hours spent per week selling or in sales-related activities) to assess levels of motivation. The first and second measures correlate highly at the .91 level and are therefore interchangeable. We could not report on the revenue increases or decreases because of confidentiality agreements. Also revenue increases and decreases were the result of other factors such as changes in the economy and in marketing programs. Our primary purpose was to measure salesperson motivation and effort as precisely and accurately as possible. We believe that the time a salesperson spends on selling and sales-related activities is a clear and precise measure of motivation.

The final form of the questionnaire contained a total of 68 questions. Most of the key variables were measured by at least two items. In an effort to establish reliability, we administered a retest to a number of sales representatives from a service organization. Using a three-week time spread between the first and second test, we then examined the pairs of questionnaires, and the reliability coefficient indicated no significant variation. We also spent three consecutive days each calling on diverse customers with two sales representatives from each of the four participating companies.

Authors' note: The questionnaire was designed and produced with help from a number of different sources, including: (1) Survey Research Center, Institute for Social Research, University of Michigan; (2) Edwards Personal Preference Schedule; (3) Internal-External (I-E) Scale†; and (4) Jay W. Lorsch and John J. Morse, *Organizations & Their Members: A Contingency Approach* (New York: Harper & Row, 1974), methodological appendix.

*R.L. Oliver, "Expectancy Theory Predictions of Salesmen's Performance," *Journal of Marketing Research*, August 1974, p. 243.
†See J.B. Rotter, "Generalized Expectancies for Internal Versus External Control of Reinforcement," *Psychological Monographs*, 1966, vol. 80 (1), p. 1.

Notes

1. For a good summary of the area, see Orville C. Walker, Jr., Gilbert A. Churchill, and Neil M. Ford, "Motivation and Performance in Industrial Selling: Present Knowledge and Needed Research," *Journal of Marketing Research*, vol. XIV, May 1977, p. 156.

2. N.H. Nie, C.H. Hull, J.G. Jenkins, K. Steinbrenner, and D.H. Kent, *Statistical Package for the Social Sciences*, 2d ed. (New York: McGraw-Hill, 1975), p. 404.

3. See, for example, Gilbert A. Churchill, Neil M. Ford, and Orville C. Walker, Jr., "Organizational Climate and Job Satisfaction in the Sales Force," *Journal of Marketing Research*, vol. XIII, November 1976, p. 323.

4. David Mayer and Herbert M. Greenberg, "What Makes a Good Salesman," *Harvard Business Review*, July–August 1964, p. 119; E.E. Ghiselli, *The Validity of Occupational Aptitude Tests* (New York: John Wiley, 1966); and David C. McClelland, *The Achieving Society* (Princeton, N.J.: Van Nostrand, 1961).

5. David C. McClelland, "Business Drive and National Achievement," *Harvard Business Review*, July–August 1962, p. 99.

6. Harry R. Tosdal, "How to Design the Salesman's Compensation Plan," *Harvard Business Review*, September–October 1953, p. 61.

7. "Sales Compensation" (Mount Kisco, N.Y.: Research Institute of America, 1975).

8. John P. Steinbrink, "How to Pay Your Sales Force," *Harvard Business Review*, July–August 1978, p. 111; and Richard C. Smyth, "Financial Incentives for Salesmen," *Harvard Business Review*, January–February 1968, p. 109.

9. Tosdal, "Salesman's Compensation Plan."

10. Walker, Gilbert, and Ford, "Motivation and Performance in Industrial Selling," p. 157.

11. Gene W. Dalton and Paul R. Lawrence, *Motivation and Control in Organizations* (Homewood, Ill.: Richard D. Irwin, 1971), p. 291.

2
Make the Sales Task Clear

Benson P. Shapiro and Stephen X. Doyle

In an earlier HBR article we reported that sales task clarity has a greater impact on the motivation of field salespeople than ego drive or compensation method.[1] In addition, we reported that sales task clarity can reinforce the effects of good recruiting and selection because it can make recruits with high ego drive work harder and better. Furthermore, it can reinforce a performance-oriented compensation system. On the other hand, an imprecise task can prevent even the most clever sales compensation system from working well.

Some sales tasks by their nature are less distinct than others. A drug detailer who calls on a doctor to suggest that she prescribe a particular medicine, for example, receives delayed feedback. Without a later audit of prescriptions written by the doctor for that product and competing ones, it is hard to discover whether the sale was ever made. Another example of low task clarity comes from selling electricity-generating equipment. The sale takes months or years and involves many people.

In this sequel to the 1980 article we turn our attention to three important aspects of sales task clarity: its definition and measurement, its impact on motivation and performance, and ways to enhance it so as to improve sales force motivation and performance.

Definition and Measurement

A task is clear if the relationship between a salesperson's effort and the reported results of that effort is not ambiguous. Clarity is a function of the impact of a person's efforts on sales results, of the timeliness of performance feedback, and of the accuracy of the feedback.

We designed a questionnaire to measure these three aspects and administered it to salespeople and their supervisors in four companies. Two of the sales forces sold business products, the other two sold transportation services. All the companies were profitable and were industry leaders with national reputations and respected products.

The business products salespeople received clear and accurate feedback weekly about their performance, which was relatively easy to measure (by dollar volume of orders booked). The transport services companies had no definite, objective measures because of the difficulty of correctly crediting the revenue from millions of (usually small) shipments to the various salespersons. It was hard to discover whether a sale was made through the shipper or the receiver of the merchandise. Moreover, the time between a sales call and a purchase of the service by telephone—not directly through the salesperson—varied considerably.

Motivation and Performance

Motivation is difficult to define and hard to measure. Consequently, in trying to determine whether differences in sales task clarity are associated with differences in sales force motivation, we used multiple measures. They were sales performance against goal, supervisor's performance evaluation, amount of time worked per week, and strength of salesperson's belief that effort would be rewarded.

Salespeople in the two business products organizations scored 30% to 60% higher on the motivation measures than did their counterparts in the transportation companies. All four companies looked for recruits with a strong need to achieve and big ego drives, so the differences in motivation evidently came from differences in sales task clarity, not recruiting and selection practices.

(As our previous article explained at length, the type of pay plan—incentive versus straight salary—also had less impact than the clarity of the task. Task clarity was 50% more important in determining motivation than personality, and nearly three times as important as type of pay plan. We therefore are confident in saying that clarity of task is the most important element in salesperson motivation.)

When the elements of the job were indistinct, the salespeople did not know where they stood and could not get reinforcement from news of their performance. A sales representative of one of the transportation services companies said, "Selling in this industry is like living in a dream. Getting ahead is a matter of luck and politics. It's discouraging."

In the business products companies, the sales reps remained an average of 3.3 years, versus 1.1 in the transport services organizations. A district sales manager of one of the latter commented, "Turnover is a real problem. We hire aggressive young trainees and fire them up with training. When they get out on the street, however, frustration becomes a problem. These people want to know how they are doing and how competitive they are. Many of the reps who quit are uncomfortable with our type of selling."

Ways to Enhance It

Judging from our research, there are four areas where management can make tasks clear.

DEPLOYMENT. Often salespeople are assigned territories with only geographic boundaries and are given little more than "hunting licenses" within those boundaries. We suggest that important parts of task clarity are a limitation on the number of accounts for which each person has responsibility and specification of goals for each of these target accounts.

Few sales representatives can regularly handle more than about 50 accounts in a situation in which a real sales effort, instead of a cursory presentation effort, is necessary. Yet some companies assign several hundred accounts to each salesperson or give them "all" the accounts in a geographic area. Doing so can only lead to frustration as the salespeople realize they have no set priorities and are powerless to control their performance.

The more specific the account coverage, the better. It is important, for example, to list the accounts for each rep. If necessary, a part of the defined task can be the salesperson's responsibility to add to the list some number, perhaps five, of qualified prospects.

The important thing is that the salespeople understand which accounts they are responsible for and will be judged by.

ACCOUNT MANAGEMENT.   The salespeople must be charged with clear goals to accomplish at each account—total sales goals, activity goals, sales goals by product, and so on. As we have seen, the more measurable the goals, the clearer the task definition and the greater the motivation. Goals can, of course, go beyond sales to include matters such as presentations, placement of promotions, and penetration to specified members of the buying organization.

Another criterion, attainability, deserves note. It is dysfunctional to include in a person's goals tasks over which he or she has little or no control. Frustration and anxiety are the result. If, for example, salespeople are judged by shipments to accounts (not by orders or bookings) and the shipping schedule varies with the production control organization's ability or inclination, the salespeople will be disgruntled because the task is unclear.

INFORMATION SYSTEM.   The information system furnishes the connection between actual performance and reported performance. A poor information system will destroy the salesperson's perception of an unblocked linkage between effort and results.

The information system, more than any other tool, determines the timeliness and accuracy of feedback, which are vital to task clarity. An element of randomness added by the system to the quality of the performance reports ruins the accuracy of the feedback. Delay in the information flow reduces the salespeople's ability to remember their effort (at both an intellectual and an emotional level) and to relate it to the reported results.

FIELD SALES MANAGEMENT.   To ensure task clarity for each salesperson, the field sales manager can use a variety of management mechanisms and processes. Most of these center on the goal-setting, feedback, coaching, and appraisal cycle. They include management by objectives, performance appraisal, and monthly reviews.

Of course, they require a commitment by the field sales managers, which begins with deployment and account planning. The manager tailors the task to the particular salesperson, sales territory, and accounts. Perhaps even more important from a motivational point of view, the manager ensures through a dialogue with the salesperson that he or she understands and accepts the task as laid out. In the case of goods like the aforementioned generating equipment, the challenge of clarifying the sales task will test the cleverness and ingenuity of any sales manager.

At the other end of the cycle—appraisal—the manager helps the salesperson to interpret the results and relate them to the defined task and the salesperson's effort. So, the sales manager helps to clarify and amplify the definition of the task and the measurement of results.

Naturally, an organization's sales managers must understand *their* task and be trained to accomplish it. But no sales manager, regardless of ability or training, can work effectively with a poor information system or a compensation system that rewards people haphazardly instead of for clearly defined results.

Sales task clarity is generally controllable by management. Moreover, it may be one of the most powerful motivational tools available to policy-level sales and marketing executives.

Note

1. Stephen X. Doyle and Benson P. Shapiro, "What Counts Most in Motivating Your Sales Force," *Harvard Business Review*, May–June, 1980, p. 133.

3
Job Matching for Better Sales Performance

Herbert M. Greenberg and Jeanne Greenberg

When sales and marketing executives get together, the high turn-over and poor productivity of salespeople are probably the two most widely discussed topics. Unfortunately, they rarely talk about or challenge the hiring criteria that, more than any other factor, cause this waste.

The very basis on which hiring judgments are made helps explain why high turnover of sales personnel in most industries persists and why throughout industry, even where the turnover is relatively low, approximately 20% of the salespeople account for 80% of the sales. Basing hiring decisions on myths rather than reality is, according to our research, the reason that about 55% of the people holding sales positions have little or no ability to sell, while another 25% have sales ability but are attempting to sell the "wrong" product or service.

The remaining 20% are doing precisely the job that is appropriate for them and for their companies. These people prove to be, for the most part, the same 20% who produce nearly 80% of the sales.

Sales and marketing executives accept this situation, and corporate management continues to seek the young married white male with experience and (of course) a college degree. The result continues to be high turnover and poor productivity.

In this article we focus on such persistent hiring tenets to show that they are myths and to suggest an approach that can lead to selecting successful salespeople and sales managers from all sectors of society. The findings we report are based on our study of more than 360,000 individuals in the United States, Canada, and Western Europe since 1961. The study covers 14 industries:

Automobiles
Chemical manufacture
Life insurance
Media and publishing
Pharmaceutical manufacture
Real estate
Stock brokerage and mutual funds

Banking and finance
Business forms manufacture
Data processing
Farm equipment
Heavy manufacturing
Printing
Property and casualty insurance

The seven industries in the first group characteristically have a high turnover of salespeople, while those in the second group have a low turnover.

For this study we selected at random 5% of the 360,000 from the 14 industries. After completing our analysis of these 18,000 individuals, we selected an additional 18,000, again at random, for spot comparisons to assure ourselves that we were indeed dealing with a representative sample of each industry's personnel. The second group differed in no significant way from the first, so it can be said with a high level of statistical confidence that the findings are representative.

To the appropriate managers (mostly sales managers) at the companies concerned we sent questionnaires requesting performance information pertaining to each person selected for analysis. We received usable replies for 53% of the test samples.

The respondents reported the data in quartile form so that each person could be evaluated in terms of his or her performance relative to the rest of the sales force in the particular company. This approach avoided the almost impossible task of qualitatively equating sales performance in, for example, real estate, pharmaceuticals, and heavy manufacturing. We broke the group down by industry and by the different variables we were examining in order to see which variables actually affected performance.

There were virtually no statistically significant differences among the 14 industries. The only difference appeared when we grouped the low-turnover industries and the high-turnover industries and compared them. Therefore, for the sake of simplicity, we have divided the data for the entire group into high-turnover and low-turnover fields.

On-the-Job Performance

In comparing performance, we broke the groups down as follows: (1) people under 40 versus those over 40; (2) men versus women; (3) blacks versus whites; (4) individuals with no sales experience versus those with two or more years of experience; (5) people with high school diplomas or less versus individuals who had earned one or more college degrees; (6) people hired on the basis of matching with jobs versus people hired without being job-matched.

UNDER-40S VERSUS OVER-40S

The worship of youth has long been recognized as a feature of the American culture. The myths relating to the value and attributes of youth have done wonders for clothing designers and cosmeticians. Few others, however, have benefited from our neurotic obsession with youth. It is not our purpose, however, to deal with the tragedy of setting aside people at the very time that they can contribute most to society. Rather, let us focus on the sales talent that industry loses in the over-40 age group.

When comparing the on-the-job performance of people over 40 with that of their under-40 counterparts, we found no statistically significant difference. Nearly the same percentage of individuals in the older and the younger groups performed in the upper quartile of their sales forces in 6-month and 14-month periods (see Exhibit I). The same similarity between the groups held for second-, third-, and fourth-quartile performance.

Even in turnover rate, the two groups remained extremely close, although the older group did turn over at a slightly lower rate. Six

Exhibit I.   Sales Performance According to Age

Measurement period after hiring	Performance quartile			
	1st	2nd	3rd	4th
6 months				
Over 40	9%	38%	32%	7%
Under 40	10%	39%	30%	6%
14 months				
Over 40	7%	26%	25%	5%
Under 40	8%	25%	24%	4%

Note: Sample sizes—after 6 months, 1,679 in over-40 group and 3,928 in under-40 group; after 14 months, 1,058 in over-40 group and 2,397 in under-40 group.

months after hiring, 14% of the over-40 salespeople and 15% of the under-40 salespeople had either quit or been fired. After 14 months the proportions were 37% and 39%, respectively.

MEN VERSUS WOMEN

For a number of years, of course, it has been illegal to discriminate in employment according to sex (as well as race, age, natural origin, and so on). But women continue to be substantially barred from many occupations that they could fill perfectly well. Real estate is one of the few industries that over the years have offered women excellent opportunities to actualize their potential in sales and management.

Can women be the same rich source of talent in other fields? How well do they perform in sales in comparison with their male counterparts? The results show, beyond statistical question, no performance difference between men and women, even in industries such as stock brokerage and auto sales, which until recently were considered exclusively male bastions. Virtually the same percentage of women and men performed in the top quartile of their sales forces after 6 months and 14 months (see Exhibit II).

Moreover, the two groups had virtually the same failure rates, whether failure is described as fourth-quartile performance after 14 months or as termination because of poor performance. Six

Exhibit II.   Sales Performance According to Sex

Measurement period after hiring	Performance quartile			
	1st	2nd	3rd	4th
6 months				
Women	11%	36%	35%	5%
Men	9%	38%	32%	7%
14 months				
Women	8%	28%	21%	4%
Men	9%	26%	14%	7%

Note: Sample sizes—after 6 months, 1,069 women and 4,227 men; after 14 months, 652 women and 2,494 men.

months after their employment, 13% of the women and 14% of the men had left for various reasons; after 14 months, 39% of the original group of women and 44% of the men had departed.

BLACKS VERSUS WHITES

The law and a sense of justice tell us we cannot discriminate against individuals because of race. The data indicate clearly that it is not good business to do so, if for no other reason than self-interest. Blacks perform on the job as well as their white associates (see Exhibit III). Turnover was virtually identical: 12% and 38% among blacks in the two periods, 13% and 37% among whites.

We should point out that the blacks in these sales forces are essentially middle class, so this group is not representative of all American blacks. But the group is representative of black individuals applying for or holding jobs in the cross section of industries presented in this study. What would be the results of a study of a less advantaged group of blacks—say, participants in an antipoverty program who have little work history, little schooling, and little exposure to the middle-class world?

The answer, based on our experience with more than 7,000 individuals in federally sponsored programs in the 1960s, is that, when placed in positions suited to their real abilities, less advantaged blacks perform at high levels. Of the more than 3,000 persons

Exhibit III.   Sales Performance According to Race

Measurement period after hiring	Performance quartile			
	1st	2nd	3rd	4th
6 months				
Blacks	8%	39%	30%	11%
Whites	9%	37%	21%	10%
14 months				
Blacks	6%	25%	24%	7%
Whites	7%	24%	26%	6%

Note: Sample sizes—after 6 months, 271 blacks and 2,014 whites; after 14 months, 168 blacks and 1,269 whites.

placed in jobs under an antipoverty program, less than 3% were fired because of inability to perform. True, others left for a multiplicity of reasons; but the fact emerged clearly that, when they were placed appropriately in jobs suited to their abilities and were given proper training, counseling, and supervision, people from disadvantaged groups did well on the job.

From our sales force data and our research on the "hard-core unemployed," we conclude that blacks possess the same range of abilities as the more advantaged and that companies tapping this source of talent will benefit greatly.

EXPERIENCED VERSUS INEXPERIENCED

Experience is usually a principal criterion for making hiring decisions. Someone with experience in a particular industry, in selling any product or service, or even in doing unrelated work in the same industry, enjoys a great advantage in applying for a sales or a management position in that industry. Yet we found little difference in performance between these experienced individuals and those with no experience. The person with no experience, given training and supervision, is as likely to succeed as the person with two or more years of experience (see Exhibit IV).

As in the results previously discussed, turnover was high and marked by no discernible differences. The attrition rate for the

Exhibit IV. **Sales Performance According to Experience**

Measurement period after hiring	Performance quartile			
	1st	2nd	3rd	4th
6 months				
Inexperienced	10%	33%	36%	6%
Experienced	11%	37%	33%	5%
14 months				
Inexperienced	9%	25%	20%	5%
Experienced	10%	27%	18%	5%

Note: Sample sizes—after 6 months, 3,721 inexperienced and 6,934 experienced; after 14 months, 2,195 inexperienced and 4,161 experienced.

inexperienced was 15% over 6 months and 41% over 14 months; for the experienced, 14% and 40%, respectively.

There is an old saw that 20 years' experience reflects one year's bad experience repeated 20 times. Our findings confirm that this is often the case. Too many people cling tenaciously to their unsuitable jobs and do just well enough not to be fired. Thus they accumulate years of "experience." It is these individuals—the 80% in the wrong jobs referred to earlier—who make the value of experience nil as a prime criterion for the selection of successful salespeople.

COLLEGE- VERSUS HIGH SCHOOL-EDUCATED

As a value to be cherished and encouraged in our society, education cannot be challenged. The use of formal degrees as *the* criterion for judging someone's potential effectiveness in a sales or a sales management job, however, must be challenged.

Obviously, in certain specialized fields complex technological knowledge is required to sell the product. The computer salesperson must know the technology necessary to deal with the specialist in the company that may purchase a new system. Of course, intimate knowledge of the product or service is necessary in all sales situations. And such knowledge is obtained through the company's training programs; a college degree is not sufficient. The results of

Exhibit V.   Sales Performance According to Education

Measurement period after hiring	Performance quartile			
	1st	2nd	3rd	4th
6 months				
High school diploma or less	7%	38%	31%	8%
College degree or more	8%	38%	30%	9%
14 months				
High school diploma or less	10%	23%	22%	5%
College degree or more	11%	24%	21%	6%

Note: Sample sizes—after 6 months, 2,694 with high school diploma or less and 7,348 with college degree or more; after 14 months, 1,616 with high school diploma or less and 4,556 with college degree or more.

our probing show that people with little education can do the job as effectively and as readily as those with college degrees (see Exhibit V).

Unlike the four other criteria discussed earlier, we found some industry-to-industry variations according to levels of education. The college graduate and the multidegree recipient slightly outperformed the less educated competitor in industries characterized by big-ticket, highly technical sales and by sales requiring lengthy follow-up. These differences, however, seldom reached 5%.

As in the examination of the other hiring criteria, virtually no differences surfaced in the proportions of salespeople who were fired or who quit during the two periods. These proportions also were high: 16% of the less educated group in 6 months and 40% in 14 months, and 15% and 38% of the better educated group in the two periods, respectively.

Job-Matching Approach

In view of these findings, an obvious question arises: If these long-used criteria are invalid, what criteria can industry use that would better predict job performance? The answer is: criteria that make a better match between the person and the job.

The management of the company doing the hiring must first

consider the requirements in doing the particular job. In filling a sales position, for example, management must think about such aspects as:

How important the close is on first contact.

Whether the salesperson must organize his or her work and time, or whether this is accomplished through close supervision.

Whether a great deal of detail ability is required in the sales presentation.

Whether teamwork (with technicians, for instance) is the norm.

Whether a high degree of conceptual ability is necessary.

Such elements are rarely seen in sales job descriptions. To give these elements their due, the company should study the day-to-day function of the job to determine what qualities a person must have to perform well and be happy doing the work.

The second step in the job-matching process is the evaluation of the applicant. It should focus on:

Whether the person has ego drive—that is, a strong need to persuade and convince—and, if so, how much.

Whether the applicant has empathy—the ability to tune in on a prospect or a subordinate and to accept feedback from that person.[1]

Whether the individual has ego strength—the ability to rise above the rejection that often comes in sales situations.

Whether the candidate can be forceful without being perceived as pushy.

How quickly the person reaches decisions.

Whether the individual can handle detail work.

How open the person apparently is to new ideas.

How well the candidate communicates with others.

If most of the applicant's personality dynamics match the key functional requirements of the job and none is so disparate that it guarantees failure, there is probably an appropriate job match. The experience of companies that have tried to match applicants with their sales openings shows distinct differences in performance. A final aspect of the survey was a comparison of new hires in terms of whether they were job-matched. The results for the same two periods are laid out in Exhibit VI (showing low-turnover industries) and Exhibit VII (showing high-turnover industries).

Exhibit VI.   Sales Performance in Low-Turnover Industries According to Job Matching

Measurement period after hiring	Performance quartile				Quit or fired
	1st	2nd	3rd	4th	
6 months					
Job-matched	9%	40%	32%	14%	5%
Not job-matched	2%	17%	25%	31%	25%
14 months					
Job-matched	22%	48%	16%	6%	8%
Not job-matched	1%	9%	21%	35%	34%

Note: Sample sizes—1,980 people who were job-matched and 3,961 who were not job-matched.

Both exhibits indicate that persons who had been matched in the first 6 months with open sales positions outperformed, to a statistically significant degree, those who had not been matched. Moreover, the differences widened after 14 months. Finally, the turnover rates of job-matched individuals were much lower in all cases.

While the job-matching approach is far superior to the standard tack of hiring according to experience and education, it does not approach perfection. As Exhibit VI reveals, the 14-month results indicate that 24% of the salespeople who had been matched with

Exhibit VII.   Sales Performance in High-Turnover Industries According to Job Matching

Measurement period after hiring	Performance quartile				Quit or fired
	1st	2nd	3rd	4th	
6 months					
Job-matched	11%	28%	23%	14%	24%
Not job-matched	2%	10%	18%	24%	46%
14 months					
Job-matched	19%	42%	7%	4%	28%
Not job-matched	1%	6%	14%	22%	57%

Note: Sample sizes—4,362 people who were job-matched and 8,740 who were not job-matched.

their jobs (and who still held them) were below-average performers. In the high-turnover fields (Exhibit VII), nearly 16% of the job-matched salespeople who still held their jobs were performing below average after 14 months.

In the low-turnover industries, 8% of the job-matched employees had quit or been discharged at the end of 14 months, while 28% of the job-matched were no longer with the high-turnover companies after that period. In both cases, however, the majority had left their positions voluntarily, while the majority of the unmatched salespeople who had left had done so involuntarily.

While error-free personnel selection will remain an impossible dream, this study points out a direction business can take to reduce such errors. The preliminary interview or interviews can provide another means of improvement.

A thorough understanding of the functional requirements of the job will help the manager maximize the data gathered in an interview. To the applicant the manager should lay out, clearly and honestly, everything he or she knows about what the work actually entails.

The interviewer(s) should quite closely study the applicant's reactions to these specifics. Of course, the applicant is likely to say, "Yes, that's what I like to do," to everything; but subtle reactions can often be picked up. Sometimes when the applicant is confronted with the realities of the job function, the person will make the decision that this, after all, is not the job for him or her.

An interview can also be used to discuss the applicant's personal qualities in relation to the functional requirements. For example, if teamwork is critical in the particular job and the employer's assessment indicates that the applicant is too much the individualist, the manager should point out this disparity. The applicant's reaction could be important both as a validation and as an indicator of willingness to adjust to the work.

If the manager enters the final interview with a thorough knowledge of the requirements of the job and the strengths and weaknesses of the applicant, the interview can contribute greatly to bringing mistakes in selection down to a minimum.

The Method Isn't Important

It is more important to assess the personality qualities of a person applying for a sales position than to gauge appearance or consider what he or she happens to have done. There are, of course, hundreds, if not thousands, of assessment methods, ranging through biographical analysis, in-depth multiple interview techniques, and psychological tests and assessment center approaches. These approaches range from totally invalid to highly effective.

How the assessment is done is not important, however; what is important is whether the technique employed does indeed measure the person's key job attributes. If the candidate possesses the appropriate personality qualities motivating him or her to perform well, the employer can provide the needed product knowledge and functional skills. But when the individual lacks the essential dynamics, training cannot fill the gap.

Instead of seeking sales personnel only among the experienced, well-educated, young white males, business has the opportunity to tap the potential of the one person in four throughout the population who possesses sales ability. Here is a limitless source of potential talent, much of which has not begun to be tapped.

Note

1. For extensive discussion of empathy and ego drive, see David Mayer and Herbert M. Greenberg, "What Makes a Good Salesman," *Harvard Business Review*, July–August 1964, p. 119.

4
How to Pay Your Sales Force

John P. Steinbrink

Any discussion with sales executives would bring forth a consensus that compensation is the most important element in a program for the management and motivation of a field sales force. It can also be the most complex.

Consider the job of salespeople in the field. They face direct and aggressive competition daily. Rejection by customers and prospects is a constant negative force. Success in selling demands a high degree of self-discipline, persistence, and enthusiasm. As a result, salespeople need extraordinary encouragement, incentive, and motivation in order to function effectively.

The average age of today's industrial salesman is 36 years, and about 60% have some college training or are college graduates. Today's salesman wants a challenging job with good prospects as well as payoffs now.

A properly designed and implemented compensation plan must be geared both to the needs of the company and to the products or services the company sells. At the same time, it must attract good salesmen in the first place and then keep them producing at increasing rates.

In this article, I will focus on the basic types of compensation plans, current levels of pay, and the compensation-related areas of expense practices, additional incentives, and fringe benefits. The main source of data used throughout is *Dartnell's 19th Biennial Survey of Salesmen*.[1] The data are based on studies of 380 companies in 34 Standard Industrial Classifications throughout the United States and Canada which employ a total of more than 15,000 salespeople.

Exhibit I.   *Companies Using Various*
             Compensation Plans

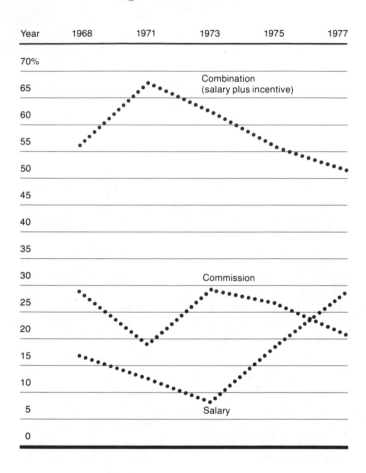

| Year | 1968 | 1971 | 1973 | 1975 | 1977 |

Basic Kinds of Plans

Three basic compensation plans are available to sales management: salary, commission, and combination (salary plus incentive) plans.

Exhibit I shows the use of the three basic plans in recent years. While the combination plan continues to be most favored, the commission plan has been declining in recent years. For example, 1971, a recession year, was a poor commission year, while the boom year of 1973 produced commission earnings that, in many cases, were totally out of proportion to the sales effort put forth. Exhibit II shows selective use of the three basic plans in 34 SIC industries.

SALARY PLAN

This kind of plan, in which salesmen are paid fixed rates of compensation, may also include occasional additional compensation in the form of discretionary bonuses, sales contest prizes, or other short-term incentives. The plan works well when the main objective is missionary work or requires a lot of time for prospecting, or if the salesman's primary function is "account servicing." Secondary objectives of increasing sales from existing accounts and opening new accounts require special incentive treatment.

The salary plan is appropriate where it is difficult to evaluate who really makes the sale, where a salesman's contribution cannot be accurately separated from the efforts of others in the company such as inside personnel and technical service persons. Sales of technical products commonly involve this form of team selling. When management finds it difficult to develop adequate measures of performance against which an equitable bonus or commission can be paid, a salary plan is desirable.

The position description for a field engineer on salary with a West Coast industrial equipment manufacturer illustrates the difficulty of measuring sales performance for incentive reward. The field engineer calls on distributors. His duties include:

Developing and executing sales and product training programs for distributors' sales forces.

Doing missionary work with selected manufacturers and major oil companies to encourage them to recommend his products to their dealers and mention them in their service and installation manuals.

Participating in national and local trade shows; conducting occasional training programs for trade groups and associations.

Suggesting ideas for new products and promotional programs; recommending changes or improvements in existing products.

Many durable goods industries experience cyclical sales patterns, which makes a salary plan more compatible with the salesman's efforts and avoids the sharp swings in income that can occur in a commission plan.

Exhibit II.   Type of Compensation by Industry, 1977

Industry	Number of com-panies	Salary	Com-mission	Com-bination
Aerospace	5	60%	—	40%
Appliance (household)	8	25	25%	50
Automobile parts and accessories	12	34	16	50
Automobile and truck	10	30	30	40
Beverages	6	50	—	50
Building materials	23	17	13	70
Casualty insurance	5	20	20	60
Chemicals	13	23	23	54
Cosmetics and toilet preparations	9	33	34	33
Drugs and medicines	12	25	25	50
Electrical equipment and supplies	19	26	10	64
Electronics	21	19	9	62
Fabricated metal products	26	26	19	55
Food products	14	43	14	43
General machinery	26	19	15	65
Glass and allied products	8	60	20	20
Housewares	12	25	25	50
Instruments and allied products	10	30	20	50
Iron and steel	10	20	—	80
Life insurance	5	20	20	60
Nonferrous metals	6	50	—	50
Office machinery and equipment	7	14	29	57
Paper and allied products	12	33	—	67
Petroleum and petroleum products	4	50	25	25
Printing	17	24	47	29
Publishing	14	10	30	60
Radio and television	7	—	—	100
Retailing	4	50	25	25
Rubber	8	25	—	75
Service industries	21	15	40	45
Textiles and apparel	6	33	33	34
Tobacco	4	—	100	—
Tools and hardware	11	18	36	46
Transport equipment	5	100	—	—

After close examination of the salary plans of many companies, I have identified the following basic advantages and disadvantages of the salary plan approach.

The salary plan has advantages for both salesmen and their companies because it: (1) assures a regular income, (2) develops a high degree of loyalty, (3) makes it simple to switch territories or quotas or to reassign salesmen, (4) ensures that nonselling activities will be performed, (5) facilitates administration, and (6) provides relatively fixed sales costs. However, the salary plan does have disadvantages, in that it: (1) fails to give a balanced sales mix because salesmen would concentrate on products with greatest customer appeal; (2) provides little, if any, financial incentive for the salesman; (3) offers few reasons for putting forth extra effort; (4) favors salesmen or saleswomen who are the least productive; (5) tends to increase direct selling costs over other types of plans; and (6) creates the possibility of salary compression where new trainees may earn almost as much as experienced salesmen.

The two lists do not necessarily cancel each other out. Every compensation plan is a compromise. Determination of marketing and sales objectives, which will in turn determine the role of the sales force, will indicate to the sales executive whether the salary plan is best for achieving his goals. Exhibit III shows that the average earnings of experienced salesmen on this plan have increased from $9,700 in 1964 to $20,950 in 1977.

COMMISSION PLAN

In this type of plan, salesmen are paid in direct proportion to their sales. Such a plan includes straight commission and commission with draw. The plan works well at the start of a new business where the market possibilities are very broad and highly fragmented. In such situations, territory boundaries are usually rather fluid and difficult to define. Therefore, quota and customer assignments are difficult to determine, making other types of compensation plans too costly or too complex to administer.

When management desires to maximize incentive, regardless of compensation levels in other company functions, or prefers a predictable sales cost in direct relationship with sales volume, the commission plan is appropriate. However, use of the straight commission approach has declined in popularity over the past several

*Exhibit III.   Average Earnings and Median Range
                 of Experienced Salesmen, by Compensation Plans*

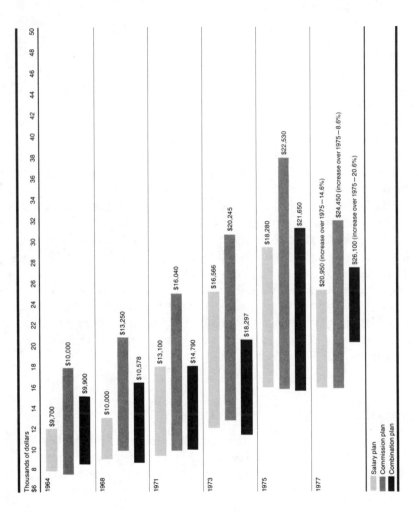

years and is not currently preferred, as the data in Exhibits I and II show.

Following are the advantages of the straight commission plan: (1) pay relates directly to performance and results achieved, (2) system is easy to understand and compute, (3) salesmen have the greatest possible incentive, (4) unit sales costs are proportional to net sales, and (5) company's selling investment is reduced.

The disadvantages of this plan are: (1) emphasis is more likely to be on volume than on profits, (2) little or no loyalty to the company is generated, (3) wide variances in income between salesmen may occur, (4) salesmen are encouraged to neglect nonselling duties, (5) some salesmen may be tempted to "skim" their territories, (6) service aspect of selling may be slighted, (7) problems arise in cutting territories or shifting men or accounts, (8) pay is often excessive in boom times and very low in recession periods, (9) salesmen may sell themselves rather than the company and stress short-term rather than long-term relationships, (10) highly paid salesmen may be reluctant to move into supervisory or managerial positions, and (11) excessive turnover of sales personnel occurs when business turns bad.

Commission plan salesmen have historically earned more than their counterparts in a salary or combination plan. However, this trend was reversed in 1977, with commission men earning an average of $1,650 less than combination plan salesmen, as shown in Exhibit III.

We note in these data that from the eight-year period of 1964 to 1971 the average yearly gain was 7.5%. However, the unusual boom year of 1973 produced a 26% increase in earnings over 1971. Several sales executives cited examples of extraordinary commission earnings for that year which they felt were undeserved and totally disproportionate with sales effort expended. The swift economic swings from 1971 to 1973 forced sales executives to seek more stable compensation arrangements, as shown in the decrease in use of commission plans and the increase in combination plans previously referred to in Exhibit I.

If a commission plan is desired, the disadvantages must be offset. To accomplish this, some elements of guarantee must be added to the compensation package, especially for new salesmen. These can include guaranteeing a monthly minimum income, generous draws, and starting new men on a salary-plus-commission plan until commissions reach a desired level. The effect of possible personal economic fluctuations should be balanced by strong, security-ori-

ented fringe benefit packages, including surgical and medical insurance, pensions, and educational assistance. These stabilizing
elements should help in recruiting and keeping men.

COMBINATION PLAN

This type of plan includes all variations of salary plus other
monetary incentive plans. The variations include base salary plus
commission on all sales, salary plus bonus. On sales over quota,
salary plus commission plus bonus, and so on.

There are many sound reasons for installing a salary-plus-incentive plan. It permits greater incentive than a salary or commission
plan and provides better control of the incentive or variable income
than is possible with the commission plan. Also the much greater
degree of flexibility with a wide variation in incentives to work
with allows management to develop practically tailor-made plans
for each salesman.

But these plans have liabilities, too. Salary-plus-incentive plans
tend to be more complex than the other two methods. Thus they
involve more paperwork, control, and administrative work. They
need more frequent revision because of the interaction of the elements that comprise the total plan. In making individual adjustments over the years, one should be careful to avoid a gradual loss
of uniformity in the plan.

The most important determination in building a sound salary-
plus-incentive plan is the split between the fixed portion (salary)
and the variable portion (incentive). The split is usually determined
on the basis of historical sales performance and compensation
records. Competitive analysis of other company programs, the base
salary needed to keep good men, and an estimate of incentive
potential should also be considered. Ceilings on incentive payments
are usually part of combination plans.

The most frequent percentage split reported in the Dartnell study
was 80% base salary and 20% incentive. A close second was a 70%/
30% split, with a 60%/40% split being the third most frequently
reported arrangement. As the rewards are closely tied into sales
or gross margins, closer supervision and control of the plan are
needed as the incentive portion of the plan increases.

Structuring the salary portion of the plan requires establishing
salary grades for the sales force. The three grades used in the
Dartnell study are trainee, semiexperienced (one to three years),

and experienced (more than three years). Each salary grade should be supported by a job description and each salesman assigned according to experience and ability.

In the incentive portion of the combination plan, three basic forms of reward can be considered: a commission, a bonus, and a commission plus bonus.

Commission incentives are the most popular. Companies pay by one or more of these typical methods:

1. A fixed commission on all sales.
2. At different rates by product category.
3. On sales above a determined goal.
4. On product gross margin.

The rationale of paying commissions on gross margin dollars is the assumption that such an arrangement will motivate salesmen to improve both product and customer mix and therefore to improve territory gross margin.

A good example of a sound compensation plan incorporating the elements of base salary and incentive pay of a percentage of gross profit and gross sales generated in a territory is one set up by the sales executive of an eastern electrical component manufacturer.

In his plan, a base salary level is determined on a discretionary basis. Gross profit is defined as the difference between the selling price of an item and the cost to purchase the goods, freight to transport, labor and/or materials that must be added to make the goods salable as represented to the buyer, and other costs directly related to the transaction. Gross sales are those of new and/or used equipment invoiced to a buyer within a period of a calendar month.

Each territory has a minimum requirement for gross profits and gross sales. The following three-step formula is applied:

Step 1: Sales volume up to $18,000 a month. Base salary plus 7% of gross profits plus 1/2% of gross sales.

Step 2: Sales volume from $18,000 to $25,000 a month. Base salary plus 9% of gross profits plus 1/2% of gross sales.

Step 3: Over $25,000 a month. Base salary plus 10% of gross profits plus 1/2% of gross sales.

Base salary is paid every two weeks. The earned percentage of gross profits and gross sales is paid monthly.

One great advantage of the commission incentive is the frequency and regularity of the reward, usually monthly. Salesmen are more quickly motivated to keep or exceed performance levels with the rapid tie-in between performance and reward.

Bonus incentives are usually paid as a percentage of salary and vary by goal performance levels. Bonuses are paid on a variety of sales results, but gross margin goals are used most frequently. Other factors used as a measure for bonus goals are market share, product mix, new accounts, nonsales activities, higher unit sales, and increased sales from existing accounts. Some companies simply make bonus arrangements on a discretionary basis.

Goals may be based on an analysis of the potential of the territory and expected performance against the potential. They may be developed from a moving average of historical sales or gross margin for two or three years plus a one-year forecast averaged into the moving base.

Bonus payments should be structured to begin at the 70%- to 75%-of-goal level to motivate salesmen to achieve goals. A lower threshold level works against sustained sales effort. Conversely, by not receiving bonuses until sales effort of 100% goal is achieved, many persons become discouraged along the way. While payment rates may be uniform both under and over the 100% goal, increasing the rate beyond the 100% mark adds an additional incentive with a lower cost factor.

Because bonus incentives are usually paid quarterly, it is not recommended that the full amount be paid when due. Withholding a small percentage due each quarter until the end of the year avoids a possible overpayment for the total year bonus. A proper adjustment is made with the final quarter payment.

A bonus incentive plan is more difficult to establish and administer than a commission incentive. Also, rewards paid on a quarterly basis are not as effective motivators as weekly or monthly commission payments.

Another variation of the combination plan is one which pays *salary, commission,* and *bonus.* While this approach offers more flexibility than the other two types, it is more complex and more difficult to administer than any other plan.

Here are the elements of a good salary, commission, and bonus plan used by a midwest fabricated metal products company:

1. Base salary, company car, and all business expenses.
2. A 5% commission, based annually and paid quarterly, on all sales volume over predetermined sales base.

3. A bonus on attainment of quota. Annual quota is divided in two parts: first six calendar months and last six calendar months. If quota is attained for the first half, bonus of 1% of all sales during that period is paid in July. This is repeated for the second half with bonus paid in January.
4. If quotas for both halves of the calendar year are attained, an additional bonus of 1/2% of all sales for the year is paid. Thus a total of 1 1/2% of annual sales is paid as a bonus.
5. If quota for either of the six-month periods is not achieved but annual quota is achieved, 1/2% for the year is paid but not the 1% for period in which quota is not achieved.
6. "House" or "divisional manager" accounts are excluded from quota, commission, and bonus calculations.

Take another look at Exhibit III to see how the experienced salesperson on a combination plan has fared historically. Survey data covering the period from 1964 to 1977 are shown.

Two observations about these data are worth noting: average total earnings have increased 163% in the past 13 years; and total earnings in 1977 increased 20.6% over 1975, showing the highest increase of the three basic compensation plans for that period.

Also, average earnings of the combination plan salesperson exceeded the average earnings of the salaried person by $5,150 and the average earnings of the commission man by $1,650. This trend should continue. This fact of earnings plus relative advantages of the combination compensation plan, which follow, reinforces the continuing popularity of this plan.

Advantages are that the combination plan:

Offers participants the advantages of both salary and commission.

Provides greater range of earnings possibilities.

Gives salesmen greater security because of steady base income.

Makes possible a favorable ratio of selling expense to sales.

Compensates salesmen for all activities.

Allows a greater latitude of motivation possibilities so that goals and objectives can be achieved on schedule.

Disadvantages are that the plan:

Is often complex and difficult to understand.

Can, where low salary and high bonus or commission exist, develop a bonus that is too high a percentage of earnings; when sales fall, salary is too low to retain salesmen.

Is sometimes costly to administer.

Can, unless a decreasing commission rate for increasing sales volume exists, result in a "windfall" of new accounts and a runaway of earnings.

Has a tendency to offer too many objectives at one time so that really important ones can be neglected, forgotten, or overlooked.

To round out the basic compensation data, it is worth noting that in the past 25 years, average earnings of the experienced salesperson have more than tripled, rising from $7,200 in 1952 to $24,500 in 1977. Perhaps of more significance, earnings have doubled in the past 10 years. These data are shown in Exhibit IV. The average annual compensation broken down into the seven distinct varieties of compensation is shown in Exhibit V.

Related Areas

Other policies besides direct compensation have an impact on both the salesperson's total pay package and the company's financial position. These are sales expenses and extra incentive plans.

EXPENSE PRACTICES

The need for keeping a tight rein on sales-generated expenses, which have a direct effect on profits, was never more evident than in the recent turbulent economic years. With the cost of sales calls constantly rising and with increased traveling and lodging costs, companies must periodically examine their expense policies and procedures and make adjustments in order to draw that ideal fine line where expenses are kept under proper control and reimbursement to salesmen is fair and reasonable.

Respondents to the Dartnell survey indicate that 92% of the companies paid all or some of their salesmen's expenses—in addition to compensation payments.

Eight major expense categories are covered in Exhibit VI, which shows the percentage of companies paying all or part of salesmen's expenses by compensation plan.

Exhibit IV. *Average Earnings of Experienced Salesmen, All Plans,*
1952 to 1977

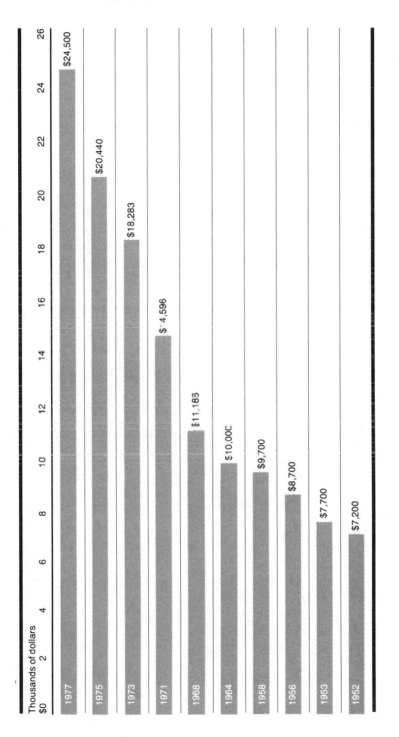

Exhibit V. Average Annual Compensation and Median Range, by Compensation Plan, 1977

Thousands of dollars

Compensation Plan	Average	Median Range
Straight salary	$19,250	$15,000 – $24,000
Straight salary and discretionary bonus	$23,330	$16,400 – $27,000
Straight commission	$24,750	$18,000 – $30,000
Commission and bonus	$23,700	$13,500 – $32,500
Salary and commission	$27,700	$20,900 – $28,000
Salary and bonus	$22,950	$20,000 – $24,700
Salary and commission and bonus	$25,250	$20,200 – $26,800

Scale: $10, 11, 12, 13, 14, 15, 16, 17, 18, 19, 20, 21, 22, 23, 24, 25, 26, 27, 28, 29, 30, 31, 32, 33, 34

Exhibit VI. Percentage of Companies Paying Expenses, by Compensation Plan, 1977

Expense	All companies	Salary	Commission	Combination
Automobile (company-owned, leased, personal)	91%	97%	73%	99%
Other travel (commercial airlines, railroads, company plane)	84	88	63	88
Lodging	86	90	69	90
Telephone	87	89	75	91
Entertainment	80	86	58	86
Samples	73	75	71	75
Promotion	76	72	71	77
Office and/or clerical	73	63	73	77

A few significant observations regarding expense practices should be noted:

More salesmen are using air travel, with 84% of all respondent companies authorizing commercial flights. Additionally, 26% have company planes which are available to all their salesmen for sales calls based primarily on the function of territory coverage.

There has been virtually no change in expense policies in the past six years—80% of the companies pay all or part of their salesmen's entertainment expenses. Many companies noted that these expenses must have prior authorization or are "luncheon only" types of expenses. Expense limits are usually set. Salesmen rarely have "carte blanche" on entertainment expenses.

Promotion expenses usually cover the cost of meetings, local publicity, and other merchandising activities.

ADDITIONAL INCENTIVES

No matter how well a compensation plan is formulated and executed, another dimension is necessary to achieve best results. What I am talking about are the incentives that make a salesman work harder all around. And again, let us consider the unique aspects of the salesman's job: limited personal contact with his manager; extended periods of travel which brings loneliness and inconvenience; decisions that require a high level of motivation (when to make the first call of the day, how many calls to make, objectives to be achieved on each call, when to quit for the day); and emotional swings between the elation of obtaining a large order and the frequent frustrations of orders lost to competitors and missed shipping dates.

Motivation calls for creating a climate in which the salesman can motivate himself with the incentives provided by management. These incentives can be financial, nonfinancial, or a combination of the two.

FINANCIAL INCENTIVES

Short-term sales contests are popular. Costs are predictable, results are usually successful, and rewards are immediate. Contests usually run for one or two months, but some as short as a week can produce results. The awards that are most favored in contests are money, trips, merchandise, and personal recognition.

A successful sales contest should include these basic elements: well-defined objectives, simple rules, short duration, goals attainable by most salesmen, inclusion of wives and families when possible, and follow-through program to sustain enthusiasm.

Contests are like a double-bladed sword. Improperly used or used for the wrong reasons, they can create dissension and dissatisfaction within the ranks. Properly used, contests can create a competitive atmosphere that will stimulate sales and provide additional rewards.

In addition to the usual contest objectives of increased sales volume, more sales calls, new accounts, and so forth, contests can serve to build off-season business, increase the use of displays, stimulate various dealer tie-ins, revive dead accounts, and reduce costs.

NONFINANCIAL METHODS

Techniques that principally provide salesmen recognition, status, and a sense of group belonging are generally referred to as "psychic income."

This is an area in which the industrial psychologists have made positive contributions. Though many of the successful techniques have been available for a long time, it has just been within the past 10 to 15 years that sales executives have begun to realize their importance.

Over the years, as the role of the salesman has been redefined and enlarged, many companies have conferred more meaningful titles on members of their sales forces to improve their status with customers, to give them personal status symbols, and to more aptly describe their functions. Companies commonly use such titles as regional, area, or zone manager, field sales engineer, account executive, and staff associate.

Other productive ways to recognize individual good performance or encourage effectiveness are: distinguished salesman awards, honorary job titles, publicity, personal letters or telephone calls of commendation, face-to-face encouragement, and individual help with responsibilities.

Exhibit VII.   Percentage of Companies Using Nonfinancial Methods of Compensation, by Compensation Plan, 1977

Nonfinancial method	All companies	Salary	Commission	Combination
Distinguished salesman awards	44%	31%	49%	47%
Honorary job titles	13	16	16	12
Publicity	37	39	37	36
Personal letters of commendation	59	56	54	63
Telephone calls of commendation	42	42	40	43
Face-to-face encouragement	88	90	81	88
Individual help with responsibilities	64	69	61	62
Sales meetings	91	86	88	92
Training programs	70	64	63	75
Honor societies	7	3	11	8
Published sales results	57	44	61	59
Management by objectives	43	44	32	46

Exhibit VII shows the percentage of companies (by compensation plan) using broad nonfinancial methods of motivation. The low percentages in most categories indicate that many companies are missing a good bet in not using these highly effective techniques. All these methods are inexpensive and convey a sense of personal communication that salesmen value highly.

Fringe Benefits

The cost of maintaining medical, accident, life, and dental insurance programs on a personal basis is significant, so fringe benefits constitute an important part of the "total income" of every company employee, including the sales force.

Adding up the costs of personal use of the company or leased car, memberships, and educational expense assistance that many companies provide, the basic benefit package would cost a salesman a minimum of $1,500 a year.

Currently, many companies in most industries are paying part or all of the costs of 12 major benefits: hospitalization-surgical insurance; life, accident, and dental insurance; educational assistance; profit sharing; pension plans; stock purchase; personal use of car; club or association memberships; moving expenses; and salary continuation program. Exhibit VIII shows the participation by companies broken down by the three basic compensation plans and for all companies responding to the survey, regardless of compensation plan used.

The salary plan and combination plan salesmen fared about equally in all benefit provisions. As was to be expected, commission plan salesmen lagged in all categories. However, in comparison with previous studies, the commission man has made dramatic gains. As I said earlier, many companies are seeking ways of increasing company loyalty and of providing competitive advantage to attract and retain the commission salesman on the payroll.

To dramatize the significance of fringe benefits for salesmen in the total compensation package, I compared current data with that of 1958, 19 years ago. The percentage of companies providing hospital insurance increased by 16%, life insurance by 10%, educational assistance by 36%, and club or association memberships by 14%. Dental insurance, stock purchases, profit sharing, and salary continuation programs have been added to the benefit package since 1958 at an increasing rate. As general company benefits to all employees increase in scope, the salesman's benefit package will likewise increase.

Compensation plans have become more complex—the three basic methods of paying salesmen have stretched into at least seven kinds of plans, and possibly more will be designed tomorrow.

Combination plans dominate the compensation package makeup despite the complexity of administration and control. The disadvantages are far overshadowed by the flexibility in providing meaningful incentive pay tied more directly to sales performance—that is, applying commission and bonus to single and/or multiple sales goals. In addition, a combination plan provides the salesman with a greater range of earnings possibilities based on a steady base income.

The salesman expense policies I have examined over the last five years indicate that sales executives are exercising good judgment in controlling and administering field expenses.

In the area of nonfinancial motivation, sales executives should be doing a better job with the available techniques. Personal contact, recognition, and encouragement are needed to sustain a positive attitude and a high level of morale.

Increasing amounts of fringe benefits add to the total income

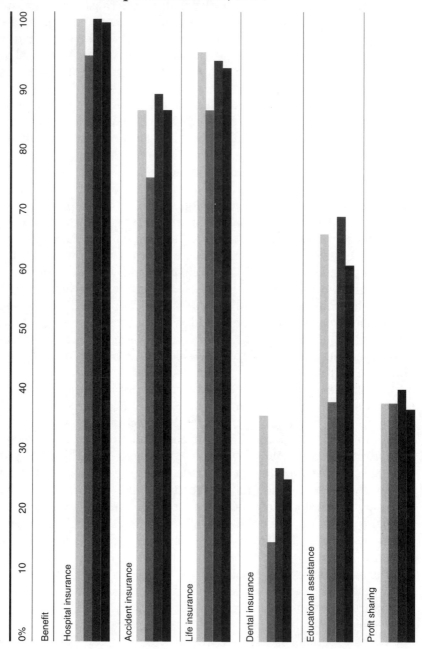

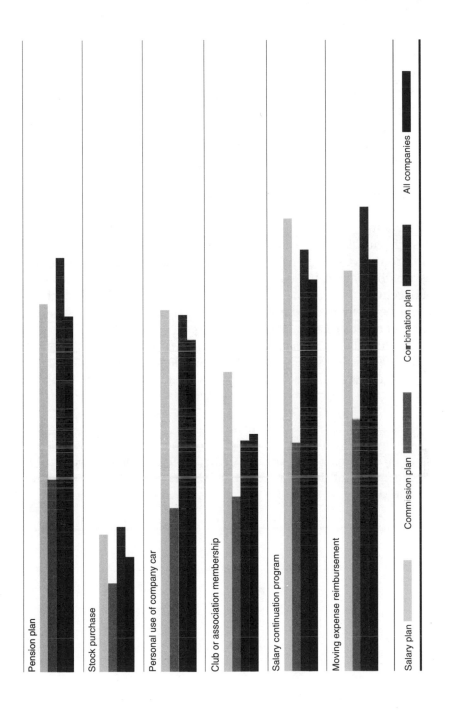

Pension plan

Stock purchase

Personal use of company car

Club or association membership

Salary continuation program

Moving expense reimbursement

Salary plan   Commission plan   Combination plan   All companies

package of a salesman. Employees, including salesmen, no longer regard such benefits as fringe offerings, but rather as a basic part of the terms of employment. Additionally, the salesman has been gaining special "perks" of his own, such as personal use of a company or leased car and club or association memberships.

In my many discussions with sales executives over the past two years, the subject of "profitability of sales" kept coming up. While sales executives should never lose sight of their primary objectives—to increase sales—top management pressure for profitable sales increases. It demands new rules and definitions of the cost of doing business in a given sales territory.

The trend toward obtaining profitable sales, as opposed to sheer sales volume, could well lead to defining a sales territory not only as such but also as a profit center with the salesman as the sales *and* profit producer in a given territory. This might be an awesome responsibility, but it would certainly be a new dimension in sales management and in the salesman's job responsibility. The effect would be to increase the influence of a profit factor in the salesman's compensation package.

The sales executive will have to educate and reeducate himself in this expanding sphere of profit consciousness. This is his challenge in the years ahead, and he must meet it if he is to survive.

Note

1. *Compensation of Salesmen: Dartnell's 19th Biennial Survey* (Chicago: Dartnell Institute of Financial Research, Dartnell Corporation, 1978).

PART

VI

Manage the Selling System

Introduction

For many companies, the sales force is the primary mechanism for seeking customers. In today's complex selling environment, however, companies are increasingly complementing, supplementing, and in some cases, even replacing their own sales forces with distributors, resellers, and other vendors. Distribution channels have a major impact on profits. On the one hand, they can significantly increase the efficiency with which products can be delivered to the market. On the other hand, they can account for large discounts and commissions, and they require expensive servicing and support. Moreover, vendors and distributors vary greatly in their effectiveness in meeting sales goals and performing sales-related functions.

In this section, we consider both the advantages and the challenges of managing relationships with outside vendors and distributors. The primary challenge is learning how to deal with the dual nature of these relationships: at one level, distributors and other agents are a channel to *sell through* to the ultimate customer (or sometimes to another level in the distribution chain on the way to the customer); at the same time, they behave in many ways like customers to *sell to*, requiring similar commitment of resources and attention.

As the complexity of the sales and distribution channels increases it is difficult to maintain focus. IBM, for example, uses about two dozen different channels to reach its prospects and customers. Multiple channels lead to delicate trade-offs. What is, for example, the relationship between keeping customers happy and keeping distributors happy? Are these conflicting or complementary goals? And how does one manage conflicts among the various types of distribution channels?

Relationships are very important to distributors. They value their relationships with their principals (their suppliers) as well as their relationships with the end customers. In fact, there is often great conflict between the producer/supplier and the distributor over who "owns" or "controls" the relationships with customers. In order to avoid, or at least manage, such conflicts producer/suppliers must learn to create strong relationships with distributors.

In "Turn Your Industrial Distributors into Partners," James Narus and James Anderson provide straightforward guidelines for developing such relationships. The article emphasizes three elements of this process: (1) understanding distributors, (2) building working partnerships, and (3) managing the partnerships. Within this framework, the authors provide a wide variety of specific recommendations that can lead to deep, enduring distributor relationships. In many ways, these recommendations echo those expressed earlier in this book for forging satisfying customer relationships. For example, the partnership approach advocated by Narus and Anderson is similar to the strategic-account relationship described in "Close Encounters" (Part III). Moreover, like the articles in Part I, Narus and Anderson argue that establishing two-way channels of communication between a manufacturer and distributors is a necessary precondition for developing satisfying and productive relationships.

As the number of players and subplayers in the distribution system grows, the challenge of effectively and efficiently managing them also grows. In "Managing Hybrid Marketing Systems," Rowland Moriarty and Ursula Moran argue that "in recent years, as managers have sought to cut costs and increase market coverage, companies have added new channels to existing ones." With a hybrid system, a manufacturer can call upon a wide array of vendors to perform different tasks in the sales process, from lead generation to account management.

But managing this network of relationships brings a new set of challenges: "The appearance of new channels and methods inevitably raises problems of conflict and control—conflict because more marketing units compete for customers and revenues; control because indirect channels are less subject to management authority than direct are." Nevertheless, as the authors argue, "a company that can capture the benefits of a hybrid system—increased coverage, lower costs, and customized approaches—will enjoy a significant competitive advantage over rivals that cling to traditional ways."

The authors contend that hybrid systems will become the dominant design for going to market in the 1990s. To create the most effective and efficient system for reaching customers, however, the producer/supplier must carefully think through the roles of every participant. In this regard, Moriarty and Moran provide a workable framework for mapping the hybrid system, bounding and managing conflict, adding channels, orchestrating the hybrid system, and capturing the benefits.

"Managing Hybrid Marketing Systems" provides a fitting conclusion to this collection. In an increasingly complex and competitive marketplace, hybrids offer a creative and dynamic approach to profitable selling. Developing and managing a hybrid system, however, demands the full set of resources developed and advocated throughout this book, from building channels of communication to energizing the sales force (and associated distributors and vendors). Managing hybrids requires commitment to profitable selling, focus, and relationship building, through a combination of science and art.

1
Turn Your Industrial Distributors into Partners

James A. Narus and James C. Anderson

When the president of a small chemical distributor phoned a major chemical producer requesting expedited delivery of a specialty chemical for an important customer, the manufacturer's inside salesperson did not recognize him and told the distributor that a credit check would have to be run first. "Our company's dealt with this manufacturer for over 50 years, and they don't even know my name, our credit history, or how important this kind of order is to our business," the distributor lamented afterwards. "And they wonder why my salespeople don't go all out to sell their chemicals."

A veteran distributor sales manager for a major fastener manufacturer called on an industrial supply distributor only to discover it had a new president. "Here we go again," the sales manager said to himself. In the past five years, almost half the principal owners of his company's distributors had sold out, died, or retired. "It seems as though we have to start from scratch when one of our distributors changes management," he said. "For years, I'd visit this guy's dad every six months to see how things were going. To gain his cooperation, all we had to do was give competitive discounts, keep him well stocked, and run an occasional sales incentive program. But his son insists on knowing what we're doing to improve his company's ROI, how we plan to help him develop a new market, and what computer software his company should be using. I wonder if we're losing touch with our distributors."

A bushing manufacturer's sales rep called on a distributor for the first time in a year. The sales rep's prime concern was to learn why the distributor's sales of the manufacturer's product had remained flat during that period. The question was particularly vexing to the rep because her company had given the distributor a new and costly set of merchandising aids "proven" to boost sales. The sales rep found the materials unused—stacked up in a remote corner of the distributor's warehouse. When asked about them, the distributor responded that they were very elaborate and too technical. More important, he said, no one from the sales rep's company had taken the time to demonstrate to the distributor how to use them in a sales presentation.

These situations show that for manufacturers to effectively plan and implement industrial distributor programs they must:

Gain a deep understanding of distributor requirements.

Build working partnerships with distributors.

Actively manage these partnerships.

Building working partnerships has become a priority for many manufacturers because of industrial distributors' expanded role in the U.S. economy. In 1982, sales by all wholesaler-distributors topped $1.1 trillion. Of this total, $20 billion was accounted for by industrial supply distributors that sell primarily to maintenance, repair, and operating supply accounts; another $314 billion can be attributed to other types of distributors that sell the majority of their products to industrial and/or commercial businesses.[1]

According to a recent Arthur Andersen & Company study, wholesaler-distributor sales are expected to grow in real terms at a rate faster than the economy over the next ten years.[2] And a recent McGraw-Hill survey found that only 24% of all industrial marketers sell their products directly to end users exclusively; the remaining 76% use some type of intermediary, of which industrial distributors are the most prominent.[3]

Understanding Distributor Needs

How can manufacturers, especially those unfamiliar with distribution, determine their distributors' most important needs? The key appears to be in continuous, routine information collection. Here are some common practices:

MONITOR DISTRIBUTORS.   The best way to learn about distributor requirements is to get out into the field periodically and listen carefully to what they have to say. It is the field salespeople who must perform this important task on a continuing basis. Timken Corporation, the leading manufacturer of tapered roller bearings, requires all its outside sales representatives to make calls on various officials of each of their distribution companies, including general managers, purchasing managers, and inside and outside salespeople.

Each contact contributes bits of information about the distributor's current opportunities, problems, and changing needs. Timken sales reps also call on end users and other individuals connected with the industry to learn about market trends and competitive actions that may affect distributors. Based on their observations, Timken sales reps recommend program changes to their national sales manager that are designed to improve distributor effectiveness.

One way that Square D, a leading manufacturer of circuit breakers, switchboards, transformers, and controller equipment, keeps in touch with its distributors' and customers' needs is through its "counter days" program, whereby Square D field salespeople spend a day at the distributor's location "working the counter"—answering customer questions and demonstrating Square D products. The "counter days" program is an excellent way to learn about distributor needs and reinforces to both distributors and customers Square D's commitment to a working partnership.

LEARN FROM COMPANYWIDE EXPERIENCES.   Du Pont has established a distributor marketing steering committee, consisting of 35 divisional distributor marketing managers, to discuss common distribution problems, share market information on trends affecting the function, and ponder changing distributor requirements. Committee meetings often include presentations by market research analysts, consultants, and the distributor marketing managers of noncompeting companies.

CONDUCT MARKET RESEARCH STUDIES.   Parker Hannifin Corporation, a major fluid power products manufacturer, has developed two comprehensive research programs to monitor distributor needs. The first is an annual mail survey that asks distributors to rate each Parker division on key performance dimensions and recommend program improvements.

The second program uses the Parker distributor agreement, which requires each distributor to forward to Parker's market research division a photocopy of every invoice for the sale of a Parker product. The invoices are sorted and analyzed by industry, product, and customer to enable Parker to develop distributor programs that mirror changing market conditions. One such program produces a series of market research reports tailored to each distributor. The reports analyze the distributor's sales and recommend customers that should be targeted for greater sales effort, products that should be promoted to various potential customers, and types of marketing techniques the distributor should use.

ESTABLISH A DISTRIBUTOR COUNCIL. Although some executives believe that distributor councils are little more than banquets and tennis or golf outings for a manufacturer's best distributors, this need not be the case. Dayco Corporation, a manufacturer and distributor of engineered plastic and rubber products, uses its council to keep up with its industrial distributors' changing needs. Selected to represent the entire network, about 10% of Dayco's distributors comprise the council and serve on a rotating basis.

Prior to the annual four-day meeting, Dayco asks council members to write suggestions for improving policies and programs; Dayco uses the responses to draft an agenda for the meeting. The council sessions are then largely taken up with discussion of proposed policy changes and new programs, distributor problems and concerns, the competition, and other pressing issues. Within one month of the council meetings, Dayco sends its distributors a written report outlining the suggested policies and programs that will be implemented. Historically, Dayco puts about 75% of distributor proposals into effect.

Building Working Partnerships

Building effective partnerships usually takes two to three years because they must be earned, not merely declared. The manufacturer's distributor programs are the basic implementation tools. These programs should be designed to meet distributor requirements and furnish benefits that surpass those of the competition.

Companies seeking to initiate or resuscitate distributor relationships can take any of three approaches to develop distributor programs:

1. *Get the benefit of industry experience.* Several years ago, a Du Pont division decided to start selling Tyvek, a spun-bonded olefin that can be used for home insulation, through building products distributors. Rather than assume that the division had all the answers on steps to take, management obtained from a building products distributor association the name of a consultant who had been a distributor for many years. The consultant helped Du Pont draft a distributor marketing plan, select the distributors, and implement initial programs. The division has been pleased with the results.

2. *Establish a position in the distribution marketplace.* In the early 1980s, Cherry Electrical Products, a manufacturer of electrical switches and electronic keyboards, displays, and components, noticed a dramatic rise in sales through electronics distributors, while its own sales through distributors plateaued. Determined to improve its productivity, Cherry hired a new distributor marketing manager and charged him with revamping its distribution network.

He set to work by calling on end users, distributors, and manufacturers' reps. He gathered information on how distributors marketed electronic components, distributor requirements, and on what programs competitors were using. Thereupon the new manager rewrote company policies, revised the distributor discount system, and devised a set of marketing programs. These efforts created Cherry's reputation not only as a manufacturer of quality products and first-rate services but also as a company committed to its distributors. Cherry maintains its position by making every effort to meet changing distributor needs and by offering an array of superior distributor programs.

3. *Devise a formal distributor marketing plan.* This plan should be written for the whole network and then broken down individually. The plan should include the following: a situation analysis, describing the network's makeup and activities; an opportunities and threats section, identifying the business situations the company should capitalize on or avoid; an objectives section, detailing sales quotas, products, and markets to receive special attention; a basic requirements analysis, spelling out the kinds of support distributors will need in the coming year to meet objectives and seize market opportunities; a distributor programs section, describing

all the manufacturer's marketing actions for the coming year designed to meet distributor requirements; and finally, a control section, charting a timetable for program implementation and assigning responsibilities for execution.

If the manufacturer takes the time to obtain distributors' input for the plan, they will be likely to perceive it as their plan and work hard to implement it.

DEVELOPING SOUND COMMUNICATION

An essential ingredient for successful partnerships is sound, two-way communication between a manufacturer and its distributors that occurs at multiple levels and uses a variety of communication means. Communication between the manufacturer's order center or inside salesperson and the distributor's purchasing manager is extremely important since these individuals deal with each other more often than any others in the partnership. The manufacturer's order center personnel or inside salespeople, therefore, should be well qualified and trained.

These employees must take distributors' orders accurately and cheerfully, comprehend and work to resolve their problems, respond quickly to distributors' requests, know the names of their counterparts, be familiar with the distributors' history, and use their contacts to gather market information. Cherry Electrical Products assigns each distributor to a pair of inside salespeople. Although one person has primary responsibility for the distributor's orders, both are familiar with the distributor and can take orders and respond to problems.

Contacts between the manufacturer's outside salesperson and the distributor's top officers, purchasing managers, and salespeople should be nurtured. When visiting a distributor, the outside salesperson should help explain policy changes, gather distributor suggestions and market information, demonstrate products and merchandising tools, solve problems, train distributor sales and technical people on proper procedures and product applications, and conduct joint sales calls.

Because outside salespeople often get promoted, change territories, or quit, the distributor marketing manager should make periodic calls on the president or CEO of each distributorship. The manager should explain major policy changes, review mutual performance, plan joint marketing programs, and generally reinforce the working partnership. Dayco takes this approach one step further. Each year, all its distributor marketing managers, the president, and even the chairman of the board make selected calls on distributors to demonstrate the importance of each distributor to Dayco.

While face-to-face contacts have the greatest impact on distributors, they are obviously the most expensive communication option. They should be used mainly to resolve differences, explain new products or policy changes, or review performance. Timken, for instance, makes a point of announcing all of its major policy and program changes to the distributor in person to permit full explanation and full responses to questions.

Quite a few manufacturers (Du Pont and Dayco, for example) use newsletters to inform distributors about new products and applications, personnel changes, distribution news, and human interest stories. Finally, with the boom in VCR sales, many manufacturers such as Parker Hannifin are communicating via videotape. The cassettes can contain messages to distributors from the manufacturer's senior management, training programs, and promotional information (such as new product application stories).

SIGNALING COMMITMENT

To gain the benefits of a productive working partnership, manufacturers must demonstrate that they are committed to distributors for the long term. Companies boasting successful distributor partnerships usually have the most competent and best-trained field sales forces in their industries (signaling by this that they expect the best from their distributors).

Lincoln Electric, a manufacturer of arc-welding equipment and supplies, hires graduate engineers for its field sales positions. As part of their eight-month training program, they attend welding school and become certified welders. Before promotion to a field sales position, each trainee also must do what generations of sales trainees have done, demonstrate his or her ability to find a welding-related potential cost reduction at the company's production facility. When placed in the field, these knowledgeable salespeople are a useful resource to Lincoln Electric's distributors and customers on efficient welding technology and applications.

Another way to communicate confidence in distributors is to refer all customer inquiries and requests to them. Timken, for instance, encourages customers to seek technical assistance on minor difficulties from distributors. Timken handles only major problems. Du Pont's Chemicals and Pigments Division does not publish a less-than-truckload price list; LTL quantities are sold exclusively by distributors. Du Pont refers callers asking for an LTL price quote to distributors, thereby demonstrating that the company will not take business away from them.

Finally, manufacturers that limit the number of distributors per trading area are indicating that they want their distributor partners to be successful. When selective distribution is used, authorized distributors gain status and an enhanced local reputation, which can motivate them to sell aggressively. Square D and Parker Hannifin are just two examples of manufacturers whose distributors prominently display their authorized distributorship signs and strive to perform up to the manufacturers' reputations. Of course, multiple distributors are justified when a trading area's potential sales are extremely large; similarly, different types of distributors may have to be used when a market contains radically different types of customers. The key for the manufacturer is to be aware of the level of sales potential per trading area.

PASSING THE CRITICAL INCIDENT TEST

Incidents in which the distributor critically needs the manufacturer's assistance eventually come up in all relationships. For a working partnership to evolve, the manufacturer must respond decisively and meet this critical need so as to reinforce the importance and quality of the partnership in the distributor's mind.

Manufacturers excelling in marketing through distributors can usually cite stories of situations in which they came through in the clutch. Dayco provides an excellent example. Several years ago, an industrial distributor needed to place an emergency order but could not get through to Dayco's order center. He was, however, able to phone Dayco's chairman of the board because the chairman makes a point of being accessible to all the distributors.

Rather than turn the distributor over to a subordinate, the chairman listened carefully to him, worked up a three-page order, and later made sure that the order had been filled. This story sent a loud and clear message to everyone in Dayco's organization and distribution system. To be able to deal with critical incidents, a manufacturer must train its personnel, especially sales and order center people, to be sensitive to distributors' key concerns, including product delivery, pricing, and credit.

Managing These Partnerships

What action can manufacturers take to improve the productivity of their distributor partnerships? The main short-run task is to ensure that operational promises are kept. Distributors want delivery within stated lead times, quality products that are not defective, adequate promotional and merchandising support, and rapid technical problem-solving assistance. Manufacturers must coordinate sales activities with those of the transportation and manufacturing people so that delivery promises will be kept. To facilitate problem solving, Cherry Electrical Products has a policy of rapid, in-kind response (for example, if distributors call, Cherry responds by phone).

Over time, a manufacturer must develop a reputation for equitable policies that are consistently and uniformly implemented. Policies that are grounded in marketplace realities, that are in tune with distributor requirements, and that are well publicized will accomplish this. To underscore its consistent and uniform dealings with all its distributors, Square D in the mid-1960s published portions of its distributor policies in full-page advertisements in *Electrical Wholesaling*.

Manufacturers must be able to defuse the occasional disputes that inevitably arise. The key to turning problems into opportunities is launching an immediate resolution attempt. If after investigation you determine that the distributor has caused the problem, present its executives with your conclusions supported by the facts. If the problem is your fault, tell the distributor what you plan to do to resolve it. Be sure also to check whether the problem is widespread, and if it is, determine how to solve it systemwide. Inform all distributors of any policy or program changes needed to resolve the issue.

Look at how Lincoln Electric works with its distributors to meet the challenges of a changing marketplace. To deal with intense price competition, the company has devised what it calls the "Guaranteed Cost Reduction Program" for its distributors; whenever a customer requests that a distributor lower its prices on Lincoln supplies and equipment to meet those of competitive manufacturers, the company and the particular distributor guarantee in writing that they will find cost reductions in the customer's plant during the coming year that meet or exceed the price difference between Lincoln's products and the competition's. The Lincoln sales rep and distributor counterpart together survey the customer's operations, identify possible cost reductions, and help to implement them.

At the end of the year, the customer independently audits performance. If the cost savings do not match those promised, Lincoln Electric and the distributor pay the customer the difference (Lincoln contributes 70%). All the customer has to do is continue buying Lincoln Electric products from the distributor. To date, individual customers have reaped up to $100,000 in annual cost savings and, more important, Lincoln has reinforced its relationships with its distributors.

Finally, in sustaining long-term working partnerships, manufacturers should plan for the future. Dayco uses an intriguing program, called "Aftermarket 2000," to accomplish long-term continuity in its partnerships. Each year, Dayco sponsors a week-long retreat for 20 young distributor executives and 20 young Dayco executives that features notable speakers, seminars on future economic and market trends, and most important, plenty of time to interact. In this way, the future senior executives of Dayco and its distributors have an opportunity to get to know each other and develop over time the mutual trust and understanding that will be critical to the continued success of Dayco and its distributors. Such a program can help to alleviate the problem of starting all over again when managements change.

Building productive partnerships with industrial distributors takes years of effort. When the effort is successful, the partnership can be expected to yield the following results:

Motivation for superior effort and performance from both parties.

An atmosphere of goodwill that produces a willingness to overlook inevitable mistakes.

A reduction in the distributor turnover rate and a consequent lowering of the manufacturer's costs of bringing new distributors into the network.

Coordinated performance in the marketplace, with satisfied end users who are loyal to both the manufacturer and the distributor.

Clearly, building sound partnerships is worth the effort.

Notes

1. Calculated from "Preliminary Report," *1982 Census of Wholesale Trade*, U.S. Department of Commerce: Washington, D.C., May 1984.
2. Arthur Andersen & Company, Inc., *Future Trends in Wholesale Distribution* (Washington, D.C.: Distribution Research and Education Foundation: 1983), p. 7.
3. "Industry Markets Goods Through Dual Channels, Says McGraw-Hill Study," *Industrial Distribution*, April 1985, p. 15.

2
Managing Hybrid Marketing Systems

Rowland T. Moriarty and Ursula Moran

There was a time when most companies went to market only one way—through a direct sales force, for instance, or through distributors. But to defend their turf, expand market coverage, and control costs, companies today are increasingly adopting arsenals of new marketing weapons to use with different customer segments and under different circumstances. In recent years, as managers have sought to cut costs and increase market coverage, companies have added new channels to existing ones; they use direct sales as well as distributors, retail sales as well as direct mail, direct mail as well as direct sales. As they add channels and communications methods, companies create hybrid marketing systems.

Look at IBM. For years, IBM computers were available from only one supplier, the company's sales force. But when the market for small, low-cost computers exploded, IBM management realized that its single distribution channel was no longer sufficient. In the late 1970s, it started expanding into new channels, among them dealers, value-added resellers, catalog operations, direct mail, and telemarketing. IBM had built and maintained its vaunted 5,000-person sales force for 70 years. In less than 10 years, it nearly doubled that number and added 18 new channels to communicate with customers.

Apple Computer also started out with a clear and simple channel strategy. It distributed its inexpensive personal computers through an independent dealer network. But when the company began to sell more sophisticated systems to large companies, it had to change. Apple hired 70 national account managers as part of a new direct sales operation.

In adding these new channels and communications methods, IBM and Apple created hybrid marketing systems. Powerful forces lie behind the appearance of such hybrid systems; all signs indicate that they will be the dominant design of marketing systems in the 1990s. At the same time, smart managers recognize the high risks of operating hybrid systems. Whether the migration is from direct to indirect channels (such as IBM) or from indirect to direct (like Apple), the result is the same—a hybrid that can be hard to manage.

The appearance of new channels and methods inevitably raises problems of conflict and control—conflict because more marketing units compete for customers and revenues; control because indirect channels are less subject to management authority than direct are. As difficult as they are to manage, however, hybrid marketing systems can offer substantial rewards. A company that can capture the benefits of a hybrid system—increased coverage, lower costs, and customized approaches—will enjoy a significant competitive advantage over rivals that cling to traditional ways.

Examples of hybrid marketing systems extend beyond high-tech businesses such as computers to older industries such as textiles, metal fabrication, and office supplies and to service industries such as insurance. Many of the examples in this article are high-tech companies because the accelerated pace of high-tech industries foreshadows trends that tend to occur more slowly in other industries. The trend to hybrid systems, however, appears to be accelerating in many industries. According to one recent senior manager survey, 53% of the respondents indicated that their companies intend to use hybrid systems by 1992, a dramatic increase over the 33% that used those systems in 1987.

Two fundamental reasons explain this boost in the move to hybrids: the drive to increase market coverage and the need to contain costs. To sustain growth, a company generally must reach new customers or segments. Along the way, it usually supplements existing channels and methods with new ones designed to attract and develop new customers. This addition of new channels and methods creates a hybrid marketing system.

The need to contain costs is another powerful force behind the spread of hybrid systems, as companies look for ways to reach customers that are more efficient than direct selling. In 1990, the loaded cost of face-to-face selling time for national account managers can reach $500 per hour; for direct sales representatives, the average is about $300 per hour. Selling and administrative costs often represent 20% to 40% of a company's cost structure and thus have a direct effect on competitive advantage and profitability. For instance, Digital Equipment's selling and administrative costs in 1989 were 31% of revenues; for Sun Microsystems, the figure was only about 24%.

Given such economics, many companies are pursuing techniques such as telemarketing, which costs about $17 per hour, or direct mail, which runs about $1 per customer contact. A marketing strategy built on such low-cost communications methods can yield impressive results. Tessco, a distributor of supplies and equipment for cellular communications, emerged as one of the industry's fastest growing competitors by relying on low-cost communications methods. Tessco generates leads through direct mail and catalog operations; it uses telemarketing to qualify sales leads, make its sales pitch, answer questions, and close the sale. It then follows up each sale with service telemarketing and maintains accounts through an automatic reordering process. The result: Tessco enjoys significantly lower costs than most of its competitors, which continue to rely on traditional methods such as direct sales.

Wright Line's Problems

Despite the proliferation of marketing methods, few companies pay sufficient attention to the design of marketing systems or seek to manage them in ways that optimize coverage and costs. Indeed, most companies decide to add new channels and methods without a clear and realistic vision of an ultimate "go to market" architecture. These decisions are usually made separately and independently—and often swiftly as well. As a consequence, companies can find themselves stumbling over their hastily constructed, overlapping hybrid system.

Consider how an ill-conceived and mismanaged hybrid system contributed to the 1989 hostile takeover of Barry Wright Corporation. Many factors made the Massachusetts-based company vulnerable, but a principal cause of its troubles was the performance of a major subsidiary, Wright Line, Inc. A leading supplier of accessories used to store, protect, and provide access to computer tapes, diskettes, and other media, Wright Line was struggling vainly to halt the erosion of its market position.

Wright Line's troubles stemmed from a decision made in the early 1980s to reorganize its marketing and sales functions. Previously, the company had sold its products exclusively through a direct sales force. Although the company had been growing rapidly and adding new sales reps every year, Wright Line's management was alarmed by several trends: inability to increase market penetration, declining sales productivity, high turnover of sales reps, and what appeared to be a fundamental shift in the market away from the company's traditional stronghold in large, central computer installations.

After analyzing these trends, Wright Line supplemented its direct sales force with additional marketing channels and communications methods.[1] The company formed two new units: a direct marketing operation to handle midsize accounts through direct catalog and telephone sales and a unit to serve small accounts and to attract nonusers through indirect channels. Management's goals were to combine the advantages of high-quality personal selling to major accounts with lower cost, increased coverage of smaller accounts.

Signs of trouble appeared almost immediately. By 1985, the reorganization had yielded declining growth rates, diminishing market share, and plummeting profits. Inside the company, strife over account ownership was rampant, and turnover among the direct sales reps reached an all-time high. Worst of all, Wright Line's customers grew confused and angry after encountering different sales offerings of the same products under widely disparate terms and conditions. Wright Line's best customers became alienated, and its margins shrank as major accounts ordered the company's products from discount suppliers.

By the time new leadership tried to untangle the mess, it was already too late. Its stock weakened by Wright Line's rapidly eroding market position and declining profitability, Barry Wright Corporation was taken over in 1989.

The Barry Wright story is an extreme example of an increasingly evident problem. Fewer and fewer major industrial or service companies go to market through a single channel or a "purebred" channel strategy that matches a specific product or service to an exclusive segment. Rather than designing an ideal distribution strategy, companies tend to add channels and methods incrementally in the quest to extend market coverage or cut selling costs.

Unfortunately, such actions typically result in conflict and morale problems inside the marketing organization and confusion and anger among distributors, dealers, and customers on the outside.

Mapping the Hybrid

At the heart of the problem of designing and managing hybrid systems is the fundamental question of what mix of channels or communication methods can best accomplish the assortment of tasks required to identify, sell, and manage customers. The trick to designing and managing hybrid systems is to disaggregate demand-generation tasks both within and across a marketing system—recognizing that channels are not the basic building blocks of a marketing system; marketing tasks are. This analysis of tasks and channels will identify the hybrid's basic components and permit managers to design and manage the system effectively.

A map of tasks and channels—what we call a hybrid grid—can help managers make sense of their hybrid system. (See Exhibit I.) A hybrid grid, for example, can be used to illustrate graphically what happened at Wright Line and what might have happened differently.

Before its reorganization, Wright Line used direct sales for all demand-generation tasks and all customers (see Exhibit II). When it reorganized in 1982, Wright Line wanted the direct sales force (unit 1) to perform all demand-generation tasks for big customers; the new direct response unit (unit 2) to concentrate exclusively on midsize customers (using catalogs and telemarketing); and the new third party and resale unit (unit 3) to market to small customers and nonusers through indirect channels (see Exhibit III).

Instead, Wright Line wound up with a marketing system that was neither what it wanted nor what it needed (see Exhibit IV). The three marketing units were performing all of the demand-generation tasks for many different types of customers. Units 1 and 2 bickered constantly over account ownership. To avoid losing accounts, for example, some sales reps improperly classified accounts to hide them from the direct response marketing division. Those who complied were frustrated by guidelines that prohibited them from calling on smaller and midsize accounts in their territories and growing with them. The activities of unit 3 added fuel to the fire. Among major customers, purchasing managers who read

Exhibit I. The Hybrid Grid: The Elements of a Hybrid Marketing System

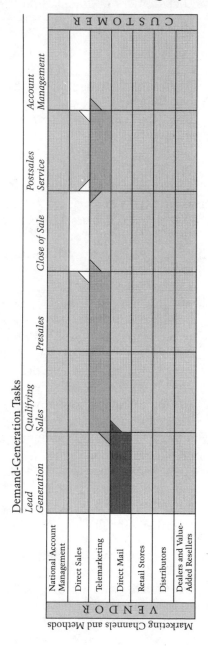

Exhibit II.   Wright Line's Marketing System: What It Had

Demand-Generation Tasks

Marketing Channels and Methods (VENDOR)	Lead Generation	Qualifying Sales	Presales	Close of Sale	Postsales Service	Account Management
National Account Management						
Direct Sales			ALL CUSTOMERS			
Telemarketing						
Direct Mail						
Retail Stores						
Distributors						
Dealers and Value-Added Resellers						

CUSTOMER

Exhibit III. Wright Line's Marketing System: What It Wanted

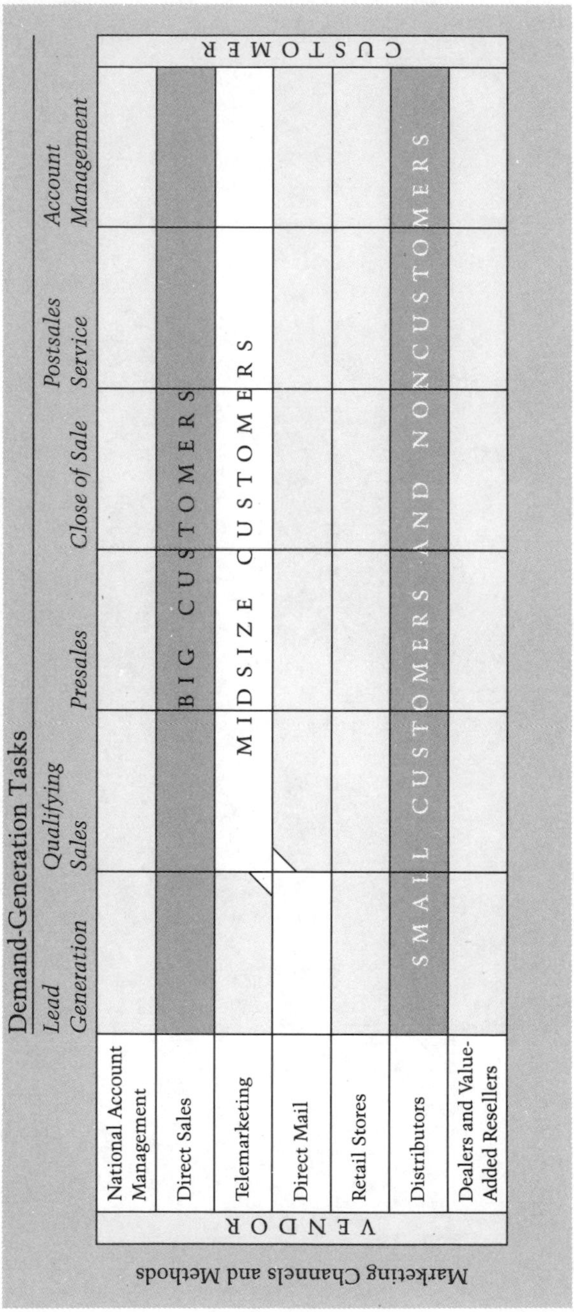

Demand-Generation Tasks

Marketing Channels and Methods (VENDOR)	Lead Generation	Qualifying Sales	Presales	Close of Sale	Postsales Service	Account Management
National Account Management						
Direct Sales	BIG CUSTOMERS					
Telemarketing	MIDSIZE CUSTOMERS					
Direct Mail						
Retail Stores						
Distributors	SMALL CUSTOMERS AND NONCUSTOMERS					
Dealers and Value-Added Resellers						

CUSTOMER

Exhibit IV. Wright Line's Marketing System: What It Got

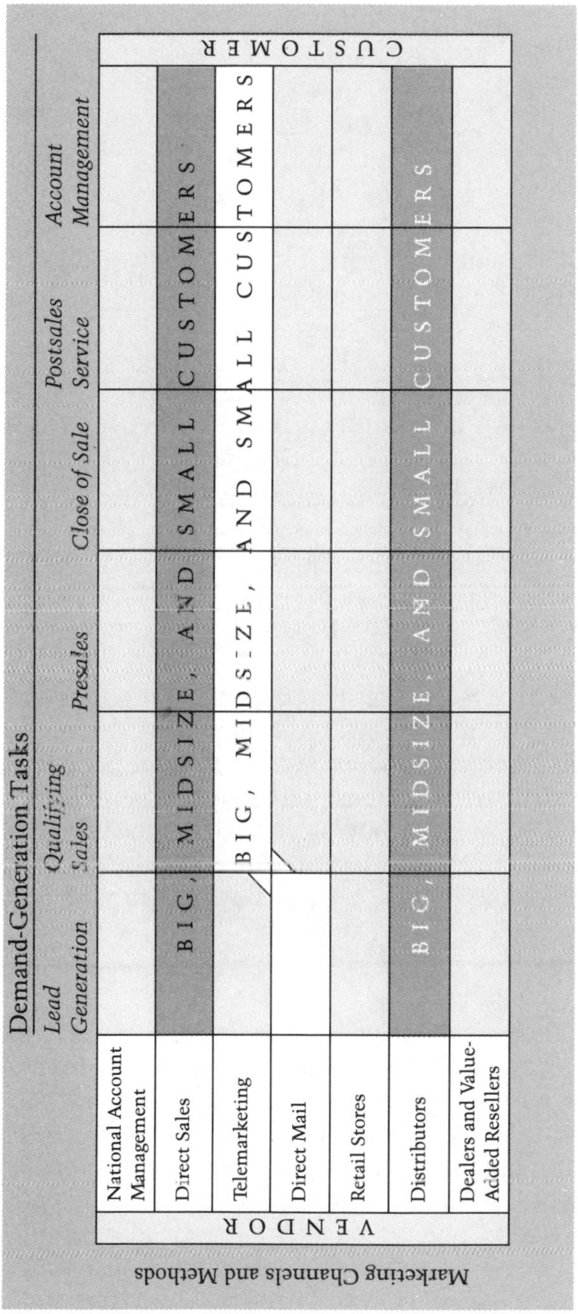

Demand-Generation Tasks

CUSTOMER

Marketing Channels and Methods (VENDOR)	Lead Generation	Qualifying Sales	Presales	Close of Sale	Postsales Service	Account Management
National Account Management						
Direct Sales	BIG, MIDSIZE, AND SMALL CUSTOMERS					
Telemarketing	BIG, MIDSIZE, AND SMALL CUSTOMERS					
Direct Mail						
Retail Stores						
Distributors	BIG, MIDSIZE, AND SMALL CUSTOMERS					
Dealers and Value-Added Resellers						

catalogs and received visits from the sales reps of office supply vendors found that Wright Line products were available at a substantial discount off the direct sales price.

In many respects, Wright Line's experience was typical, both in terms of the problems the company faced and its approach to solving them. Management's effort focused on identifying new channels that could be added to or substituted for all of the marketing tasks performed by the existing direct sales force channel. But this approach incorrectly assumes that each channel must perform and control all demand-generation tasks. The hybrid grid forces managers to consider various combinations of channels and tasks that will optimize both cost and coverage.

In addition, the company assumed that certain channels could best serve all the needs of certain customer segments. Hence, units 1, 2, and 3 were aligned with big, midsize, and small customers. The process of aligning high-cost channels—that is, the direct sales force—with big customers and low-cost channels with small customers is very logical, if that is the way customers buy. In Wright Line's case, however, customers bought from multiple sales channels. The attempt to use a single channel to reach a single customer group resulted in severe channel conflicts, along with customer confusion.

The design of an effective hybrid system depends not only on a thorough understanding of channel costs but also on a thorough understanding of buying behavior. When a new channel is added to service a particular customer segment, the segmentation scheme must clearly reflect the customer's buying behavior—not just the channel costs of the company. The design of an effective hybrid system requires balancing the natural tension between minimizing costs and maximizing customer satisfaction. In Wright Line's situation, the hybrid design was driven by costs, without regard for buying behavior.

Wright Line's fatal flaw was basing its marketing strategy on what was best for the company, not what was best for its customers. In focusing its costliest marketing resources on the targets with the highest potential payoff and devoting less expensive resources to less promising accounts, it ignored the buying behavior of its customers. Too late, Wright Line discovered that its customers could not be segmented so neatly, nor would they conform docilely to the company's perception of its most efficient channel structure. Its hybrid system was intended to lower costs and increase coverage. Instead, Wright Line lost control of both its channels and its customers.

The hybrid grid illustrates how Wright Line might have successfully designed and managed its hybrid system (see Exhibit V). The company could have used direct mail and response cards to generate leads among potential customers of all sizes and to perform most other tasks for small accounts. It could have used telemarketing to qualify leads among big and midsize prospects and determine approximate order size. It could have routed qualified prospects interested in buying a certain amount of equipment to direct sales reps. (Qualified prospects that turn out to be current national accounts would be turned over to the appropriate national account managers.) To midsize customers, it could have made phone calls to close sales and handle accounts; a direct sales rep or a national account manager could have performed these tasks for larger customers. For all customers, telemarketing could have been used for postsales tasks like reordering.

This version assigns demand-generation tasks to various channels, balancing both cost and customer buying behavior. Distributors were a principal part of Wright Line's setup. But this approach avoids using indirect channels, thereby allowing the company to maintain broad coverage without sacrificing control of pricing and product policy. (Of course, indirect channels are appropriate and necessary in many situations.) By establishing boundaries around genuine segments and building bridges across tasks, Wright Line might have gained the advantages of expanded market coverage and cost-effective marketing management without losing control of its marketing system and its customers.

Managing Conflict in Hybrid Systems

Conflict is an inevitable part of every hybrid system. When a company adds a channel or substitutes a new communication method within a channel, existing stakeholders—sales reps, distributors, telemarketers—invariably resist. And why not: each faces a potential loss of revenue as well as competition for ownership of customers. In seeking to build and manage a hybrid system, therefore, companies must recognize and communicate the existence of conflict as the first and most important step.

The next step is to assess the magnitude of the conflict, asking

Exhibit V.   Wright Line's Marketing System: What It Needed

Demand-Generation Tasks

CUSTOMER

Marketing Channels and Methods (VENDOR)	Lead Generation	Qualifying Sales	Presales	Close of Sale	Postsales Service	Account Management
National Account Management			BIG	BIG		BIG
Direct Sales						
Telemarketing		BIG AND MIDSIZE	MIDSIZE	MIDSIZE	ALL	MIDSIZE
Direct Mail	ALL	S	M A	L		SMALL
Retail Stores						
Distributors						
Dealers and Value-Added Resellers						

some simple but penetrating questions: How much revenue does the company have in conflict? (Revenue is in conflict whenever two or more channels simultaneously attempt to sell the same product to the same customer.) Where is this conflict? How do channels and customers react to it? How much management time is devoted to dealing with the conflict?

The answers to these questions will vary by industry and by company, but some generalizations are possible. Clearly, a company with no revenue in conflict may be sacrificing coverage, failing to attract new customers by focusing too narrowly on a particular segment. Indeed, a certain amount of conflict in a hybrid marketing system is not only inevitable but also healthy. On the other hand, as the Wright Line story illustrates, conflict that is pervasive across channels is debilitating and potentially destructive.

Of course, the concept of having revenue in conflict is alien to many CEOs and senior managers, particularly those who are accustomed to using only a single channel. They should seek a point of balance where conflict is neither too little nor too much. Although the location of this point depends on many variables—as a rule of thumb, destructive behavior occurs when 10% to 30% of revenues are in conflict—managers can estimate it by monitoring feedback from customers and marketing personnel. When phone calls and letters become angry, or when a significant portion of management time is absorbed in mediating internal disputes or dealing with customer complaints, warning bells should go off.

Bounding the Conflict

After they determine the amount and location of conflict, managers can establish clear and communicable boundaries and specific and enforceable guidelines that spell out which customers to serve through which methods.

Most companies observe some natural boundaries in the marketplace—areas defined by the interaction between buyer behavior and channel costs. Typically, companies target the largest and most profitable customers for some form of direct personal selling and serve smaller, less profitable accounts through less expensive methods. The problems arise with those customers residing somewhere in the middle: midsize accounts or markets with fuzzy boundaries, such as large national accounts that use a combination of centralized and decentralized purchasing practices that vary by product, location, or order size.

In this no-man's-land, neither the customer's buying behavior nor the company's transaction economics indicates definitively which method is the most effective way to serve the customer. Because no single method is clearly superior or appropriate, several may compete with each other—an example of a situation where clear boundaries will not work. These no-man's-land customer segments should be identified and clearly communicated to all marketing units so they know they will have intracompany competition.

Once the "jump ball" selling situations are identified, it is easier to construct barriers where natural segments exist. Boundaries between classes of customers are frequently couched in terms of sales, but effective boundary design involves much more than spelling out who makes which sale. It should instead indicate who owns and who doesn't own certain customers. Boundary mechanisms that help achieve this goal are generally based on customer characteristics, geography, and products.

CUSTOMER CHARACTERISTICS.   Customer size is a familiar boundary criterion. One large computer manufacturer specifies that, for its banking customers, its value-added resellers (VARs) should sell to small community financial institutions with less than $250 million in assets. For larger institutions, the manufacturer should sell through its direct sales force or some combination of that group and a third-party software supplier.

Order size provides another standard for drawing boundaries. A leading maker of PCs, for example, specifies that orders for more than 25 units must go through its direct sales force and orders of less than 5 units through independent dealers. Either direct or indirect channels may handle orders in the no-man's-land between 5 and 25 units.

Customers can also be classified by decision-making process or decision-making unit. A manufacturer of specialty and commodity chemicals uses a direct sales force to sell specialty chemicals because the purchasing process for these products is complex and requires several engineers to develop specifications and participate in supplier selection. The company's commodity products, however, are most often bought by a purchasing agent, and price is the key consideration. Hence, commodity chemicals are handled by distributors.

Finally, customers can be categorized by industry, particularly when there are genuine differences both in the product, price, and service package and in the expertise demanded of salespeople. The paper industry is a good example of differences in end use or applications. A different channel serves each of the four major end-use groups—newsprint, magazines, office products, and business forms.

GEOGRAPHIC BOUNDARIES. Bounding by geography is clear and easy to enforce. A major manufacturer of computer-aided design/computer-aided manufacture (CAD/CAM) systems sells its offerings in the United States and Europe through a direct sales force; in Japan, it uses an exclusive distributor. The company has little difficulty preventing major conflict (except in global accounts) because the channels are physically separated. Many companies serve large, urban markets through some form of direct sales and use distributors or reps to cover less densely populated areas.

PRODUCT BOUNDARIES. Xerox used product boundaries when it entered the personal copier market. It sells mid-range and high-end machines through a combination of direct sales and dealer distribution; it sells low-end machines exclusively through retail channels. Electronics and appliance stores, mass merchants, department stores, and an American Express direct mail program are all sources of Xerox personal copiers. The company has tried to avoid excessive conflict among these different retail channels by producing distinct models for each. The basic model 5008 personal copier was designed in three different versions so retailers would not compete with one another over an identical product.

Boundary mechanisms will help contain and control conflict when it arises, but they do not—and should not—eliminate it. It is impossible to hermetically seal each segment or customer group. Astute marketers identify and communicate to their channels not only those areas where clear boundaries exist but also those where they are either impossible or impractical.

Managing Channel Additions

Maintaining order in a hybrid marketing system is a complex administrative challenge. The addition of new channels and meth-

ods inevitably requires modifications to existing reporting relationships, organization structure, and management policies with
respect to motivation, evaluation, and compensation. The stakes
are high since organizational moves issue a strong signal about the
direction of change and top management's commitment to it. In the
past decade, for example, Wang Laboratories struggled through
three separate attempts to create an indirect sales organization to
supplement direct sales of its products. Each new attempt found-
ered after meeting entrenched resistance inside the company. Indeed, Wang's inability to solve this problem is a hidden cause of
its much-publicized troubles in recent years.

Although each hybrid system presents unique challenges to managers, two general administrative guidelines may be helpful. First,
decisions about structure and support policies should conform to
the overall goals of the marketing system. Each potential configuration should be measured against the obvious tests: Will it satisfy
customers in the most cost-effective manner? Will it maximize the
prospect of achieving greater coverage and control throughout the
system? Will it limit destructive conflict inside the organization?

Second, the timing of changes in structure and policies should
reflect a realistic assessment of revenue flows through various channels and methods over time. In a large company, for example, it is
extremely unlikely that a new channel or method will account for
a significant fraction of total revenues in its first year. A new
indirect channel added to a system dominated by a direct channel
may account for 3% to 5% of revenues in the first year and perhaps
20% by the fifth. During such a transition, management should
weight its policies heavily in favor of the new channel to ensure its
success.

Management sends the most powerful and immediate signals
through the compensation system. Companies with hybrid systems
rely heavily on compensation policies to reinforce new boundaries
and routinely subsidize new activities during transition periods.
The most common approach involves paying personnel in the older
units to allow personnel in the newer units to make the sale. An
example reveals the reasoning behind such a tactic. A large computer company was struggling with the familiar problem of adding
low-cost direct methods and indirect channels to supplement its
direct sales force. In seeking to motivate the direct sales reps to
relinquish revenue responsibilities, the company considered three
options: a penalty, a modest incentive, and a strong incentive.

In weighing the penalty option, the company reasoned that re-quiring direct sales reps to forfeit commissions on each sale that should be made elsewhere would discourage them from stealing sales from new units. The risks of such an approach, however, seemed overwhelming: the company saw that conflict and petty rivalries were bound to erupt throughout the marketing organiza-tion as soon as it instituted the policy.

The modest incentive option would entail paying direct sales reps a portion of their normal commission when the new units made a sale. On reflection, this solution appeared too cumbersome: it would be difficult to determine appropriate compensation levels and to define and enforce a policy that would avoid sending mixed signals.

In the end, the company chose the strong incentive option—and eventually implemented it successfully. After a thorough analysis of long-term costs and benefits, the company paid the direct sales reps their normal commission for every sale regardless of whether they were responsible. Once the new units became established, the company phased out this system of double pay.

Orchestrating a Hybrid System

Once a hybrid system is up and running, its smooth functioning depends not only on management of conflict but also on coordi-nation across the channels and across each selling task within the channels. Each unit involved in bridging the gap between the com-pany and the customer must "hand off" all relevant information concerning the customer and the progress of the sale to the next appropriate unit.

A recent technical tool called a marketing and sales productivity (MSP) system can be an invaluable aid in coordinating customer handoffs.[2] Beyond this, an MSP system can help a company com-bine and manage distinct marketing approaches to produce cus-tomized hybrid channels. An MSP system helps serve customers by identifying and coordinating the marketing methods best suited to each customer's needs. In other words, it allows the development of customized channels and service for specific customer segments.

An MSP system consists of a central marketing data base con-taining essential information on customers, prospects, products, marketing programs, and methods. All marketing units regularly update the data base. At any point, it is possible to determine previous customer contacts, prices quoted, special customer characteristics or needs, and other information. These systems can significantly lower marketing costs and increase marketing effectiveness by acting as a central nervous system that coordinates the channels and marketing tasks within a hybrid system. With a fully integrated MSP system, it is now possible to know how much it costs to acquire and maintain a customer—essential data in understanding a company's marketing productivity.

Data Translation, a small manufacturer of computer peripherals, installed an in-house MSP system to manage its hybrid marketing organization. At the outset, the company could not afford to hire sales reps but instead generated leads through trade advertising that featured an 800 number. Interested prospects received the company's catalog; they were also encouraged to call and speak to an inside sales representative about products. All contacts with prospects were tracked by the MSP system. Inside sales reps were supported by a group of technical engineers who handled customer inquiries. When Data Translation later added a direct sales force, it continued to rely on its MSP system to coordinate various marketing tasks, including generating leads and dealing with customers who call.

Coordinating the handoffs within its hybrid system and knowing the cost of acquiring and maintaining its customers give Data Translation significantly lower marketing costs than its competitors. These lower costs translate directly into competitive advantage and bigger margins.

Capturing the Benefits

Staples, a Massachusetts-based office supplies company, is achieving outstanding growth through clever allocation of marketing tasks based on what it has learned about customer behavior. At its birth in the mid-1980s, Staples's founders decided to offer discounted office supplies in a retail superstore format, targeting white-collar companies with up to 100 employees. Staples encouraged customers to accept a free savings card that granted additional discounts and, more important, allowed the company to track purchases and to build up a customer data base.

Armed with this information, management discovered that its

penetration of businesses with 2 to 10 employees was good, those with 10 to 20 not so good, and those with more than 20 quite weak. Customers in the latter two segments wanted more service. In response, Staples started accepting phone orders and added a delivery service. It has also used direct mail, telemarketing, and catalogs and has considered adding a direct sales force to handle large accounts. An MSP system orchestrates and monitors the entire hybrid system and provides management with performance and productivity information on each marketing element. Staples credits much of its success to the design and implementation of its hybrid system.

Many signs indicate that hybrid systems will be the dominant design for going to market in the 1990s. How a company manages its system will help determine its fate in the marketplace. A company that designs and manages its system strategically will achieve a powerful advantage over rivals that add channels and methods in an opportunistic and incremental manner. A company that makes its hybrid system work will have achieved a balance between its customers' buying behavior and its own selling economics. A well-managed hybrid system enables a marketer to enjoy the benefits of increased coverage and lower costs without losing control of the marketing system. Further, it enables a company to customize its marketing system to meet the needs of specific customers and segments.

In sum, a company with a successful hybrid marketing system will accomplish the following:

It will recognize that the design and management of its marketing system is a powerful weapon in an increasingly competitive and continually shifting battle for customers.

It will construct its marketing system using marketing tasks, not entire marketing channels, as the fundamental building blocks.

It will anticipate, recognize, communicate, and contain conflicts inherent in the marketing system.

In designing boundaries between customer segments, it will strike a balance between too loose and too strict limits.

It will form policies and an organizational structure that allow new channels to grow, minimize internal conflict, and reinforce segment boundaries.

It will exploit information technology and other managerial tools to coordinate handoffs of customers and accounts from one channel or method to another and eventually develop customized marketing systems for each important customer or segment.

Notes

1. Channels are either direct or indirect. Methods are the communications options companies can use to reach potential customers; they may also be direct or indirect. For example, through a direct channel, a company may use account managers, a sales force, or telemarketing. The same methods may also be used singly or in combination through indirect channels.
2. For an analysis of these systems, see Rowland T. Moriarty and Gordon S. Swartz, "Automation to Boost Sales and Marketing," *Harvard Business Review*, January–February 1989, p. 100.

About the Contributors

James C. Anderson is William L. Ford Professor of Wholesale Distribution and Professor of Marketing and Behavioral Science at the Kellogg Graduate School of Management, Northwestern University. The article included in this collection, co-authored with James A. Narus, was based on their research on working partnerships between man ufacturers and distributors.

Alan R. Andreasen is professor and head of the Marketing Department in the School of Business Administration, University of Connecticut, Storrs. He has published several articles in the *Harvard Business Review* on consumerism, marketing in nonprofit organizations, and low-cost market research. He is currently involved in research on several aspects of social marketing.

Thomas V. Bonoma is president and chief executive officer of Benckiser Consumer Products, Inc., the North American subsidiary of Joh. A. Benckiser GmbH, which produces a wide variety of fragrances, cosmetics, detergents, and cleaners. At the time these *Harvard Business Review* articles were written, he was an associate professor of marketing at the Harvard Business School. His article, "The Instant CEO," was recently published in *Across the Board*, the magazine of The Conference Board.

Frank V. Cespedes is an associate professor of marketing at the Harvard Business School. He is co-author of *Going to Market: Distribution Systems for Industrial Products* (Harvard Business School

Press) and author of *Organizing and Implementing the Marketing Effort: Text and Cases* (Addison-Wesley).

Stephen X. Doyle is president of SXD Associates, a sales management consulting firm located in Great Neck, New York. He recently published an article on relationship selling in the *Journal of Personal Selling and Sales Management*, and is currently developing an article on "relationship havoc."

Robert J. Freedman is vice president of Towers Perrin, a consulting company in Stamford, Connecticut, where he specializes in sales and executive compensation.

David Green was vice president of Sales and Marketing for VideoStar Connections, Inc. in Atlanta at the time his *Harvard Business Review* article was written.

Herbert M. and Jeanne Greenberg are principals of Caliper Corporation, a Princeton-based human resources consulting firm. For nearly three decades the firm has helped develop the capabilities of more than 15,000 companies throughout the world. The Greenbergs have spoken and written extensively on the relationship between personality and job performance, including their recent publication, *What It Takes to Succeed in Sales* (Dow Jones-Irwin).

Mary Karr served as a research consultant at the Harvard Business School and as a marketing and communications manager for several high-tech companies. At the time her *Harvard Business Review* article was published, she ran a writing and research consulting firm in the Boston area.

Thomas C. Keiser is president of the Forum Corporation, a training and education consulting firm in Boston.

Harvey B. Mackay is chairman and chief executive officer of the Mackay Envelope Corporation in Minneapolis, Minnesota. He has written several books, including *Swim With the Sharks Without Being Eaten Alive* and the forthcoming *Sharkproof: Get the Job You Want, Keep the Job You Love . . . in Today's Frenzied Job Market.*

Ursula Moran is director of Retail Operations for Coach Leatherware, a division of Sara Lee Corporation, managing hybrid marketing channels for approximately 80 full-price and factory stores. Previously, she was an associate at Booz, Allen & Hamilton.

Rowland T. Moriarty is chairman of Cubex Corporation, an international management consulting firm based in Boston. Prior to founding Cubex, Dr. Moriarty was professor of Business Administration at the Harvard Business School, where he taught a variety of marketing courses in the executive and MBA programs. He has consulted to more than 75 companies worldwide, and has written extensively on the subject of marketing.

James A. Narus is associate professor of management at the Babcock Graduate School of Management, Wake Forest University. He specializes in issues of relationship management and industrial marketing.

Ronald S. Posner is chairman, president, and chief executive officer of WordStar International, a leading publicly held personal computer software company. He has been instrumental over the past 10 years in improving the performance of three other PC software companies. At the time of his article's publication, he was chairman of National Training Systems.

Clifton J. Reichard is director of Business Development at the Ball Corporation, Muncie, Indiana. At the time of his article's publication, he was vice president, Commercial Sales, of the Ball Corporation's Glass Container Group.

Benson P. Shapiro, Malcolm P. McNair Professor of Marketing at the Harvard Business School, is a well-known authority on marketing and sales management. In more than 20 years on the HBS faculty, he has taught a wide variety of MBA courses and executive programs, and has held several administrative positions, including senior associate dean for Publications and faculty chair for Strategic Marketing Management. Professor Shapiro is the author or co-author of six books and numerous *Harvard Business Review* articles.

John P. Steinbrink recently retired from Dartnell Corporation as senior vice president. At Dartnell he was author of the *Biennial Surveys of Compensation of Salesmen*. He currently heads JPS Associates, a sales and marketing consulting firm in Niles, Illinois.

John J. Sviokla is an assistant professor in Management Information Systems and Control at the Harvard Business School. His most recent research has focused on how to drive sales increases, higher prices, or superior quality through efficient management of information technology and organizational innovation. He has published widely and consulted to more than 50 organizations worldwide.

Gordon S. Swartz is a marketing doctoral student at the Harvard Business School, where his research focuses on the use of marketing and sales data bases to optimize marketing resources allocation. Before joining Harvard, he was president of Visual Thinking, an industrial film and video production company, and director of research at the Competitive Assessment Center, a computer industry research firm.

John Wyman is distinguished lecturer at the College of Business Administration, University of Florida, Gainesville, where he specializes in business strategy. At the time of his article's publication, he was vice president, Marketing, for AT&T Long Lines.

INDEX